M McLean

Echoes from Japan

M McLean

Echoes from Japan

ISBN/EAN: 9783337167936

Printed in Europe, USA, Canada, Australia, Japan

Cover: Foto ©Andreas Hilbeck / pixelio.de

More available books at **www.hansebooks.com**

ECHOES FROM JAPAN.

(SECOND EDITION.)

BY

M. McLEAN,

Author of "Open Doors in Japan."

London:
PASSMORE & ALABASTER, PATERNOSTER BUILDINGS.
1889.

[*All Rights Reserved.*]

CONTENTS

	PAGE
MAP OF JAPAN	4
INTRODUCTION	7

CHAP.
I.	A PEEP AT OLD JAPAN	13
II.	PRESENT CONDITION OF JAPAN	19
III.	HOW I HAD ACCESS TO THE JAPANESE	33
IV.	BEFORE AND AFTER CONVERSION (OF A SAMURAI)	50
V.	JAPAN PLEADING WITH ENGLAND TO BE RECONCILED TO GOD	57
VI.	AN AWAKENING AMONG THE BLUE-JACKETS	68
VII.	BRIGHT HOURS WITH MY PUPILS	82
VIII.	A VISIT TO THE SHIBA TEMPLE AND TOMBS	95
IX.	THE JAPANESE CHRISTIANS IN A DILEMMA	101
X.	VISIT TO KOBE AND OSAKA	109
XI.	SELF-HELP	117
XII.	SOCIAL LIFE IN JAPAN	126
XIII.	CHILD LIFE IN JAPAN	131
XIV.	FRAGMENTS	145
XV.	A TRIP TO THE HACONE HILLS	156
XVI.	HOW ORIENTALS IN LONDON MAY BE REACHED—HOW IT STRIKES A STRANGER	169
XVII.	OSAKA NOTES	173
XVIII.	A TRIP TO ARIMA	193
XIX.	HOTEL LIFE AT OSAKA	205
XX.	SECULAR EDUCATION	217
XXI.	MORAL CONDITION	236
XXII.	"THE ELEVENTH HOUR"	239
APPENDIX I.	JOTTINGS FROM MY NOTE-BOOK	249
APPENDIX II.	PREFACE TO THE LETTERS OF BLUE-JACKETS	274
APPENDIX III.	CRUMBS FROM THE LETTERS OF A SOUL-WINNER AT SHANGHAI	301
CONCLUSION		314

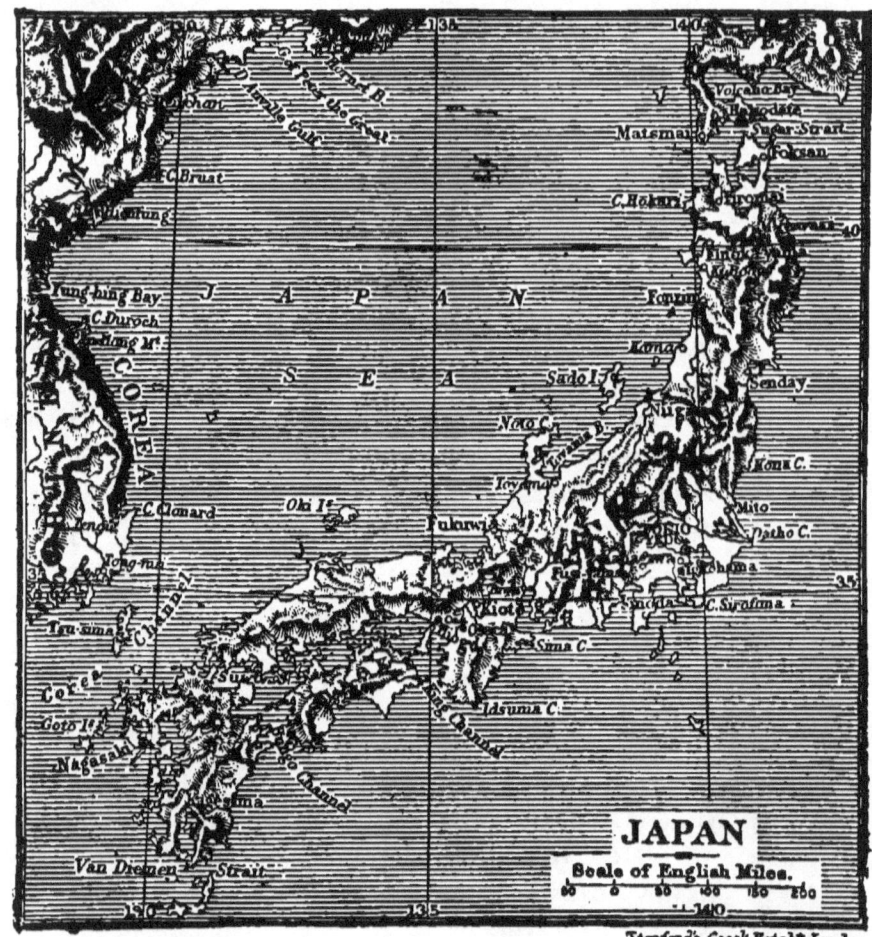

PREFACE.

―――◆―――

The following extract is taken from the letter of a Japanese gentleman who kindly read my manuscripts before sending them to the press.

I HAVE read your very interesting papers about Japan, and the Japanese people, with great pleasure. Of course, I know very well those customs and manners of the people depicted by your pen, and all the country places, except one, described by you, are quite familiar to me; so that the reading of these papers immediately aroused most happy and charming recollections in my mind. Some of them give the reader a simple and honest description of child-life in Japan; and they forcibly reminded me of the happy days of my own boyhood. Others are very faithful in telling what travellers see and feel in visiting various places of interest. They mostly give exactly what I recollect from my own travelling to those places.

I was, as you know, a student of law in the Imperial University of Japan, and am now at the Middle Temple, London. Thus, my own study is not very congenial to the cultivation of literary taste. But I do not hesitate to declare that you have surely written these papers out of the simple love of truth. You have put down, now and then, what occurred to your mind—simply because you cannot help expressing it. It is perfectly clear that you are neither one of those who praise anything which is Japanese, because they have some benefits in view; nor one of those who are anxious to find fault with other people, and who are so devoid of good taste as to expose the people of distant lands in their worst aspects. Your residence of nine years in Japan gives you a very fair insight into the feeling and thought of the people, and throughout your papers I distinctly perceive your true sympathy with my own country. I observe almost every day in London that, although there is so much talk about Japan and Japanese art, yet most people, I should say, even educated people, have only some inadequate, and often many mistaken ideas of Japan. This is just what most Japanese feel much disappointed to find. Therefore, I am very glad to find such descriptions and comments as you have given about Japan in these papers, because they are true and honest. We Japanese have no desire to have our merits exaggerated as a nation very old in her history, and now trying very hard to effect a complete regeneration to become one of the respectable modern states. But we are, at the same time, very anxious to dispel those unfairly hostile, and even monstrous, criticisms which frequently appear in books of travel.

If you are going to publish these papers, which I have had the pleasure of reading all through, I sincerely hope that they may find a good many readers; and I am very happy to supply you with some statistical facts about my country, taken from the latest returns.

I am, yours very truly,
S. UYEMURA.

THE TEMPLE, LONDON,
April 1*st*, 1889.

INTRODUCTION.

On Board the SS. "New York."

. . . "He led him about, He instructed him, He kept him as the apple of his eye."—Deut. xxxii. 10.

ON embarking at Shanghai for Yokohama, Japan—in November 1872—a friend gave me the text : "*Casting all your care upon Him ; for He careth for you.*" I was in every sense of the word a fit subject for the comfort it brought. After forty-eight hours' sail, we entered the beautiful and picturesque harbour of Nagasaki. The day was, in keeping with the reputed climate of Japan, bright and sunny. The view from deck was particularly enchanting; the calm and transparent waters of the harbour reflected hills covered with luxuriant vegetation, as well as a fleet of vessels, representing Western nations. The rock of tragic history, called "Pappenberg," is very suggestive of its name, so closely does it resemble the Pope's mitre. Doubtless in the days of Xavier the Portuguese thought so, and accepted it as a sign that Japan was destined to become a vassal of the Holy See. The nearer hills and islets were lovely to gaze upon, while the more distant ones lent enchantment to the view. The scene was lit up with the autumn tints, so that it was difficult to realize that we were only within two weeks of bleak December.

On going ashore, I steered for the C. M. S. Mission Station. I had a kind welcome from Mr. and Mrs. Burnside, who, with Rev. Mr. Ensor, pioneered the C. M. S. Missionary operations in Japan. I began to discover that the C. M. S. was doing here, what on a larger scale they had already done in China—*i.e.*, planting the Cross along its shores in the strongholds of idolatry—and by their earnestness and unworldliness, proving that they were not there for gain, ease, or luxury.*

In Japan I found that there was less religious tolerance than in China, for as yet the missionaries had but little official liberty given to them to carry on their work. There were, however, some few disciples. I also found that the ground had been broken by the American Episcopal Mission, in the person of Bishop Williams, who was one of the first Protestant Missionaries to Nagasaki; and, as in China, so in Japan, he was abundant in labours, and as much at home in the Japanese as in the Chinese tongue. His intense humility must strike and edify all that come in contact with him, and that he is an example to the flock in missionary zeal and self abnegation is universally known. One instance, to show its genuineness, is the fact that he has for more than twenty years remained at his post between the two empires, without availing himself of the rest which seems to us so necessary in order to regain strength. Such lives are for the most part shielded from the praise of men, and careful only to please Him who gave the promise

---

* At a later date (1881), I spent a pleasant week under the roof of Mr. and Mrs. Maundrell, and found that they and their co-workers had largely developed the work of their predecessors.

that "He who seeth in secret shall reward thee openly." After eight hours' halt in the harbour of Nagasaki, we got under weigh for our destination —Yokohama. Early in the morning we entered the most enchanting scene in Japan—the inland sea. Some of the hills were quite verdant, and some were emblazoned with a variety of autumn tints. I tried to make friends with some Japanese who came on board at Nagasaki. I thought them very thinly clad, for at this season—November— the Chinese are wrapped in thickly wadded clothes. Everything on board was examined by them. All that their eyes rested on seemed to be objects and subjects of interest, and remarks were constantly being made which were unintelligible to me. Notwithstanding the glory of the scene, and the novelty of my first impressions of Japanese life at this initial stage, I was glad to return to my cabin and ask that the words "Casting all your care upon Him, for He careth for you," might be made good in my experience ; for, like Abraham, I felt I was going forth, not knowing whither. On Saturday we sailed into the quiet harbour of Kobé, a most lovely spot, to say nothing of its being a place of commercial promise, judging from its position, for on the mainland behind it is an extensive network of railways projected. Already a train runs between it and Osaka, eighteen miles along the coast, and sea-ward it opens its arms to all navigators. The row of European villas on the shore, and range of irregularly shaped hills behind, brought before us familiar scenes in the far West. All the other passengers went ashore till Monday morning, but I, for various reasons, preferred remaining on board, one being that, like Ezra of old, I felt drawn to have time and quiet with the Guide of my life, to seek of Him a right way. . . . .

On Monday afternoon we weighed anchor again, and steamed for Yokohama, where our good Captain Furber said we should arrive on Wednesday morning. As I had been entrusted to his protection by my kind Shanghai friends, Mr. and Mrs. N——, he said he would take me ashore, and introduce me to some of the Missionaries. Our ship's party from Kobé was considerably augmented, for we received on board the Governor of Osaka, his wife, and long train of attendants. It was quite an interesting study for us—from the West—to see how these cultured Easterns behaved to each other—essentially polite and elegant in manners. The ladies, as to their toilette and bearing, were the pictures of grace and neatness—if adherence to simplicity in colour and ornament be indicative of good taste? The Japanese in every way present a striking contrast to the natives of China, especially the women. In China they are shy and reserved, and are difficult at first to approach ; but the Japanese women, with their gay and open manner, are as accessible as Europeans.

On Wednesday, in accordance with the predictions of our Captain, we entered Yokohama, the busiest and most important harbour of Japan.

INTRODUCTION

One of the first sights I had from my cabin window was a very familiar one—a train, flying on its way to Tokyo, the capital; and, on casting my eye in another direction, I caught sight of the matchless Fuji Mountain—Japan's pride. Though at a distance of more than sixty miles, it seemed to be only ten or fifteen miles away :—this illusion is due to the clear atmosphere, which always renders Japan a physical panorama, rarely overcast with black clouds, fogs, and murky sky.

Having had a rough passage all night, the captain went at daylight to lie down. Not caring to disturb his much-needed rest, and to prolong my stay on board, I, in imitation of my fellow-passengers, went ashore alone in a *san-pan*. On arriving at the jetty some ten or twelve unemployed men jumped on board my fragile craft, scrambling and squabbling over my luggage as to who should be its bearer. The scuffle was so tempestuous that the boat was in danger of sinking every moment. In vain, by gesture and word, I begged them to leave off. Even the boatman's furious protests in the native tongue were unheeded, and it was not until a custom-house officer was sighted by them that they made off.

On getting ashore, I found that some friends had been on the look-out for me, and I and my belongings were taken charge of. I felt I had been deservedly punished for having acted so independently of the captain's offer to see me safe off his hands. My first ride in a Jinrikisha ended, I found myself in the hospitable quarters of the American Mission Home, superintended at that time by Mrs. Pruyn, now gone to her resting-place, till sowers and reapers shall rejoice together at the great Harvest Home. Miss Guthrie, one of the party of ladies which composed this first female mission to the women of Japan, has also departed to be with Christ. I have sweet recollections of our times of refreshing, as we unitedly compassed the throne of grace.

A BIRD'S-EYE VIEW OF KANAGAWA AND YOKOHAMA HARBOUR.

CHAPTER I.

A Peep at Old Japan.

"In the beginning God created the heaven and the earth."—Gen. i. 1.

IF you were to ask a Japanese to give you a verbal outline of the history of his country, he would do so, as nearly as possible, in the following words:—In the "Jindai-no-maki" (mythology of Japan) it is said that the condition of the lower world, originally, was chaotic; from this the pure matter ascended and formed the skies (or heaven), while the impure descended and formed the earth. From this latter evolved a race of heavenly beings, called Celestial Kami, of whom Izanagi (a male) and Izanami (a female) were the last individuals. Izanagi, standing one day on the bridge called Ama-no-uki-hashi (the floating celestial bridge), he dipped his spear into the sea, and as he drew it out, the drops falling from it solidified, and formed an island called Ono-Koro-jima, which is said to be the present Awaji. This was the first island brought into existence. These celestial visitants are called, in mythology, Ten-jin-shi-chi-dai, or seventh generation of gods, *i.e.*, from Kuni-toku-tatsu-no-mikoto (lit. the God whose kingdom is everlasting). They are said to have had three children: first, Ama-no-terasu-no-mikoto (a female), Susano, and Hiruko (males). The fifth generation, and last of the gods terrestrial, was U-ga-ya-fu-ki-awa-zedzu-no-mikoto. From him, it is said, descended the primogenitor of the one hundred and twenty-three Mikados who have sat successively on the throne of Japan. The Emperor Jimmu was, in reality, a king, or chief of Kiu-Shiu. He and his army having gained a victory over the islands of Japan, he ascended the throne of that country, at a place called Kashi-wa-bara, and founded the dynasty of the Mikados. This took place when Manasseh ruled over the house of Judah. With the help of two of his provincial governors—Koku-zo and Agata-nushi—he ruled his realm with great ability.

As to a geographical sketch of the country, I feel that, in these days of enlightenment, it is unnecessary to draw your attention to a map of the world, and say that Japan is bounded on the north by the Sea of Yczo, on the east and south by the North Pacific Ocean, and on the west by the Sea of Japan and Straits of Corea.

Before giving you a few extracts from my diary, also a few stories about the Japanese, let me say that Japan is made up of four main islands, and a great many smaller ones. Many of the latter are uninhabited islets or rocks. Hondo, the largest, is in the centre; Hok-kai-do, or Yezo, in the north; Shi-koku and Kiu-shiu, in the south-west. These four main islands are divided into eight large divisions, or "do," namely, Tokai-do, or eastern sea circuit; To-san-do, or eastern mountain circuit; Hokku-roku-do, or northern land circuit; Nan-kai-do, or southern sea circuit; San-yin-do, or mountain back circuit; San-yo-do, or mountain front circuit; Sai-kai-do, or western sea circuit; Hok-kai-do, or northern sea circuit. These are again subdivided. First, into koku (provinces); second, into gun or kori (counties or districts); third, into mura and son (villages and hamlets).

Since Japan is, in every sense of the word, a progressive country, the above divisions may be undergoing a change at this moment (1889) which will make this account appear a little out of date. But the adage, "*a rolling stone gathers no moss*," must not be applied to the Japanese, even although they are so impatient for reform that they remind one of an impetuous boy turning over the leaves of an illuminated album, with which he is well acquainted himself, and saying to his curious juvenile beholders, "This is to be your last chance of getting a glimpse of this book, so be quick." Never has a nation so suddenly sat down and counted the cost, and immediately put her conclusions into practice with such startling unanimity. Japan, as everyone must see, has, for the past twenty-one years, been in favour of adopting the customs of Europe. See how she places herself in a position likely to prove conducive to a rapid development! She opens her chambers to the light of civilization, which forces itself upon her from the West, exclaiming as it were—" What plant can flourish, or flower bloom without light? At any cost let us have it!" Thus she wakes up, after the manner of Samson, and suddenly breaks away from the yoke imposed upon her by the long line of Shoguns who usurped the authority of the throne. The newly-reinstated legitimate young sovereign, seeing the loyalty of his advisers, meekly listens to what they have to say to him. He, with them, sees the folly of being shut up behind his screen, the mere shadow of a ruler, and where, too, he is made to believe that it would be fatal to the welfare of his people, as well as "derogatory to his divine origin," for mortal eyes to look upon his face. So much, then, for the light which has so far thrust its rosy finger into the Royal Palace of Japan, as well as into the lordly domains of the Daimios.

The New Régime.

Unprecedented and imposing sight! What do we see in front of that spacious, quaint palace at the old capital Kyoto (with its massive cedar pillars, its thickly thatched roof, its richly embellished panels and sliding partitions, its chastely decorated rooms, its romantic grounds and curiously constructed bridges, its ponds of carp and mandarin ducks, its dwarfed trees, including the emblems of happiness, as well as the proud, self-conscious looking stork, which seems to say, as it moves forward with measured footsteps, "*Thrones and dynasties may change, but my equanimity* * *lengthens out my days*"?) None other than the long train of hierarchies, the Daimios of the three hundred dominions, sitting in a fashion befitting the relationship which is about to exist between their sovereign and themselves. See, how the sea of heads bends simultaneously in one direction, as if swearing (by the Emperor Jimmu—founder of the Mikado's dynasty) to him who sits before them, that henceforth they and their retainers will bow to his will, as becometh filial sons and loyal subjects! Hitherto, they have been petty kings over their own domains; but, henceforth, they seem to say, "*We shall be servants to our Lord the Tenno*" (Mikado). Another profound bow, and all their richly decorated swords (emblems of distinction and power) are as good as surrendered. Hark! They unanimously and reverently groan out a final assent to what they believe to be the voice of the throne (or heaven), and they retire, bearing the name of Kwazoku—flowery family—in lieu of the more illustrious title, viz., *Daimio* (lit., great name). The Daimios have been in the habit of paying their respects to the Shoguns and

---

* The stork is the emblem of longevity in Japan.

Emperors at different intervals, *en masse*, as on this occasion : but this visit has a different significance, for they have come to formally surrender their hereditary rights to the latter, and to him they have ever since (1868) rendered that submission, if not homage, which becomes such a display of loyalty.

The present reign is called Meiji (*i.e.* enlightened era). Instead of saying " Anno Domini," as with us, they say " In the year of Meiji." At this moment, the era of Meiji may be said to have come of age ; and, judging of her future career by the past twenty-one years, we may safely conclude that Japan will, ere long, wield the same influence in the far East that England wields in Europe. But if she is to do this, with Christianity as the foundation-stone of the kingdom, the Christian Church has not a moment to wait. "*Now or never*" has never been more aptly applied than in reference to the present critical moment Japan is passing through.

CHAPTER II.

Present Condition of Japan.

(BY A JAPANESE GENTLEMAN.)

THE rumours of the British conquest of India, and the humiliation of that proud celestial empire, had already half awakened Japan, when the American fleet, with her intimidating guns and cannon, came to our shores. The sight of the terrible and merciless struggles for existence raging high between the nations of the earth gave warning to our people. To sit still and be trampled down and destroyed, to cling to the old customs and usages, is the surest way to feebleness and decay. And so, with a healthy confidence and strong resolution, Japan has decided to take the new course of western civilisation. Right or wrong, her one desire at present is to be assimilated with the community of the enlightened nations of Europe and America. No wonder that she is impatient now and then. No wonder that her measures of social reform are often carried too far. Nay, this very fact ought to awaken the deepest sympathy in every Christian soul.

A whole nation, kindled with a lofty sense of her own responsibility, struggling with all her might and strength for improvement and progress is a spectacle which cannot fail to impress her bystanders. But although it might seem that the history of Japan, in recent times, is characterised by abrupt suddenness, be it remembered that God was preparing her people for this apparently sudden transformation. Through the past centuries the history of the empire, from the time of Jimmu Tenno, the first Mikado of Japan, down to the present moment, is a gradual development of democratic ideas, changes of dynasties, transference of power from one hand to another, the rise of the Samurai—that flowery race of Japan; the revival of learning during the past three centuries, and, above all, the downfall of the military *régime* of the Tokugawa in the years of 1867-8, have been slowly, but steadily, preparing the Japanese nation for a new era of enlightenment. We have had a long history, and the present is largely the outcome of the past changes now transpiring in Japan, and neither so sudden nor so abrupt as you might imagine. God has been preparing a nation in the far East for freedom and independence, and if Japan continues faithful to her responsibilities, there is no doubt that she will come out all right and prosperous. A commonwealth without God! what could be more sad and contradictory? The only nation which may properly be so called is one whose God is the Lord. It is Christianity alone that is able to impart a taste for freedom, and facilitates the use of free institutions. Civilisation, without the benign influence of

Christianity, is a sepulchre painted in white. This solemn fact is sadly ignored by our leading statesmen. May God be pleased to open their minds to this all-important fact, viz., that one thing is needful for the all-important growth of Japan, even the Gospel of the Kingdom of Heaven. I feel more and more convinced that it is Christianity alone that will bring salvation to Japan, both spiritually and politically. The present is the most critical time of our country. The Macedonian call from the far Orient, is resounding in your ears. This naturally brings us to the missionary work in Japan; and if, in political affairs, we can trace the hand of God leading the people to changes and reforms, the same kind providence is more clearly to be discerned in the religious development of the land. Shintoism, though disfigured by childish mythology, has at least one thing to be said in her favour: she impressed on the Japanese people the idea of holiness. Buddhism, that strange mixture of superstitious shallowness and metaphysical profundity has succeeded in reminding them of the hollowness of the present evil world, and aroused a thirst for something infinite and eternal. Confucianism, the Stoic philosophy of Asia, inculcated lofty doctrines of morality, and inspired her disciples with a spirit of magnanimity, and a high sense of honour. These three religious and philosophical systems of the heathen, have been preparing the Japanese mind for the reception of the absolute religion of Christ; and, after more than twenty centuries spent wandering in the labyrinth of human wisdom, and in vain groping after the unknown God, a gleam of light from a higher source, though sadly broken by the intermixture of human errors, has, for the first time, appeared to the yearning souls of Japan.

About four centuries ago, the whole country was divided into petty factions, constantly at war with each other. The long-continued internal commotions, the wretched poverty to which the populace had been then reduced, the uncertainty of life and property, and many other woes of life, were driving people into despair, and many of them became pessimists, and others were crying out for a time of peace and happiness. Just at that time, Francis Xavier and the Jesuit missionaries came to our shore. The good tidings brought by these earnest missionaries sent a thrill of joy to the hearts of the people. Princes, nobles, and the commons crowded to hear them, numbers were converted and baptized, and Catholic churches spread through the length and breadth of the land; but before long, evil days came. Instigated by the intrigues of jealous Buddhists, and enraged by some imprudence on the part of the missionaries and their converts, a fierce and long persecution ensued. Missionaries were killed and expelled, Japanese Christians had to recant, or to submit to cruel death; and during ten years of severe persecution, it is recorded that 200,000 Christians were slaughtered. Thus you will find that our disheartened nation of Japan has already sent a host of representatives to join with that glorious throng of Christian martyrs. The government of the Shogun thought it succeeded in extirpating Christianity, but she came to our shores to stay there. No human power can stop for ever the onward march of the Kingdom. The blood of martyrs is, indeed, the seed of the Church. Roman Catholicism has never become entirely extinct in Japan. It was only waiting for better days, and to-day the Romish Church numbers her converts, not by hundreds, but by thousands. The power of the government, which persecuted the early Christians of Japan, is finished for ever; but the once suppressed gospel of Christ, in its better and purer form, is being established in Japan.

For fifteen years, the Protestant missionaries were unable to find opportunities for preaching the Gospel; but since the revolution of 1867-8, the law against Christianity became slackened, and missionaries had many reasons to hope that the time had come at last, for which they had waited so long.

First Protestant Church.

In 1872, the first Protestant Church of Japan was organised at Yokohama. This was the beginning of a good harvest. Churches arose in quick succession in the different parts of the Empire, and during the last five or six years, the velocity of our progress has greatly increased, the rate being about seventy per cent. a year. The total number of evangelical churches is more than 200, and more than one half of this number are self-supporting; that is to say, do not rely on foreign funds for sustenance. Of these (namely more than 200 churches), 130 are going to unite into one body, under the name of the CHURCH OF CHRIST IN JAPAN. Many leading men among us have been desirous of forming a union of churches, untrammelled by complicated creeds and forms. Sectarianism is a *disgrace* to Christianity. If it be possible, we want to be delivered from this special evil. The committee appointed last year to draw up a new constitution, as the basis of the union, have completed their work. This new constitution will be adopted in the coming month in the churches. The next council of churches is to meet in the city of Osaka in May, 1889. God forbid that this should be the final step to be taken against Sectarianism! No, we hope this is the mere beginning of our work, the formation of one solid body of Christians. What are the principles on which this new constitution is based? Broadly speaking, the principles unity in essentials, and diversity in non-essentials. Our creeds are, the Apostles', the Nicene, and the Nine Articles of Faith, adopted by the Evangelical Alliance. Our doctrinal standard, as you will see, is very simple and concise. We lay more stress on the teachings of the Bible. Our creed, perhaps, will not satisfy those who are bent on heresy hunting, but we believe that it is comprehensive enough to include all the essential points of Christian doctrines. As to our Church policy, we believe in the purity of ministers. Every ordained minister in the Church is a Bishop. The management of the general affairs of the Church will be committed, with a definite limitation, to a council, constituted of pastors and delegates. The government of each individual Church is left to its own choice, provided it makes provision to send a delegate to the council. A Church may be Presbyterian or Congregational in the management of its own affairs.

A Small Beginning.

I think I have spoken enough on the union of Churches in Japan. You will allow me now to dwell a little on the work with which I am more closely connected. The story I am going to tell you will help you to understand how Christian work is carried on in Japan. Twelve years ago, I was licensed to preach. In a year's time, I rented a small house, near a beautiful park; there, in a small room, 12 by 18 feet, encouraged and helped by my mother, I commenced to preach Sunday after Sunday. I had only three or four hearers, including my mother and my brother, to preach to on idolatry, expecting a devout Buddhist priest to come, but he did not. I preached about idolatry to my mother and brother, who constituted the congregation that day. Things went on for two years in that way, but at last our work became more encouraging. In 1880, I was able to organise a small church, with nineteen members. We soon numbered 200, and built a new church. Four ordained ministers, seven preachers, and thirteen theological students came out of that small congregation. Nearly five years ago, an American lady and her son asked me to come and explain the Bible to a few Japanese gentlemen and ladies,* whom they invited to their beautiful home, near the castle. The hospitality of the lady, and the preaching of the Word, did not fail to produce good results, and in about a year, we were enabled to organise a church, which now has about 180 members, thirty-six of whom were baptized on one Sunday. There are many open doors for Christian work in Japan. Dear friends, our infant churches are struggling onward, to promote the cause of Christ, with scanty means and feeble hands. We are trying to do all we can. It is my fervent prayer that God will put it into your hearts to help our humble efforts.

Progress of Christianity.

Another Japanese gentleman writes:—"In all respects, and especially in Christian work, our country has progressed wonderfully of late years; but while we have great hopes, we have also some fears regarding our future.

---

* This instance suggests the facilities there are for single workers, as well as families. Let such take with them the silver and gold which God has given them, and be daily " At home " for all who come to them for instruction in the truth.

"Our Church has no ritualistic tendency, but is characterized by great simplicity, and all denominations work together in the name of our Lord. The Roman Catholic and Greek Churches have missionaries, and in numbers, these two Churches are at present greater than all Protestant denominations combined. But fortunately, the more intelligent Japanese are most in sympathy with the Protestant missions, and this gives Protestanism a much greater influence in Japanese society, than either of the other churches. There are many educational institutions under the control of Christians, of which the most important are 'Mei-ji Gakuin' and 'Do-shi-sha.' These two colleges have several hundred students, and all graduates are working for the Lord. Christian associations for young men and young women have also been established, and a national Christian women's temperance union is in existence. All these institutions are Protestant.

"To-day, all missionaries, Roman Catholic, Greek, and Protestant, are allowed a fair field for their operations, and are doing all in their power to convert the Japanese to their respective Churches. In my opinion there are two chief reasons for the success of Protestantism :—(1) Circumstances were in its favour, and (2) the Protestant missions appealed most strongly to Japanese students.

"The Japanese are at present very anxious to introduce foreign elements, material and intellectual, into the country, and with this end in view, English,

German, and French are taught in our schools. But of these three languages, English is by far the most widely known, and many schools and colleges are in existence for its study. Lately, too, English reading has been introduced into the national schools. This gives an immense advantage to Protestant missions over those of the Roman Catholic and Greek Churches, whose languages—Russian and French—are as yet but little known.

"With respect to Church government, most intelligent Japanese are fully convinced of the importance of a complete separation between Church and State. After the restoration of the legitimate Imperial dynasty (which took place twenty-one years ago), Shintoism was favoured by our Government from motives of policy, but, before long, both Shintoism and Buddhism were entirely disestablished, under the pressure of advanced opinion. Under these circumstances, the Roman Catholic and Greek Churches, which unite the spiritual and temporal power under one head, are at a disadvantage as compared with Protestantism.

"Looking back only thirty years, we reach a time when Christianity was strictly prohibited, under penalty of capital punishment, and when missionaries first came to Japan, there were no links to connect them with the people; but many students who had been brought into contact with missionaries in secular work, were led to Christ, and soon became active workers and witnesses for Him among their own people.

"Our Church in Japan has no denominational history like the Western Churches, for the Japanese of every denomination work together in perfect harmony, and already several denominations have united, to form one body, called 'The United Church of Christ in Japan.' In this one body are included what were formerly the Presbyterian, German Reformed, and Dutch Reformed; and the Congregational Church is now entering into the union. A committee of the United Church and the Congregationalists have drawn up a Constitution, which will, I am confident, be accepted by all the churches of both.

"So far, all has been favourable, but there are dangers to be guarded against, for Satan is always active when God is working. Although the Christian influence gets stronger every year, it must be remembered that at present the whole Protestant population numbers only 20,000, while the whole remaining population of Japan, consisting of thirty-eight millions, are ignorant of the true light of Jesus Christ. Japan has undergone a sudden social and political change during the last quarter of a century, and, in consequence of this, the national ideas are unsettled and changing.

"The old religious systems of the country have been shaken and are falling, and the question is, 'What shall take their place?' The question is one of vital importance, for on it depends the salvation of the souls of thirty-eight millions of mankind.

"It is a remarkable feature of Japanese Christianity, that its converts are numerous among the young people, and comparatively rare among the older people. This can be accounted for by the fact that the old religions have taken deep root in the minds of these older people, and a strong anti-Christian prejudice exists among them. They do not distinguish between Roman Catholics and Protestants, and to them the name of 'Christian' recalls the long and eventful conflict between the Government and the Jesuits, which ended in cruel persecutions. They are, therefore, suspicious, and the Buddhist priests take advantage of these suspicions to alarm the people. But such misunderstandings will in time be cleared away, so long as our faith remains pure and untarnished.

"But there is another mistake current amongst the intelligent classes. In the East, the teachings of Confucius have formed the basis of morality, and this sage's teaching closely resembles that of the Greek philosophers, and treats mostly of relationships between man and man. Confucianism is, however, popular among the most educated, while the mass of the people are Buddhists. And since Buddhism, which treats of the other world, is confined to the lower classes in Japan, they conclude that Christianity, *which also treats of the other world*, must in the same way be confined to the lower classes in the West. The minds trained in the teaching of Confucius eagerly embrace the sceptical philosophy of the West, and already several books of this kind have been translated into Japanese, and are much read.

"The educated class in Japan are therefore divided into two sections—those supporting Christianity, and those opposing it—while the mass of the people are not taking either side. The future of Japan depends on which of these two sections can succeed in gaining the support of the people.

"The great need at present is to let the Japanese see that Christianity is not opposed to Philosophy and Science, and that its doctrines have reference to this world as well as that to come; that Christianity exercises an elevating and refining influence over society. When these facts are known and recognised in Japan, the time will soon come when the educated Japanese will accept the Lord Jesus Christ, and the people will soon follow.

"With this end in view, I have, with the assistance of some Christian friends, established a girls' school on Christian principles. At first we rented a small house, and commenced with ten or eleven pupils; but though it has only been in existence three years, already over fifty students have been baptized, and the school now consists of about 170 pupils. So we have reaped a rich harvest.

"My life has been spent in the political field; and I am fully convinced that I am right in working for social and political reforms, in the Christian spirit, for the good of our people.

"In 1890 we shall have our first National Assembly, and the time will be a very critical one in our history. I therefore came over to visit America and England, in order to see the working of Christian institutions in these countries. My time is limited, the task is great, and there is so much to be seen, that I feel my own weakness; but I pray the Lord for help, and trust Him for His power, and I am confident that I shall be able to gain some information which will benefit my beloved country, and the cause of our Lord Jesus Christ."

PRIVATE CREST OF THE MIKADO.

CHAPTER III.

𝔥𝔬𝔴 𝔦 𝔥𝔞𝔡 𝔄𝔠𝔠𝔢𝔰𝔰 𝔱𝔬 𝔱𝔥𝔢 𝔍𝔞𝔭𝔞𝔫𝔢𝔰𝔢.

(SUBSTANCE OF AN ADDRESS DELIVERED AT DRAWING-ROOM MEETINGS IN ENGLAND.)

"And when they were come, and had gathered the church together, they rehearsed all that God had done with them, and how He had opened the door of faith unto the Gentiles."—Acts xiv. 27.

JAPAN, as you are aware, was partially opened to the preaching of the Gospel at the close of the year 1872. Several American and English missionaries were there long before this, and they, in anticipation of the religious liberty about to be proclaimed, had utilised their time in acquiring a knowledge of the language, and in compiling a dictionary phrase book, teaching English, &c. No sooner was the edict of 300 years standing against Christianity abolished, than numbers of young and old hastened to identify themselves with the "new religion," so termed in those days. The door was now open, and the halls and rooms hired by the missionaries for the purpose of preaching (and teaching) the Gospel were filled to overflowing with eager and attentive listeners. English Bibles found a ready sale, both amongst the real inquirers and those who merely wished to know out of curiosity what this new doctrine was. Many had already read and heard of the Lord Jesus, and were prepared to accept His love and His offered salvation; but of the many who clustered round the missionary it was not surprising to me and others, who were lookers on, to find that a large proportion had merely followed in imitation of others, a thing especially characteristic of the Japanese as a people.

My own work was principally teaching. I had gone to Japan with only a few dollars in my pocket, and therefore deeply felt the need of casting all my care upon Him who was my only hope and refuge in that strange land. Blessed be His Name, He then, and since, abundantly proved the truth of the words, "*He careth for thee.*" I had made known my willingness to give up a few hours daily to teaching English, but for a time my faith was sorely tried. One day a missionary called on me, bringing with him a young ex-Daimio and his vassal, who requested that I would give them two hours' private instruction in English daily, for which they offered to pay me forty dollars a month. In this I saw the tender care of my Heavenly Father, for this liberal sum was twice as much as I should have asked had I made my own charges, and yet every dollar was needed to meet current expenses.

This introduction to my first pupil was to me like a great calm after a storm. The still small voice was ever and anon discerned by the ear of faith, saying, "It is I; be not afraid." "Fear not; for I am with thee." "I am thy shield, and thy exceeding great reward." Every cloud vanished, and every wave receded. My experience was such a striking contrast to anything I had known since I first set foot on heathen soil, that I was all praise, morning, noon and night. Finding myself thus situated was to me like a translation, for I only conceived the thought of coming to Japan a few weeks before, when, through failing health, my prospect of spending my life among the Chinese seemed well-nigh eclipsed. It was very cheering thus to see my way so soon paved by the loving kindness of the Lord, and lighted up with His favour.

I at once began giving lessons to the young man and his retainer at their hired apartments, which were supplied with easy chairs and table, for my special benefit. Every morning I was shown with great ceremony into the seat prepared for me in a chastely decorated clean room. The more I saw of my pupils the more persuaded I became of the greatness of the Japanese race, amongst whom I had now come to dwell. As I sat, day after day, teaching them, I felt that here were jewels which should sparkle in my Master's crown, and I felt it specially laid on my heart that God would open their eyes that they might see.

Access to the higher classes in Japan was then very hard to obtain, so that I felt how very important it was to use well this chance.

We studied English reading, grammar, geography, paying especial regard to English pronunciation. I found my pupils had a fair knowledge of classical Chinese, and they very gladly accepted the gift of a Chinese testament; and when we parted and closed our relationship as teacher and pupils, time after time they came the long distance of twenty miles or more to see me, bringing with them tokens of kindly feeling in the shape of specimens of the beautiful works of art with which that most interesting country abounds. More than once the gentleman invited me to his house, and there, in the presence of much that indicated rank and refinement, he treated me as an honoured guest. It was a rare thing in those days to have such an opportunity of seeing a first-class Japanese house. The simplicity, cleanliness, and artistic taste displayed in the furniture and decoration of their rooms are unique. To lay out all their ornaments, as we are in the habit of doing, would be a violation of good taste. On certain occasions—for example, when the good man of the house is expected home—some of the costliest and rarest bits, whether of china, bronze, or lacquer, are placed in his room to express joy at his return. My great longing for my pupil was that he should be led to a saving knowledge of the Lord Jesus. His imperfect knowledge of English, and mine of

Japanese, rendered an intelligent chat about the soul and its interests almost impossible; and much as I wished to convey to his mind those precious truths upon which my own soul feasted, I could only lift up my heart in earnest prayer to God that the darkness of superstitious belief might be dispelled, and that Christ, the Sun of Righteousness, might arise in his soul with healing in His wings.

On the dissolution of the feudal system, several young Daimios and their retainers flocked to the treaty ports, and some of them became my pupils. I had boys from nearly every province in the empire, most of them being the sons of the Samurai or gentry. Up to the year 1868, or thereabouts, this class was permitted to wear two swords as a mark of social distinction. After the above date, however, they exchanged their swords (speaking figuratively) for English books. They have been, and still are, the intellectual class, and correspond with the literati or Confucian school in China. Their ambition, of late years, has been to fit themselves for official appointments under the new form of Government. The desire to embrace Christianity was not so generally expressed by the Samurai; but they did not treat the Bible with indifference, for many of us were happily interrupted often by one or two at a time begging for explanation on certain passages already marked with tiny bits of pink paper. My pupils, of course, varied much in ability as well as proficiency. Some could not read words of one syllable, while others astonished me by the ease with which they could read Peter Parley's History, a book in the hand of every student of English wherever met; and in penmanship and spelling they were very expert.

The Bible, as may be supposed, occupied a prominent place in all the mission schools; and though much time had to be given to teaching English, in order to attract pupils, every teacher endeavoured to "seek first the kingdom of God, and His righteousness." Many of my pupils used to come daily to read the Bible with me after our secular studies were over, and on Sunday mornings, when we met especially for that object. Thus the Lord "*let fall handfuls of purpose for me,*" in order that I might prove afresh, and in no small degree, the faithfulness of Him whose loving hand was upon me for good. Although the outward chain by which Japan had been bound was snapped by the Government, I knew that unless the Holy Spirit made them free indeed, her people were still held captive by the bonds of sin. I therefore gratefully accepted the privilege of living amongst them, and the measure of access I already had to their hearts, as an opportunity for doing them good, and pointing them to Him, who still says, "Look unto me, and be ye saved, all the ends of the earth." "Come unto me, all ye that labour and are heavy laden, and I will give you rest." Though a perfect stranger among them, I never felt more at home than in the midst of this great people.

A variety of circumstances in my life among my new friends, seemed to echo, "He led them forth by the right way, that they might go to a city of habitation."

> *"The child of God must walk alone,*
> *If he would live and walk with Thee,*
> *And only to such hearts are known*
> *The joys of Thy blest company.*
> *Alone with Thee, O Master, where*
> *The light of earthly glory dies!*
> *Misunderstood by all, I dare*
> *To do what Thine own heart will prize."*

In a short time, a young Samurai named Hirano, came to me privately and said, "I have found Jesus. My heart is changed. I am filled with joy. It is wonderful, so unlike anything I have heretofore experienced." His face beamed as he went on thus for an hour, telling me, with tears, of his new-found treasure, and also of the compassion he had for his countrymen. "Once," said he, "I cared to come to your class to learn English only, but now my desire is to learn the Bible thoroughly, that I may go and teach it to my countrymen." I was greatly in need of a helper in my work, and he proved most efficient. I at once invited him to come and stay with me. All his spare time was devoted to Bible reading, and it seemed to me to be the dawn of better things for Japan, as I watched him daily poring over its contents. He occupied himself principally in writing out hymns in his clear copperplate hand for my work among the English sailors. He always accompanied me to our Gospel meetings ashore and afloat, and it cheers my heart when I think what those meetings must have proved to his hungry soul.

Having given the clearest proofs of the reality of his conversion, our sea-faring brethren gave him the right hand of fellowship, and gladly welcomed him to the Lord's table. It was an unspeakably blessed privilege to obey our risen Lord's command, "*This do in remembrance of* ME," by meeting together in my parlour on many a Sabbath evening. We indeed worshipped! Not a doubt had we that our once crucified and now exalted Lord accepted the praise which we were enabled to offer by the help of the Holy Spirit.

About a year after his conversion, Mr. Hirano showed signs of rapid consumption. He then went to his relatives, thinking a change of air might do him good, but it proved unavailing. "To depart, and to be with Christ," was his chief desire; and such being the case, he felt careful, lest any of His commands should not be obeyed. "He that believeth and is baptized," rivetted his attention, as it does that of all who search the word of God for themselves. He and his uncle came the distance of eighteen miles, to ask if I would baptize him, as it was through me he had "learnt the way." I told him women did not baptize, but that it would be easy to find a missionary who did, provided he really desired it. "The doctor says I cannot live much longer, and I am anxious to have it attended to directly," he remarked. "Will you be able to come up to my uncle's on such a day, and at such an hour?" To this I assented, and went over on the given day, and saw him surrounded by a number of his unconverted relatives, and a few Christian natives. A godly American missionary baptized him in the name of the Father, and of the Son, and of the Holy Ghost. I shall never forget the calmness with which he spoke of his approaching decease, and the joy it gave him, that so positive a command was at last complied with. A few days after, he wrote me the following letter:—

"My dear Teacher,

"I thank you for your kindness. I feel happy in Jesus every day. There is nothing pleases me only God's Word. I feel little better. I have heard from Amah (a woman servant) you do not feel well. I hope you get well soon. Please give my kindest respects to your dear sister. My uncle thanks you for sending Amah with the presents.

"Your affectionate Scholar,
"K. Hirano."

I was not at the bedside of my beloved pupil when he departed to be with Christ, but the friend who baptized him told me that his short life of testimony, and last hours, left, he believed, a lasting impression on some of his relatives.

Many of my pupils from time to time gave evidence that the truths they studied were influencing their lives; but, as I saw comparatively little of them, and could not then talk with them in their own tongue, I transferred them to some of the missionaries who could. Most of these were received by baptism into one or other of the different denominations, and showed by their lives the reality of their profession.

May many more labourers be sent to proclaim the glorious Gospel and its saving power in Japan; for the command was given with reference to that deeply interesting country, as well as to this, " Go ye into all the world, and preach the Gospel to every creature."

My experience in Japan began, as I have said, soon after the country was opened up to Western civilisation, so that I had as good an opportunity as any of seeing the eagerness with which the Japanese learn from Europeans. Money spent on the education of their children was, in their opinion, money saved in a twofold sense. The only fault ever found with me by the parents of my resident pupils was, that I charged too little for my services; but then they were rich merchants, and money with them was no object so long as their interests were furthered. Avarice is not the vice in Japan that it is in China; and so far as my dealings with them are concerned, I found the Japanese to be as honourable and generous-hearted as any Europeans within my range of acquaintance.

The friendship and confidence which spring up

between teacher and pupil in England are apparent also in Japan. It is more an Eastern than a Western custom to bring offerings to favoured friends. These are always offered with ceremony; and to appear otherwise than grateful and cordial in the acceptance of them would not only be a mark of ill-breeding, but would cause a wound which their sensitive natures would deeply resent. Handsome presents of old lacquer, bronze, china, carvings in wood and ivory, richly embroidered wrappers, webs of silk, drawings, cakes, fruit, plants, flowers, etc., are some of the things considered proper for presentation. In China, one is expected to return one half of the gifts sent. This is not the case in Japan.

Religious teaching in the government schools was then, as now, strictly forbidden; but I used to invite my pupils, at regular intervals, to my house, so as to give them opportunity for asking questions about the Scriptures; and I like to look back on the time when their eyes sparkled as light seemed to dawn on their dark but inquiring minds.

Owing to the shifting state of the country at that time (from 1872 onwards), it was very difficult to find out how deep an impression had been made on the minds of the larger number of these talented youths—each became so completely absorbed in the subject in which he wished to distinguish himself. The old adage, "Now or never," seemed to be their motto. It was touching to see how many of the most promising young men faded and drooped under the blight of consumption just when within a step of reaching the goal of their ambition.

The Japanese have been for a long time gradually paving the way for a new form of government. It is anticipated that they will soon have what will correspond to our English constitution; and many of the Japanese who are now in England, are here to learn from us what will contribute to the well-being of their country and people, in view of the approaching change. And now, February, 1889, true to promise, the news of the promulgation of the New Constitution has reached us in London.

Some of these young men, we are thankful to say, have been brought from "death unto life" through the Gospel. One of them, in the fervour of his first love, exclaims, "How nice when I can speak of the old, old story to our children in Japan, and also to the many grown people, wise in their own eyes, who constitute the intellectual class in our country!"

Is it not our privilege to plead with God on behalf of those at present at our door, that not only a few, but many may return to witness thus for Christ in their own land? May they find out that the Bible is the secret of England's greatness, and that its truths are more to be desired than gold; yea, than much fine gold.

CONVERSION.

I have already referred to a young Daimio (feudal prince), who came to me immediately after my arrival in Japan, and who received his first lessons in English from me. Some time after this, he went abroad to complete his English studies; whilst there the Lord was pleased to open his eyes. A short account of his conversion, as related by himself at the time, before an assemblage of people may be of interest to the reader. I give it in his own words.

* * * * *

"My dear Friends :—Please listen to me closely, because I am but a *little* child of the Christian world, and I cannot speak your language well. I was brought up among the heathen, did not know about Christianity but a little. I have been in this country little more than two years. I came here to get a knowledge of worldly culture, but not the knowledge of divine truth. I was placed under the influence of religion. I became soon interested in the Bible, which I read every morning, and studied almost every Sabbath. The more I studied it, the more I liked it; but during the two years I liked it not as *divine truth*, but as a moral code. Dear Christian friends, how can anyone understand the Bible with such a narrow view? He may pretend that he can understand, but it is all false; and so I went on, but not without some desire of becoming a Christian. Lately, my interest in religion was greatly increased, and I tried to attend the meetings as often as I could. On Tuesday night, week before last, after the meeting was over, I was brought to the enquiry meeting, and there one of the ministers talked with me very kindly about Jesus. He asked me how I felt. The light of the Bible seems to me like the 'sun covered with clouds. After talking a while, the minister offered a prayer for me, and asked me to pray. O my friends, I made an unreasonable excuse, I said that I could not speak English well enough to pray; but I went home with much interest, but still cloudy. Thursday was an impressive time to me. My desire to become a Christian increased very greatly. That night, when I was going home from the meeting, I was unexpectedly brought into the presence of the pastor of this Church. The clouds of my heart were then somewhat scattered, a beam of true light became almost visible to me, but still I was not a Christian. I will now tell you the hardest thing which I have ever experienced in my life in the matter of religion. When the preaching was over on Friday night, Mr. ——— asked those who believed in Christ to rise and sing, and those who did not believe in Him to keep their seats. This sharp voice pierced through my heart. I desired to rise and present myself a Christian, but O my friends, the wounds of my sin were too severe for me to stand up; and so I sank into a miserable state of despair. Are there any here who heard that precious voice that night? After the benediction was pronounced, a grey-haired gentleman addressed me very kindly, and prayed to God for me. He asked me to pray, so I prayed with all my heart. Dear friends, do you not remember the excuse of Tuesday night for not praying? Do you think I made a great improvement in English from Tuesday night to Friday night? No; it was not the improvement in the language, but the improvement in heart. After that, I went home, and soon retired to my room. After a short and restless sleep, I awoke, and the struggles of belief and doubt tortured my weak heart; so I was troubled a great deal for perhaps one hour. Then I thought while I am struggling in my own strength, I cannot see the light. I must cast away my own poor reasoning, and simply trust in Christ. So I tried to cry out, 'I am a Christian. Rejoice! rejoice!' I repeated it over and over. Behold, the unclean clouds of the earthly storm were swept away by the mighty current of the celestial air! The sparkling light of the spiritual sun shone into the depth of my heart! A cry of joy sprang up out of my lips! Claps and cheers indicated the happiness of a new-born infant! After a few minutes, I sprang up, and gave thanks to God for his forgiveness of my sin. Dear friends, I cannot tell you the hundredth part of that joy. I believe it is impossible to tell. I myself am a poor miserable sinner. I must tremble at death unless I have my Saviour through whom I can utter the happy cry, 'I am a Christian.' My friends, I do not care whether you will remember the story of my experience or not; but I entreat you most earnestly that you should not forget to think about the operation of the Holy Spirit. The week before last, struggling in my feeble heart, I stood trembling on your side, but now, under the great power of the Holy Spirit, I stand rejoicing before the smiling countenance of the Almighty" . . . . . .

Having heard, indirectly, of his conversion, I wrote to congratulate him. The following is an extract from the letter I had in reply:—

"Please allow me to return my sincere thanks for your kindness in writing so soon after you heard of my conversion. How can I express the deep gratitude which I felt for your warm-hearted acknowledgment of my becoming a servant of our Divine Master, and for your rich instruction for my duties in my new life? I feel so thankful to find in your letter that since I was first introduced to you, and instructed in the English language, you have regarded me as your pupil, and have kept your sincere desire for my conversion in your unceasing prayers; even asking your friends to pray for me. Let me now answer your request about my interest in the Christian religion. When at home (in Japan), I felt no opposition: I recollect you gave me a small Bible, and a story of the Bible for children. After I arrived in this country, I, through the family I am staying with, became interested in Christianity, and tried to understand its principles. Though I saw very good moral teaching in them, yet it was difficult for me to believe in the reality of eternity, which is not in Confucius's classics, in which I was taught from my childhood. For two years, I was in the same condition in regard to religion, though increasing in delight and interest. I felt nothing more joyful in my life than the time I found the true light, and offered a prayer in the name of my Saviour. Since then, I have had no doubts at all. I praise God I was brought to His presence, as a new-born child in Christ, and that He heard the voices of His disciples for my salvation. I pray Him, that by His grace, I may be strengthened. . . . Pray for Japan, that she may be Christianised; and for me, that I may do something for my countrymen. I am thankful for your patient work in Japan, and also that among the sailors of the different men-of-war stationed there. God bless you, wherever you may be."

SAMURAI, OR GENTLEMAN OF FEUDAL TIMES.

CHAPTER IV.

𝔈xtracts from the 𝔏etters of a 𝔍apanese 𝔖tudent at 𝔈ambridge.

"*Cast thy bread upon the waters: for thou shalt find it after many days.*"—Eccles. xi. 1.

BEFORE CONVERSION.

"DEAR Mrs.——* I received your letter dated 22nd. ... I read it with the greatest attention and interest. It is really too kind of you thus to think of me, a poor stranger from the East. But what shall I say in answer to your Christian and noble utterances, to deny or ignore a word of which seems to me as trying as to disobey the tender words of gentle parents? A whole week had already passed since I received and read your letter, and I read and re-read it many a time, and buried myself in profound contemplation about

---

* A lady in London who took deep interest in his spiritual welfare.

the grand problem over and over again; and yet I cannot say,

> "'Am I a soldier of the Cross,
> A follower of the Lamb;
> And shall I fear to own His cause,
> Or blush to speak His name?'

"I am reading the Holy Bible day by day as ever, and find it a book of deep interest and valuable information.

*   *   *   *   *

"Since I wrote to you last, I have made the acquaintance of some more friends, who are all true Christians, filled with noble sentiments, and acting towards others with disinterested kindness. I value and enjoy the friendship of these people; often I have earnest talk with them of Christ and the Revealed Religion, and prayer afterwards. Thus, as you see, I am in no way neglecting the search after the truth of the Christian religion, and with earnestness of purpose and humility of heart I am doing it. But, alas! my mind is still not cleared from its manifold doubts and difficulties. I often feel I am like a solitary ship in a wild and boundless sea. At times I think I see a haven, distant and yet not dim. Soon night comes, and all is dark again. Lo! I see a light on yonder shore. I cry; the waves dash, and the winds howl. All is lost; and I stand mute and half in despair! Such, dear madam, is often the state of my mind. Yet, believe me, I have not yet thrown off all my efforts in utter despair, nor ever shall. In this age of progress, when the minutest details of sun, moon, and stars are clearly known by the aid of ever-increasing knowledge, it surely is, or at least it seems to me to be, an apparent anomaly that man knows so little of himself! Why are we here? Whence did we come? Whither are we going? These are questions asked again and again, and still no satisfactory answer, for aught I know, seems to have been given by human wisdom. We are, after all, frail and ignorant beings, born yesterday and to-morrow in the grave." . . . . .

NOTE.—I met the writer of this after my arrival in England in the autumn of 1881. He was then deeply engrossed in intellectual pursuits, and did not seem to care much to turn his attention to that which became so dear to him little more than a year after, *i.e., the study of the Bible.* His preference for the society of intelligent and cultivated persons enabled me to introduce him to many such among Christians. Some of these took a very deep interest in him, and in a short time he became a Bible student. While at Cambridge it was evident that God was graciously dealing with him; but to light and liberty he remained a stranger till it pleased God to send Mr. Moody there in 1882. The result of that visit will be better expressed in my friend's own words.

"*They looked unto Him, and were lightened: and their faces were not ashamed.*"—Ps. xxxiv. 5.

AFTER CONVERSION.

CAMBRIDGE, *Nov.* 28, 1882.

"DEAR Miss——. The young Japanese of whom you have heard is myself. Ever since I came to this country (England), I have been entertaining *in my heart*, a great interest in the Gospel of the Kingdom of God. . . . 'Seek, and ye shall find.' Thank God I have found the dear Saviour, and nothing shall take Him away from me. Life indeed has a new meaning, and existence a new purpose. When I came back to my rooms, after having heard, and also talked to, Mr. Moody, the first thing I did was to put down the following words in my diary: 'I was dead till to-day. To-day I was born again. Henceforth I shall stand firmly under Christ's cross, and shall be ready to fight any battle against Satan and all his hosts.'

"My conversion, as I think was the case with many of the undergraduates, was a slow and gradual process. When I went, for the third time, to hear the earnest appeal of Mr. Moody, he said to us: 'Who among you, tell me, will stand up for Jesus?' I (moved by the Spirit of the Lord) raised my right hand, and exclaimed, 'I will!' Oh, it was such a heart-thrilling moment, the final moment of decision, the first beginning of a new existence! The night was cold and chilly, and yet all the way to my rooms my cheeks were hot as if in flame, and I felt as if my heart and soul were in utter joy, at having at last found a *long-missed friend.* I cannot understand how you managed to hear so soon of my conversion. I spoke to Mr. Moody of your pupil, Mr. O——. Perhaps *he* wrote and told you. However it may be, I know it is the angel, who indirectly carried the message to you! For, 'is there not joy in the presence of the angels of God over one sinner that repenteth?'"

Again he writes: . . . "I am going to see a clergyman to-morrow. I have accepted Christ as my personal Saviour, and my Lord God, just as I was, poor in heart and helpless. As yet I have learnt, it may be, but a thousandth part of what is still to be learned in future, by the grace of our Father, and by the help of the Holy Spirit. The divine truth is so immeasurably deep, that we learn more and more of it every day of our life; and after death, I feel sure we all shall learn still more."

Shortly after his conversion he went to Germany. While there, the Lord was graciously pleased to use him in bringing one, at least, of his countrymen to a saving knowledge of the truth as it is in Jesus. Opportunity was given him, among several Japanese and others there, of witnessing a good confession. On his way back to Japan, he wrote me the following letter:—

COLOMBO, *August* 2, 1884.

. . . "I am on my way home, where I hope to be during the first week in March, when I have to begin my work in the University of Tokyo; which consists in giving lectures on political economy and finance—a task by no means easy for me. But I hope and trust in Him, who has been so good to me, and I believe He will stand by me, and help me on, not merely in giving these lectures, but also in making His name, and love, and power, known to my compatriots, who, as you know too well, are in great need of such a Saviour. Please pray for me. My old friend, and now my dear brother in Jesus, who came to the Lord in Berlin, is in Cambridge, in order to pursue the study of the Christian religion still further. Please tell me whether, and when, you intend to come back to Japan again. I shall be so pleased to see you work there for the Lord. May God open your way thereto! May He abundantly bless you in every way, and in whatever you undertake in His name, and for His glory, is the wish and prayer of yours sincerely, ―――."

I trust these few pages may serve to show that God does, indeed, own and bless every effort put forth by His children, whether at home, or in foreign lands, to lead the wandering ones to Jesus. If only we thought of the many who still are "sitting in darkness and in the shadow of death"; who have never even *heard* of the Saviour's love, would not some of us seek more earnestly than ever, to find out His will for *us?* We are nowhere so happy as in His service. Our life here is the *only* opportunity given us of winning souls for Christ! How low an estimate of His love ours must be, if we refuse to do anything for Him! And I long very much that some of the Lord's dear children would bestir themselves, on behalf of the strangers from various lands, who are here only for a short time. Who can measure the results for eternity, which, under God's blessing, might follow simple, kindly efforts made on their behalf?

> *"Call them in"—the poor, the wretched,*
> *Sin-stained wanderers from the fold:*
> *Peace and pardon freely offer;*
> *Can you weigh their worth with gold?"*
>
> *"Call them in"—the Jew, the Gentile;*
> *Bid the stranger to the feast.*
> *"Call them in"—the rich, the noble,*
> *From the highest to the least.*

CHAPTER V.

Japan pleading with England to be reconciled to God.

A Sermon preached by a Japanese Student at Cambridge.

"At that time ye were without Christ."—Eph. ii. 12.
"Look unto me, and be ye saved, all the ends of the earth."—Isa. xlv. 22.

I CANNOT find words to express what my heart feels, on this, to me, most solemn, as well as very pleasing occasion, when, for the first time in my life, I am permitted to stand up before you, my fellow Christians, to preach Christ, to testify what he has done for the soul of a poor and helpless sinner, who, for these many years, was walking according to the course of this world, without the Saviour, without the Comforter, without the Life, without the Lord our God to serve; in a word, without Him who is all in all to us sinners; even Jesus Christ. Dear brethren, I would ask you to pay a brief, but earnest attention, with prayerfulness of spirit, to the few words of one who, for years past, was searching for Christ, and at last found Him; or, rather let me say, of a lost child, whom the ever-merciful Father, by His loving kindness and forbearing grace, found out and brought back to Him.

There is one thing, a very small matter in itself, yet somewhat significant to me on this occasion, which I wish to make known to you. It was just two years ago to-day that I came to this country. I can never forget the 17th December, 1880, when, after travelling over the distance of 11,000 miles, from the eastern extremity of the earth, to the western extremity thereof, I found myself, almost at this very hour of the evening, in the heart of your great metropolis. Two years have elapsed, and the same foreign sojourner, who, at that time, was without Christ, and knew nothing of the glad tidings from heaven, is now standing up amidst the happy sons and daughters of this blessed land of religion and riches, to speak of Him, and for Him, who is so dear and precious to every one of us. May it please the all-beneficent and ever-merciful Father of us all, to be present here at this moment; and may the things his humble servant utters in his name, and in his presence, go home to the innermost heart of every single soul of you assembled here this evening, and prove of spiritual benefit to your life, as faithful followers of Christ in this dark and sinful world, where, as both you and I know too well, there aboundeth on every side of us earthly pilgrims, *valleys* of sloth and carelessness, wherein our feet are too apt to fall;

and *mountains* of pride and self-satisfaction, that, but too often, conceal from our blind eyes the glory of the sacred heaven ; and *wide and crooked paths* of worldly-mindedness and vanity, that lead the passengers astray from the narrow, yet straight way, to the blessed home, where peace and holiness prevail ; and *rough places* of unbelief and sin, that must be made smooth, before the way of the Lord can be open to us. Dear brethren, I was once without Christ. My heart was full of pride, and obstinacy, and worldliness, and sin. Those valleys, and mountains, and crooked paths, and rough places, were before me, behind me, on the left and right of me. The meek, the pure, the lowly Saviour was not acceptable to me. " Look unto me, and be ye saved, all the ends of the earth." My sin was too great. I could not trust Him who thus kindly invited all the sinners of this world. But the Lord pitied me. He invited me to come to Him by day and by night. O dear brethren, I have decided for Jesus ! With holy affection I can say, " My beloved is mine, and I am his." With all my heart I can re-echo the voice of Paul, " Yea doubtless, and I count all things but loss for the excellency of the knowledge of Christ Jesus my Lord." Is there anyone here present, let me ask, who has not yet given up himself or herself to Jesus? He is beckoning you to come. He is waiting for you. He is calling you even now. " Come unto Me." " Come, for all things are now ready," saith the Lord. " Come now," saith the same heavenly voice. Alas! how often were these simple and sweet words of invitation heard and heard in vain! "Come unto Me, all ye that labour and are heavy laden, and I will give you rest." So says our Lord to you and to me, to each one of the children on earth. "Ye will not come to Me that ye might have life." Remember, brethren, without Christ we are all dead; dead in eternal death of darkness and sin. "Come near to me, I pray you." Yes, he is praying you to come near to him. Oh, what mercy! What patient, forbearing love! "Come down unto me, tarry not." Oh, do not hang back even for a moment! Again, "Come, and follow me," saith the Lord. O dear brethren, shall we not follow Him, with joyfulness and gladness of heart? Is He not the only reliable guide? Nay, is He not even the way itself? And, once more, "Wherefore He is able to save them to the uttermost, that come unto God by Him, seeing He ever liveth to make intercession for them." Thus saith an inspired apostle. These are only a few of the many and various royal invitations of the Lord our God, who is ever anxious to save even one sinner. There are more if you open your Bible and look for them. No doubt you have heard all of them, at one time or another, since your childhood, from the lips of your ministers, or otherwise, and now you have heard many of them again from the mouth of one who was brought up in a heathen land, and who, but a little while ago, was buried in spiritual darkness, and was full of enmity against

God. May you hear more of them in the time to come! These are blessed and precious words. They ought not to lose their value by becoming familiar to one's ears. Dear brethren, I heard all these invitations. I heard them constantly, within the last two years particularly. Yet, forgive me, O God; for a long time I was perfectly dead. Long before this, the devil had seized me. He appeared in a beautiful and enchanting form, and untiringly suggested one excuse and another. He even quoted Scripture. Dear brethren, I am not speaking in vain and meaningless metaphor; all this, to a believing Christian, is a dread reality, as real as that you are there, as real as that I am here. So real it is, that devils are always and everywhere trying to persuade men to ignore, nay, hate God and His Word. They may be sitting by your side at this very moment. They may, unless you are on your guard, even steal away your hearts which you have already given to Jesus, your heavenly Bridegroom. Well, the devil, I was saying, even quoted Scripture —I mean, he tried to persuade me there are so many contradictions in the Bible, and that the whole Book is nothing but a record of mythical story, or an account of old traditions that is not worthy of any serious thought; that religion, in fact, is a thing of the day before yesterday, that ought not to trouble any sensible man of this age of discovery and progress. Alas! how many in heathen countries, and how many also in Christian lands there are at this very moment listening to these seductive and dangerous words, and thus going astray from the home of our Father! Poor souls! their apparently bright and pleasant life is nothing but a dark and dreadful death in disguise. They think they see, but their eyes are blind. Sooner or later they must tumble down on the desolate and dusky ground. O my fellow Christians, shall we not endeavour to bring back those misled children to their and our own Father's happy home?

I was telling you how the devil was trying to persuade me. To some extent I will confess to you I yielded to the cunning persuasion. With eagerness I got hold of many books written by infidel writers against the sacred Bible, and against Christianity, and perused them with a certain relish. I joined also a society in London which met every alternate Sunday evening, with the object, as it was called, of spending the dull Sunday evening in a lively and more profitable way, and the members of it—sixty or seventy in number—were naturally, most of them, men without Christ. Remember, I did all this without taking any trouble to read even one book of the Bible, and without taking the trouble of going to the House of God. All this, I feel sure, was the work of devils; but, like the work of devils, it was soon destroyed by the power of one who is superior to all, in love as well as in strength. After a time, there arose a curiosity in me to know, by my own effort and enquiry, what kind of a book this Bible, against which I read and heard so much, could really be. I read, first, the four Gospels, chapter by chapter, and day by day. That which was a mere curiosity at first, now gave place to a real interest, and an increasing desire to learn more and more. I proceeded then to the several Epistles, and went on, and on, with a humble spirit, to be taught the truth, and nothing but the truth. The whole of the New Testament was thus read through in a short space of time. Then I began with the Old Testament. But it was not necessary to finish the whole of it before God opened my eyes to the solemn truth. "Look unto Me, and be ye saved, all the ends of the earth." I looked up unto Jesus, and in Jesus, and in none else, I found my personal Saviour, and I thanked God and rejoiced with joy unspeakable and full of glory. In Jesus Christ I have discovered the true Son of God, who came down upon the earth to live, even as a Man of sorrows and acquainted with grief, and to die a death of shame, in order to restore lost sinners to His, your, and my Father. Verily, "He was wounded for our transgressions, He was bruised for our iniquities." Oh, what shall we do to thank Him for this wonderful work of self-sacrifice and love? Believe on Him, brethren! Accept the royal invitation, "Come unto Me." And let me ask you again, is there any here among you who has not yet come to Jesus? "At that time ye were without Christ." Is there any among you of whom this can be said

now, as it could be said of me but a little while ago? Come to Him just as you are. "It is finished." So saith the Lord, even on the cross of Calvary. Have Him as your own personal Saviour. Have Him, and you will have with Him a new and real existence. Permit me to read to you what I wrote down in my diary on the day when I decidedly came to Christ. I wrote down this:—
"Until to-day I was dead; to-day I was born again. From henceforth I shall be ready to fight any battle under Christ's banner, against Satan and all his hosts!" Since that day Christ is revealing to me more and more of Himself and His boundless love, and He is becoming more and more dear to me. "Seek, and ye shall find." The promise of our Lord is ever faithfully fulfilled. Depend, brethren, on every promise the Lord has made. There is nothing so sure and unchangeable as God's own eternal promise. Jesus Christ—the same yesterday, to-day, and for ever. I have spoken long enough. Before I conclude, however, let me remind you once more how dear and precious Christ is to us. At this time of the holy season of the Advent, it is but proper for you to meditate earnestly and profoundly on Him. Consider prayerfully, in the depths of your heart, what were the good tidings of great joy which the angels delivered to the poor shepherds of Bethlehem keeping watch over their flocks by night. Almost 2,000 years have passed since then; but if you really and honestly love our Saviour, the

tidings of His birth here on earth are, and cannot but be to you to-day the good tidings of great joy they were to those poor shepherds then. O brethren, you cannot ponder too much on this grand and glorious subject. Have Christ for your Master. Walk always after Him. Ever love Him. Ever serve Him with all your heart, with all your soul, and with all your mind, and with all your might. Do this, brethren, and He will never forget or desert you. When distress or affliction visits you, when you mourn over the loss of any you have loved, or when health fails you, and you are stretched on a sick bed, weak and helpless; when earthly friends desert you; when the hopes of your young days are blighted; when all seems dark and dreary, and a heavy cloud of perplexity hangs over your head, call on the blessed name of Jesus, and He is ever ready to come to you, and comfort and relieve you. I love to sing these lines:—

> "Oppressed with noon-day's scorching heat,
>   To yonder Cross I flee,
> Beneath its shelter take my seat,
>   No shade like this for me.
>
> "Beneath that Cross clear waters burst,
>   A fountain sparkling free,
> And there I quench my desert thirst,
>   No spring like this for me.
>
> "For burdened ones a resting-place
>   Beside that Cross I see;
> Here I cast off my weariness,
>   No rest like this for me."

Amid the wild storms of life's rough sea here below, that we must pass through at one time or another, who is it, tell me, who can say, "Peace, be still"?

Read daily the Word of God. Whatever may be your profession in life, submit to the good, and perfect, and acceptable will of God. "Not my will, but thine be done!" In these sad and sublime words, which our Saviour uttered in the hour of his agony, He taught us how we children of God ought to be obedient to our Father's will. Whatever you do, do it for Christ's sake, and for Christ's glory; and if you really work for Him, nothing, we are assured, shall be impossible. "Who is he that overcometh the world, but he that believeth that Jesus is the Son of God?" Cling, then, to Him, always. What is there to fear, if we are with Him. Have Christ, and you are saved eternally. Who, or what, can take away from you the faith, the strength, the peace, the light, the hope, and the joy, of the everlasting life which you possess, even now! Who but a Christian can exclaim in triumph, "O death, where is thy sting? O grave, where is thy victory?" What more can you need? What more can you desire? What would you not do for Christ, who gave you all this? "At that time ye were without Christ." What a dreadful state, even to think of! Make sure, my beloved brethren and sisters, to have Christ in your heart, and that your love for Him is a true and living love, showing itself in works of faith, and labours of self-denial. Christ gave Himself for us. What would you give to Him? Oh, be steadfast and immovable in your faith; forget not for a moment, what a grand and glorious thing it is to be called the children of God. "At that time ye were without Christ." You cannot do without Christ. Stand for Him, live for Him, work for Him, suffer for Him, and if need be, die for Him. Never forsake Him.

God forbid that it should be said of a single soul among you assembled here this evening, "At that time ye were without Christ."

" Look unto Me, and be ye saved, all the ends of the earth." So says our Christ. Oh, be you saved, be saved, by all means!

Now to God the Father, Son, and Holy Spirit, the God of Holiness and Love, the God of the Bible, be honour and glory, for ever and ever Amen.

CHAPTER VI.

An Awakening among Blue-Jackets.

The awakening among the sailors commenced in Shanghai in 1872, when two missionary ladies, having deeply felt the need of a revival in their own souls, and the power of the Holy Ghost for the conversion of the unsaved around them, waited on God until the need felt was supplied exceeding abundantly above all they could have asked or thought.

The way in which I, for one, became a happy sharer in this blessed work, was first of all through the visit to Yokohama of H.M.S. *Cadmus* from Shanghai, and subsequently of many other American and English men-of-war, on which blessing had rested (*see Appendix*).

SUBSTANCE OF AN ADDRESS GIVEN AT DRAWING-ROOM MEETINGS IN LONDON.

"Be not afraid, but speak, and hold not thy peace: for I am with thee, and no man shall set on thee to hurt thee: for I have much people in this city."—Acts xviii. 9, 10.

IT is to me like a refreshing breeze on a sultry summer's day, to recall the good use both sailors and marines made of a room, which I set apart for them, in my little home at Yokohama. The voice of prayer and praise was heard there, generally, between the hours of 3 and 9 p.m., when the few or many dropped in, as their "leave" permitted. All of a sudden, I felt introduced to an atmosphere of life and power, which I had not before, or since, witnessed. The work spread from ship to ship, and not only did the captains of vessels permit me to have Bible readings on board, but the men were allowed special leave to visit me at my own house.

When a sailor breaks his leave, he has to pay the penalty by being denied the privilege of coming ashore for a given time, and under certain circumstances, the transgression may lead to his confinement as prisoner. In those days there was but little of this among a certain "set." Under the sobering and solemnizing power of the Holy Spirit, they were true and faithful in the carrying out of their respective obligations, and with a purer and stronger motive than formerly, fulfilled them to God, and not unto men. Of this their officers took knowledge, and attributed it to the "influence brought to bear upon them on shore."

One day is remembered by me with the freshnes of yesterday. When the late Lady Parkes, wife of the late Plenipotentiary to Japan, and latterly to China, stopped her carriage in the street to tell me, with an air of gratification and satisfaction, that the captain of H.M.S. *Thalia*, while dining at the Legation the previous evening, had told her, that since he had entered the navy, he had not had *such an easy time of it as then*, more especially as it was Christmas, a season when defaulters' names are numerous on the non-commissioned officer's list; for, said he, "It was the first time a clean sheet was brought before me" (*i.e.*, no culprits among his men). I could only praise God, and ascribe it all to the power of His grace, and go on in the blessed work, both ashore and afloat, with fresh heart and courage. When I say ashore, I refer to a battalion of 300 marines then stationed in Yokohama. It was much laid on my heart to visit the camp, but how to get in seemed an impossibility. Time after time I seemed like one labouring under a delusion, yet the more I mused, the more the fire burned. For days I felt captive bound to the throne of grace, for light and permission to act, when at length, the words of the Lord to the apostle Paul, on a perplexing occasion, came with convincing power: "Be not afraid, but speak"; and again: "Go with the name of Jesus to the dying." Very soon, I found myself in the presence of the Colonel of the battalion of marines, who received me most cordially, on being introduced by a lady friend of his own, who accompanied me.

The Colonel felt both surprise and pleasure at my request for his permission for having Bible classes among his men. He said, "The spiritual charge of the battalion was in the hands of the chaplain, and if he were willing to grant permission, he (the Colonel) would give orders at once, to get the lecture-room ready for me, as often as I wished to have it." Without any loss of time, I called on the Chaplain, making known to him my desire to have Bible readings with the marines, to which he at once responded with kindness and cordiality, adding that he hoped I should be more successful than he was, for, after several attempts to get them together for Bible study, his only audience on each occasion was "the orderly, big Bible, and two penny candles." When he had commended me and my happy project to God in prayer, I left, feeling the Lord's hand with me for good. The Colonel, on hearing that I had the Chaplain's consent, sent me a note stating the pleasure he felt in placing the lecture-room at my disposal, on every Tuesday and Friday evening, as desired. The following Tuesday found me seated with some thirty or forty of the marines, and a few blue-jackets. A zealous American missionary lady accompanied me, and played some inspiring hymns on the harmonium. We read that evening, from Luke xix., the story of Zacchæus. That same evening, God was pleased to clothe the Word with power, and use it to the conversion of some of those present. It seemed that all that was needful was the kindling spark, so prepared was the material for the holy flame. One of a few who stood listening at the door, was not ashamed to be seen bitterly crying, from the piercing conviction which he felt on listening to the Word; while he said he feared his case was hopeless, for of all publicans and sinners he was the chief. But the Word which condemned, also spoke peace to the troubled soul. Next day he came with others to see me, declaring, with sunlit face, that the darkness had passed, and that the true light was now shining.

The fields on every hand are white to the harvest, and our duty does not *so much* lie in pleading with others to go and labour, as in our choice we are apt to make mistakes; but in *praying the Lord of the harvest that* HE *would send forth labourers into* HIS *harvest*. God is in all directions looking for men and women who count not their own life dear to them, and who count all things loss for the excellency of the knowledge of Christ; who desire nothing so much as to make known the savour of His name, whose attitude of soul is "Here am I; send me."

My memory goes back at this moment to a band of twenty or more men, whose field of action was their ship, a spot where they had to wage war with the foe face to face, from early dawn till late.

"None can be a hypocrite on board a man-of-war," said a sailor one day, referring to the red-hot tests brought to bear upon them in their respective posts. The privilege and duty of witnessing for Christ acted on them as steam to an engine, impelling them forward despite adverse circumstances. Oh, how thoroughly they stood out at once for Christ! And how squarely and fairly they turned their backs on the world and faced Christ! Thus, by gazing and looking unto Him, they were lightened, and their faces were not ashamed. The lecture-hall, full with 200 or more men, also comes before my mind, as I reflect on the work of grace which was witnessed in Yokohama in those days, when the groans and sighs of the distressed souls gave place to the songs of liberated captives. "I will praise Thee, for Thou hast loosed my bonds."

By the power of the Holy Ghost, nets were dragged to shore full of great fishes ; for they soon became fishers of men themselves, and used to compare notes between the great vices and sins from which they had been delivered, and the great love which saved them. Night after night, that band of freed men marched from my door to their respective vessels, singing as redeemed ones only can sing, "Sweeping through the gates," "Safe in the arms of Jesus," "Jesus paid it all." Many would rush to their doors, and throw open their windows, to catch the refrain of these immortal songs of men, who were no longer drunk with wine, but filled with the Spirit, singing and making melody in their hearts to the Lord. Many objected to this new form of revelry; while, with others, it passed as "Jack's" mode of letting off steam. But to me it was the "Hosanna to the Son of David," which of old rivetted His ear, and of which He said, "If these were to hold their peace, the very stones would cry out."

It is not necessary, that I should turn over the photographs I possess of my dear sailor friends, to recall the face of one, who on meeting me, one day, and saluting me, said, "Miss, I could not keep in my hammock last night, the love of the Lord made me that happy, that I had to 'turn out,' and pace the deck all night."

It is indeed soul-reviving, to see, in the retrospect,

many of these dear men forming themselves in groups close to the houses of landsmen, in order to herald the Gospel message in peals of song. But the record of those red-letter days is on high; we can at best but touch the surface, and that *only* to declare the praises of Him, to whom be the glory now and for ever.

* * * * *

The following lines in acrostic, composed by a sailor on board H.M.S. *Thalia*, were given me by the Christians on board, when they left Yokohama.

Time's chariot swiftly bearing us—His smiling face to see,
Has in the past deep impress left, sweet to our memory.
A backward look to view the scene, and great that mystic sight,
Life issuing forth in victory, dispelling nature's night.
In all life's wanderings will we cherish dear,
A name by Him so blessed, to us so dear.

* * * * *

"Offer unto the Lord thanksgiving; and pay thy vows unto the most High."

On every Sunday evening, weather and "leave" permitting, the party, which soon became styled "the Christian band," were in the habit of meeting for the express purpose of remembering the Lord's death among themselves. The simplicity of this meeting had a beauty of its own, which I find it impossible to describe. They met *in the name of Jesus*, and His alone, and I always felt it a privilege to be permitted to be one with them. In the light of the Holy Spirit, shed on them at that time abundantly, they saw from the written Word, that the believers' feast should not be cumbered with the "stand in awe" of sacerdotalism, nor be desecrated by recognising as one with them those who gave no sign, and made no profession of having "passed from death unto life," who could not say, "The Spirit itself beareth witness with our spirit, that we are the children of God."

This form of worship was as spontaneous and as free as air. There was no strained teaching or exercising of gift, but worship, prayer and praise out of the fulness of each heart. We imitated no party of Christians, although we did not escape being dubbed *Plymouthists* occasionally. But it was a *bonâ fide* children's reunion, where the Elder Brother seemed to say, "Children, have ye any meat?" Our souls responded, "Lord, evermore give us this Bread."

One touching incident worthy of note might be mentioned here, if only to show the reality of the Divine presence among us. One sailor brother, in a moment of unwatchfulness, yielding to temptation on board his ship, left himself open to the reproof of his brethren, as well as to that of a self-accusing conscience. On a Sunday evening, when, as was their wont, he and a roomful of his shipmates came to remember Jesus in his dying love, I observed him rise and retire to an adjoining room; and while we sat and feasted in the presence of the King together, we overheard the agonizing sobs of our repentant brother, reminding us of Peter, when the eyes of his suffering Master fell on him, and he went out and wept bitterly. It was to myself, and to us all, a lesson never to be forgotten; and though the lesson was dearly bought at the expense of the Master's honour, yet we understood each other, while we said, "Blessed fall, that has left us such an example of self-discipline!"

No doubt the reader would like to ask the writer what it was that led to so singular a manifestation of unity and whole-heartedness among those young recruits. The simple and only answer to the question is, that they inscribed "JESUS ONLY!" on their banner, as in practical acts they had each day to take up the Cross and step in His footprints: their circumscribed quarters on board forming the arena on which they had to run their race, play their part, and go outside the camp unto Christ, bearing His reproach. They had often read the fascinating stories of the three companions, who were thrown into the seven times heated furnace, and of the man who was confined with the lions; but now they had true experience of their meaning, while others had opportunity of looking on, and learning that "no other god than the God of Shadrach, Meshach and Abed-nego could deliver after this sort."

Before their conversion many of them were given to the two common, evil practices of smoking and drinking. On one occasion a band of twenty or more took their stand in front of the British Legation in Yokohama to sing some of their favourite hymns, by way of saying, "Thank you," and bidding

'Farewell" to the inmates—the late Sir Harry and Lady Parkes—who were removing to their new house in Tokyo the capital of Japan *(see Appendix)*. Sir Harry, yielding to his characteristic good-nature and large-heartedness, begged that the serenaders might be served with refreshments; but on no account would we allow our mode of saying "sayonara" (good-bye) to impose on them thus. The sailors were so happy to have this opportunity of telling in their simple way that they recognised in dear Sir Harry and Lady Parkes the friends whom God had raised for them on a foreign shore: they were also glad of an additional opportunity of showing they had abandoned wine and tobacco, and that "*All for Jesus*" was their motto. In vain Sir Harry, in his bright, cheery manner laughingly pleaded that "tobacco was good for sailors" being "anti-scorbutic!"

They also added, "The day on which we received Christ, *grog, tobacco,* and *pipe* were flung overboard." Thus they saw the way in which they had to "cleanse themselves from all filthiness of the flesh and spirit," dispensing thus with indulgences, if not with vices, which prove so detrimental to a flourishing Christian life in the case of many. The Word of God was their meat and their drink, the man of their counsel, and by it they became rooted and grounded, and like trees planted beside a river.

It is not needful to say that the Church afloat had power, and prevailed at the throne of grace; the bedside of a sick messmate, where they ministered the Word, proved a wide and effectual door of usefulness, as they went from ward to ward in the little hospital for naval men. They had also a lively sense of the danger of becoming self-sufficient and leaning on any human arm.

One who had devoted her time to sailors at Shanghai once cautioned them thus against leaning on false supports. Instead of spending her time with them, as was her wont, she sent them the following letter:—

"My dear Friends,

"I feel strongly led to leave you this evening to yourselves. I think this first day of the week a fitting time to begin a season of prayer; indeed, I would venture to say that the whole week of evening hours might be thus spent before God with the certain result of much blessing; I will join you in spirit. I am certain that it is not *talking*, *teaching*, or even *reading* of the Scriptures that is of first consequence, it is the condition of heart which is indispensable to our taking the impression which the Holy Spirit has to make. Thus the soul would go on to apprehend divine things for which it has been apprehended, so that coming to stand-still points in our Christian life should never characterize us; so only will it come true for us; "The path of the just is as the shining light, that shineth more and more unto the perfect day." I greatly feel the need of giving myself unto prayer; and when we are unitedly before God, to keep silent before Him, and only pray audibly when distinctly led of the Spirit to do so. Our souls need getting into a prostrate attitude before God, refusing to rise in the strength of the flesh, but by the uplifting of the Holy Ghost. I shall be with you in spirit : may you as on outstretched wing, reach out your souls to the living God. Ever your servant, for Jesus' sake, J. ——."

This rather novel way of being received by their friend did not disturb them, but rather commended itself; for the result was an overshadowing sense of the presence of God, furthering their condition of soul, and much blessed time subsequently spent over the written word. Time after time after the vessels had left for distant shores, letters like the subjoined extracts reached us, giving us cheering accounts of some who kept on running the race, and telling of others, who, sad to say, had stumbled and fallen; but over these the Good Shepherd kept a watchful eye, for only very recently I heard of the restoration of the greater number of those belonging to one vessel, while of another band one of the men, who all along acted as spiritual father to many of his mates, and as true yokefellow in his co-operation with me, wrote as follows :—

" Though now some years have passed since last I wrote to you, yet I can assure you I have often thought and spoken of you in connection with the very, very happy time we spent together in Japan. We know the Lord was graciously pleased to stamp with his approval the feeble efforts put forth in

His name and strength, so that at the present time many who were first taught the preciousness of the name of Jesus, and the wonderful love of our God as displayed in Him, are still treading the wilderness journey with joy, and with their hearts stayed on Him, and the eye of faith looking forward and upward to the blessed resting-place above. There were some who seemed overtaken by the adversary, drawn aside from following the Lord; yet I firmly believe the Lord began a good work in them; and we know what He once sets His hands to, He will accomplish (Phil. i. 6). So we may hope the work begun at Yokohama may go on till the coming of the Lord. Since last I saw you, till the present moment, the Lord has been leading me along very tenderly and graciously. I must speak well of Him, and testify to the blessed fact that His compassions fail not, they are new every morning; great is His faithfulness. In all my wanderings and departures from Him, His grace has restored me; and in all my unfaithfulness He has proved Himself the unchanging one, the God of my salvation, and my rock of defence, and still continues to be gracious; for all the way by which He has led us tends only to increase our confidence in Him.

"Yours in Christian love."

Another of these early friends writes:—"I cannot express the joy it gave me to see your signature at the bottom of your letter; and strange to say, it was only two nights ago we were talking of you, and of your labour in Japan, and of the stormy trips to the dear old *Thalia* to convey the glad tidings to our shipmates. I felt carried back to the old spot, my birthplace, where I revelled in my first love; and although you have been lost sight of these past six years, yet both you and your dear sister have often been on our hearts. We feel very thankful to the Lord for preserving so many of our party on arriving in England, and for His sustaining grace from that time till now." . . .

Of five who for a time ran well, our friend writes sorrowfully, but believes the Good Shepherd will restore His own.

CHAPTER VII.

Bright Hours with my Pupils.

"Whatsoever thy hand findeth to do, do it with thy might."—Eccles. ix. 10.
"In all labour there is profit."—Prov. xiv. 23.

I SHALL never forget my dismay when, day by day, my adult Japanese pupils brought their "Peter Parley's History and Reader" with page after page decorated, as I at first thought, with tiny bits of red paper. "What does all this mean?" I inwardly exclaimed. A closer glance, and I at once perceived that this was one of the ways by which young Japan aided her memory. All the difficult words *only* were marked thus, and my work, of course consisted in taking my seat side by side with my pupil, as he asked me, with a princely bow, the meaning of *this* and *that* word. The explanation given was at once carefully written over each word, and the pronunciation underneath. As soon as he felt satisfied about his enunciation, he removed the bit of red paper, and went on to the next difficult word ; and this was repeated until a whole page, if not more, was gone over. He would then wind up with a succession of bows as he retired ; then, stepping into his shoes (or geta), which are always left at the door in Japan, he would make another profound bow, and trot off as happy as a child. If by any chance he should turn round at the outer gate and catch my eye, it would be to bow again. One is obliged to say to oneself, "No wonder they claim to be a cultured race, for their whole bearing suggests it."

* * * * *

Inosuke-San is announced. He bows, and says, "How do you do, madam?" "Well! How do *you* do?" He draws my attention to a prettily-trained shrub, full of tiny buds. He tells me that it is a species of plant much admired by the Japanese; that its name is "*Ume*" (plum), and the little yellow flower, which seems to be sheltered under its branches, is called the "*fuku-juso*," and, like the plum, is one of the emblems of happiness. I admired the quaint wooden flower pot, and the way in which each tender twig of the dwarfed tree was carefully trained, and twisted so as to resemble a pyramid. "In a few days," said he, "all the buds will burst, and it will then look like 'Fuji-San' (Sacred Mountain of Japan), covered at that season (January) from summit to base with snow." "It is an exact imitation of 'Fuji!' Clever contrivance!" I exclaimed, while I admiringly looked at it. I had in my little sitting-room a small American stove, so that the heat was sufficient to make "Fuji-San" in *horto* burst open in a few days into a snow-white object of attraction, while its sweet scent filled my little bungalow. But I must say that my pupil, Inosuke-San, read a little, and got assistance in learning the meaning of a few difficult words and their pronunciation before he left me. He, as well as myself, felt not a little relieved when we saw the last of a few dozen bits of red paper which illuminated one or more pages of his "Third Reader," which he carried carefully in his silk fukusa (wrapper). He, in saying good-bye, left with me a small translation of a Japanese story, which he wished me to correct by the time he paid me his next visit.

Subject—THE DOCTOR AND HIS PATIENT.

A certain person, having become ill, went to a physician, and said, "Oh! doctor, give me some physic, for I shall die of a pain in my interior." The doctor asked him what he had eaten that day. The man replied, "All I have eaten is burnt rice." The doctor carefully examined his eyes, and called out to his servant, who stood in the doorway, "Bring me the medicine for eyes!" On hearing this, the sick man cried out, "Oh, doctor, is this a time for joking! What connection is there between the eyes and a pain in the chest?" The doctor's calm rejoinder was, "I wish in the first place, to make your eyes sound. You were unable to distinguish black from white, otherwise you would never have eaten burnt rice."

Another pupil approaches me, with a few sheets

of the beautiful silky paper, used for letter writing in Japan, He bows, and says, "Please correct my theme." "With pleasure, Yamasaki-San," I reply, as I take it out of his hand.

Subject—THE NEW JERUSALEM.

"Oh, holy and pure city! which God himself governs; there is not a single bad man there, but all are true followers of Christ, who have loved Him, or who have been martyred for His sake. But in that city, their scars are washed away by the Living Fountain, and all are happy. They sit around the throne of God, and sing praises to Him. Pain and sickness cannot enter there.—Y. S."

The writer of the above had a copy of the sacred Scriptures at this time, which we read every day together.

Here comes Tawara-San. "Good mornings!" are mutually exchanged. He unties a prettily done up parcel. He bows, and says, "Pray be so kind as to accept this Japanese kasutera (cake)." I tell him it seems selfish of me to be accepting so much kindness from him, especially as it was only last week he presented me with a box of eggs. "This," he adds, "is a present from my mother, and she wished me to thank you for your teaching me so kindly." He puts his hand into his capacious sleeve, this being the pocket in Japan; he brings out a roll of silky paper, and hands it to me, saying,

"I am sorry that pressing business prevents my taking a lesson to-day, but I beg that you will correct my exercise, and I will call for it to-morrow." He then bows, and retires. Amah (servant), enters, and says, "Sensei (teacher), Terami-San called to say 'Ikaga' (How do you do?), but as you were engaged, he said he would come another day; in the meanwhile, he would feel deeply grateful to you, if you would correct the mistakes which this theme contains." She hands me the paper with a bow, which was her attempt at impersonating the absent writer—a thing she did creditably. "I wonder what the plodding Terami-San has produced," thought I to myself, as I unfolded his script.

Subject—STORY OF A MISER.

A miser said to one of his friends, "I have got a thousand dollars, which I will bury under a tree in my garden, and I will not tell this secret to any except yourself." In a short time they went out together, and buried the money under a large tree. Five or six days later, the miser went to the tree alone, but there was no money. He said to himself, "No one, except that friend could have taken it away; but if I question him about it, he will not confess." So he went to his friend's house, and said, "A great deal of money has come into my hands, which will be buried in the same place; if you can come to-morrow, at such an hour, we can go together." The friend, coveting this larger sum, replaced the money. The miser went to the spot next day, before his friend had arrived, and was delighted to find his treasure. . . . .

Temporary Appointment.

I have accepted a temporary appointment in a Government school. Some of my pupils come to see me each Sunday morning, when an opportunity offers for Bible readings in English, which they seem to enjoy. The questions they ask about the sacred Scriptures show how entangled they are in the meshes of their Shinto, Confucian, and Buddhistic theories. It is laid on my heart to pray that *Jesus*, the " *Way*, the *Truth*, and the *Life*," may soon become a living reality to them. My pupils at Nogé-Yama School are principally *Samurai*. The difference between them and the *Heimin* (common people) consists in their being more refined, and being, as a rule, book-worms. Their sketchings on the blackboards, as well as their neat figures and legible writing, give, at once, an idea of their capabilities. I am not allowed to teach the Bible during school hours, but I read it to myself at my dinner hour, when a bevy of them flock around me, to ask questions about it. I tell them it is to my soul, what the food I eat is to my body. I enjoy God's presence to such an extent in this schoolroom, that I would give the world to be able to proclaim it to the whole of Japan.

> " *Oh, this is life! Oh, this is joy!*
> *My God, to find Thee so;*
> *Thy face to see, Thy voice to hear,*
> *And all Thy love to know.*"

Many of my pupils have procured Bibles, and are reading them. They mark the difficult words with bits of red paper, and in the most courteous way, come and ask for my assistance when at my lunch; they know it to be the only hour when they can count on my help in this way; and an hour, too, at which teacher or pupil cannot be charged with transgressing the rules of the school.

A lad left a note on my table one day, stating, in broken English, what he felt too diffident to say orally, viz., "*Verily, verily, I say unto you, I believe in Jesus. I want you to baptise me.*"

"My dear Teacher," writes an invalid pupil,

"Your visit of last day made me very happy, and I am glad you love me much. I am under great obligation to you, for sending me your books often. There are many amusing stories in them. The Bible is very interesting also, and I am praying to our Lord Jesus Christ every day. I wish you to excuse me, for the letter is written very badly, and not in accordance with the rules of grammar.

"Your affectionate pupil,
"Y. S."

A VISIT TO THE HOME OF ONE OF MY PUPILS.

T. K. called, to take me to see his mother, now that the days for mourning for her husband are over. As on a former occasion, I was most kindly treated. His mother received my expressions of condolence with respectful bows, and the usual sipping of the air (inbreathing). The garden, so quaintly laid out, was not at this late season (Nov.) devoid of interest. Beautiful chrysanthemums were in their prime. He told me that the name given to this flower in Japan was Kiku. That it was adopted as the emblem of royalty. This at once explained the prominence which that emblem obtains in connection with the Government offices, despatches, etc. Even the tiles, which give a decorative finish to the roofs of all the Imperial residences, have this symbol stamped on them. The house was small, but prettily shaped. The rooms had niches and recesses, which suggested great taste. Some of the boards were perforated artistically with patterns of various favourite plants, flowers, fruits, birds. The light shining through these designs had a pretty effect. He drew my attention to several articles of value, which were heirlooms, and had been handled and admired by many of his predecessors. The use to which these were applied was carefully explained to me, also much more that was interesting. The Kakemono recess contained a pretty scroll, called bunji, *i.e.*, such pictures as are admired by literary men. They are produced by shadings of ink, called by us, Indian ink. The different shades of clay, with which parts of the walls were plastered, interested me as much as anything. Joints of pine, bamboo, and other trees, with bark left on, relieved the clay at regular intervals.

A basin of white dumplings, served in the liquor in which they were cooked, was placed before me on a curiously shaped tray, more like a small square

WIFE OF A DAIMIO.

table than anything else. In Japan, each member of the family is served with a separate tray, which is four-legged, and about a foot in height, and from one to two feet square. The largest is for the head of the house, and the smaller for the wife and younger members. I need not say that a pair of chopsticks were put at my disposal, so that I had no difficulty in keeping my friends company, although not quite as *au fait* in the use of them as they were perhaps. On retiring, my pupil told me that if he had a dozen children, he would gladly let me have them to educate. After thanking him and his mother heartily, we bowed and took leave.

EX-DAIMIO MIZUNO AT HOME.

The son of ex-daimio Mizuno and his Chief Vassal come to me every afternoon for private instruction. Both are as perseveringg as they are intelligent. They do not get tired of repeating the same lesson for an hour or more, so determined are they to pronounce English correctly. They are quite willing to sit an hour longer than is expected of me for teaching English, in order to read the somewhat easy first chapter of St. John's Gospel, and they come every Sunday afternoon regularly, to go over the same ground. I feel that the soil of their minds is very sterile, but as was often the case in China, so it is here. The lines come seasonably to my memory :—

> "*Sow, though the rock repel thee,
> In its cold and sterile pride.*"

They have given me an invitation to their home in Tokyo, and are quite willing that my friends from China, Mr. and Mrs. E——, should accompany me. We travelled seventeen miles by rail, and two by Jinrikisha. In order to get on to the raised verandah of their house, we had to step on a somewhat large stone. We were received into a prettily matted room, ornamented, as usual, with cleanliness, and chaste decorations. The heads of the house, several daughters, and my pupils, received us with bows and prostrations, which we returned as well as we knew how. This first act of courtesy over, my pupils invited us to take a stroll in their garden before the darkness set in. It had a somewhat large and deep pool with gold fish and lotus flowers. The maple tree was conspicuous among a great variety of others, the names of which I did not know. The vermilion tint of the maple makes it a universal favourite, so that not a garden is without it. The family shrine was covered with black lacquer on the outside, and gold on the inside. Its doors were thrown open, and there stood in array a large group of tablets of some deceased relatives, containing their names, date of birth, death, etc. There were besides small steel looking-glasses in little frames, facing each miniature shrine. Small branches of evergreen were in brazen vases, and the Gohei (*lit.*, August offering), and various white papers of curious and significant device, occupied their appropriate places. Mr. H—, the chief vassal, courteously begged of us to discontinue inspecting the dumb occupants and emblems, of what was, to say the least, full of historic interest to my friends. Shintoism is peculiar to Japan, so that a fresh field of research presented itself to them. But false worship in any shape or form has a saddening effect on those who have turned to God from idols, and who can from experience exclaim, "*Lord, to whom shall we go but unto Thee? Thou hast the words of eternal life.*" On re-entering the house, we observed a tall, venerable-looking, and well-dressed Japanese blind gentleman conducted by a servant into the reception room, where he took his seat on the cushion. Five or six young ladies, exquisitely attired, followed, and seated themselves on prettily quilted silken cushions, before which were placed elaborately inlaid guitars. The aged, blind teacher, seated in front of the ladies, tapped his knee with a closed fan, which he carried in his hand ; and more like a ventriloquist than a vocalist, he gave out in a weird tone the keynote to a somewhat prolonged performance — sometimes lively, and sometimes more of a requiem than the melody our English ears are disposed to appreciate on festive occasions. But the exquisite quality, texture, and cut of the ladies' dresses, to say nothing of their uniformly glossy, dark hair, so artistically dressed, attracted and entertained me more than the music. And then I could not get rid of the feeling which I so inadequately impressed upon them, viz., the deep obligation we were under to them for treating us to an entertainment which would repay any skilful artist coming a long distance to describe, if possible, with pen or brush. I have seen gaudily dressed Eastern women, and chastely attired ladies, but in this instance I saw nothing but what a better judge of dress and its combinations than I, termed *superb*. No powder or rouge was seen on their fair complexions on this occasion. After having partaken of a very choice dinner, which was cooked and served in French style, the young ladies handed us a few mementos of our visit. It was getting late, and we bade each other farewell We were shown into our Jinrikishas and taken to our destination, which was on that night only a mile or two off. That God may be the rewarder of such singular acts of disinterested kindness is an oft-breathed prayer. *They* saw that we meant much more than we could express, and *we* saw from their bright, open countenances, that they understood and felt that true kindness looks for no reward, save the privilege of seeing that it is appreciated.

CHAPTER VIII.

𝔄 𝔙isit to t𝔥e ℭelebrate𝔡 𝔖𝔥iba 𝔗emple.

"And the times of this ignorance God winked at; but now commandeth all men every where to repent."—Acts xvii. 30.

ACCOMPANIED by Mr. and Mrs. E. of the L. M. S. Pekin, China, and our guide, we proceeded to the celebrated Shiba temple and tombs of the Shoguns.* The day was bright and fair. On arrival we found that the cathedral was thronged with worshippers, who sat in orderly rows facing the preacher. We entered thoughtlessly with our shoes on to the spotless mats; but suddenly we were stopped by the verger, who indignantly drew our attention to a board bearing the notice, "*Leave your shoes outside this sacred place.*" There was what answered to a reading desk and altar. The officiating priest was dressed in gorgeous canonicals, suited to the high day or solemn festival. Each time the appointed lesson was read the congregation would bend forward as if assenting

---

* Since writing the above this temple has been burnt and rebuilt.

in solemn silence, or saying *Amen* to it. The priest at intervals stepped up to the high altar at the further end of the temple, bowed and clapped his hands, elevating them in the meantime, and muttering prayers, unintelligible to us. The choir sat opposite to the desk. All were dressed in sombre attire, which, including their simple head-coverings, were quite a contrast to the cardinal or bishop, for the latter wore vestments of gold cloth, and stole of different colours. My lady friend whispered, " Does it not remind you of Ritualism?" I nodded assent, having never before seen a more striking resemblance. The choristers performed their part by means of stringed and wind instruments. The notes of the latter, " sho," were solemnly plaintive. It is in shape suggestive of an organ. The instrument itself, however, is very small in comparison.

The temple or cathedral was beautifully matted. The shrines and furniture of each were so brilliant that they reflected every object that stood near them. The gold, red and black lacquer seemed to be of the best quality. There were many objects calculated to arrest the eye of the stranger; but nothing could come up to the solemn, yet dissatisfied, look of the worshippers, too devout on this occasion to be distracted by the presence of three "barbarians!" In front stood a prettily-shaped belfry, from which was suspended a bronze bell said to have been cast 200 years ago, and to be one of the largest and most celebrated in Japan.

This bell is sounded (not rung) from without by a ponderous wooden mallet, suspended from the

A BUDDHIST TEMPLE BELL.

ceiling, and so adjusted that a child can manage it, but the custodian of the bell performs this office. The day of casting such bells used to be a Red-

Letter-Day. Ladies from all parts brought and sent their silver hair pins, and steel looking glasses: and presented them to the master of ceremonies, to be put into the crucible, along with various other metals calculated to produce the rich mellow sound which, for many generations, has rippled from the centre to a circumference of many miles. Such bells all over the country bear on the surface inscriptions in Chinese characters, and sometimes in Sanscrit.

When a worshipper arrives, the bell is sounded to draw the attention of the deity; and it is said that prayers are offered by each vibration, *tone*, and *moan*, of the bell on behalf of those who, ages ago, contributed to its existence. They also say that it would be desecrating to the metal were a man or woman to touch it, and in order to avert the indignation of the god, costly offerings have to be presented by the desecrator. Oh, that an apostle might be sent with the burning message of St. Paul to the Athenians:—"*Ye men of Japan, I perceive that in all things ye are too superstitious. God that made the world and all things therein, seeing that he is Lord of heaven and earth, dwelleth not in temples made with hands.*"—Acts xvii. 22.

Tombs of the Sho-guns.

Our next move was towards the bronze tombs. The gorgeous mass of rich foliage is in itself a sight. The cryptomeria trees are gigantic. Some of the temples attached to the tombs are very large. The outer courts are full of costly bronze "toro," more like little light-houses than lamp-stands. The ground is covered with large oval and round pebbles, and shaded with umbrageous cedars, pines, and other trees. The tombs, which are made of fine bronze, show at once the wealth, power, and esteem which each silent inmate obtained among his contemporaries. Objects of interest meet the eye everywhere, in nature and in art. Our survey of each temple was short, as there were several to see. In one temple we saw an elaborate gold lacquered shrine, which contained articles of great value, including the sacred tablets, on which were descriptions of the names, dates of birth and death of the posthumously-honoured rulers. The spacious hall in front of the shrine of one large temple, was occupied by Buddhist priests, who were performing their devotions, which consisted of chanting prayers, bowing, and beating with a padded mallet a sweet-toned bell, and an embossed wooden gong. Each bonze had a rosary, as like the string of beads carried by the Romanist, as possible. The massive pillars of the temples are also overlaid with gold lacquer. The lamp-stand and candlesticks on the altar are made of brass and bronze respectively, and not very unlike those sold in London shops for use in ritualistic churches. Here, as at the Shiba temple, every object was mutually reflected on account of the excellent quality or polish of each. The ceilings seemed like a net-work of burnished panels, finished at each end with cunning work. Carvings of gorgeous lotus leaves, peonies, dragons, and other fictitious objects, decorated the ceilings of the verandahs and eaves, as well as the wooden pillars. But to do such a sight justice one would require to spend a few days there, and then he would need to be able to wield the pen of a ready writer. This is one of the many places to come to in order to get a right idea of the tight hold the superstitions of Japan have on the thirty-eight millions of her people, judging from the sacrifices they are willing to make to express their loyalty and affection to the supposed founders of their religion, as well as to the memory of their rulers.

CHAPTER IX.

The Japanese Christians in a Dilemma.

"Now ye are the body of Christ, and members in particular."—
1 Cor. xii. 27.

A SMALL party of Japanese Christian young men called upon me one day in 1874, to petition me, in common with other missionaries, to join the newly-organised Japanese Church, and sign a paper to that effect. I deeply sympathised with them; but, without considering the subject, I could not at once comply with their wishes. I was asked to what sect I belonged? I told them I belonged to the Free Church of Scotland, if to any; that I was taught from childhood to believe it to be the most in accordance with Scripture, but, as years rolled by, I could see that excellent Christians of the various denominations thought the same was true of the system with which they were identified. Divisions I knew were contrary to the Word of God, and the mind of Christ, and it seemed to me that it must be a question of choosing the sect most to our minds.

It was deeply touching to see how thoroughly in

earnest they were, and their look of disappointment as they turned away without my signature. From that moment I had heart-searchings, to which I had previously been a stranger. The more I read the Word of God, the more the ecclesiastical ground on which I stood seemed to be cut from under my feet. The Church that was formed at Pentecost was not, corporately, to be seen. I traced the Tower of Babel confusion which now prevails to man's presumption, and felt at rest. God's method can bear inspection.—1 Cor. i., xii. and xiii.

No wonder the Japanese are ready to say to us:—"Your methods do not agree with what we find in the Holy Book, touching *oneness* and *unity*; you do not teach the *same* thing; there are *divisions* among you; you are not *perfectly* joined together in the same mind and in the same judgment, for one saith, I am an Episcopalian, another a Presbyterian, a third a Methodist, a fourth a Unitarian, a fifth a Quaker, a sixth a Plymouthist, and a seventh a Dutch Reformed."

As time went on, the newly-organised Native Church became stronger, and several of the American and Scottish missionaries merged their sectarian differences, and co-operated with their Japanese brethren. Such a movement as this, having originated with the Japanese themselves, must commend itself to every reasonable Christian. Simultaneous with this movement, a tidal wave of blessing washed against the shores of Japan. God was mightily at work among the sailors on board the different men-of-war in the harbour, and it seemed to me that, from their midst, the Holy Ghost had called to the front a sample of that primitive simplicity and *reality*, which existed in the days of the apostles, when great grace was upon them all. (See Appendix.)

The following incident may be worth relating:—

AN EARLY CALL.

The pupil, to whom I refer on page 43, having heard of the newly-organised Church, felt that he must join it; but on learning that, if baptized by Mr. ———, he must consider himself a member of *his* Church, and not feel at liberty to identify himself with any other, he felt bewildered. This was too mysterious a problem to the guileless inquirer. His large-hearted uncle, who took the deepest interest in that which was a matter of profound concern to his nephew, proposed that they should go early the next morning to Yokohama, and see me and get the matter cleared up; for it was not for a moment suspected that I could have any difficulty in answering their questions. They travelled about eighteen miles, and were announced about nine o'clock, when they at once poured forth their troubles with reference to the public rite of baptism. This young disciple, and most eligible candidate for Christian baptism, felt instinctively that there could not surely be anything so shackling in the Christian religion as that the rite of baptism should create a barrier between brother and brother; for, as they had no such strictures in their own heathen systems, he insisted that Christianity must be a *levelling*, and not a *creating* of barriers. I must confess that I was utterly incapable to grapple with the subject, and how to evade it I knew not; but to prove to them that I was not alone in all I endeavoured to explain, I called in my sister, who at the time was with me on a visit, and she, seeing how they hung on our words, steered clear of touching the sectarian tangle, but exhorted our young brother to go to any of the Protestant missionaries, and simply state that it was his wish to be baptized in the name of the Father, and of the Son, and of the Holy Ghost; that baptism was the outward expression of an inward change, and the thing of supreme importance to him was, that already his soul was washed in the precious blood of Jesus; consequently, he had a new nature, and, if called to quit the frail body in which he suffered, the pearly gates of heaven would welcome him.

We further pressed on him the importance of exhorting his brethren to follow the example of the noble Bereans, who would not even accept the verdict of the apostles, until they had proved it by the *Word of God*, and to keep clear of our cumbersome Church machinery; that the Bible laid down no rigid rule, but broad principles; for different nations and peoples would always have different customs, so that all must seek the help of the *Holy Spirit*, who was now with us, to guide us into all truth.

Surely, nothing can more forcibly break down barriers, than that the gospel should be preached to the Japanese in the power of the Holy Ghost by the foreign and native evangelists conjointly. They are like sheep in the desert who need *feeding* and *leading*.

RÉSUMÉ.

1. On reviewing what I have written, I feel some reserve, lest anything I have said should look like reflecting on those who have watered in the field, and others who failed to do anything for Japan; and as to this, I would only say, "I would not sit in judgment on any." "*Who am I that I should judge the servants of my Lord? to Him they stand or fall:*" neither do I feel biased to speak for or against any church, mission, sect, or name.

2. I admit that I am somewhat carried away with my theme, viz., *Japan!* How her Spiritual condition is *now* to be helped forward by our entering on the openings made to her homes and educational centres by the wedge of western light, is a matter which exercises me greatly. I am thankful that we did not force our way among them with the sword or opium, a thing the Chinese are constantly and reproachfully reminding us of. Opium, let it be said, is held by the Japanese in eternal reprobation and abhorrence.

3. It may be well to say here that fifteen years of

association with, first, the Chinese, and latterly the Japanese, has, I think, led me to understand a little of the large and impartial heart of the Saviour, which could not embrace a less limited sphere than the whole world; and of how it must pain Him to see us so divided. And, as a member of the whole family in heaven and on earth, I am more and more disposed to love all those who love the Lord Jesus Christ in sincerity. To love one believer more than another, because he belongs to one's church party, or holds the same views, is un-Christ-like. "We are members *one of another*," and are united to Christ our Head.

4. As a home or foreign worker, I believe I ought to enter by every door, which I recognise the hand of God to have thrown open, and carry out the Scriptural principle: "*Whatsoever* thy hand findeth to do, do it with thy might."

5. Although we entered Japan with clean hands, yet I must say that civilisation, as a *pioneer* of the Gospel, has rendered that country less the virgin soil for apostolic methods than the world was for the heralds of the Cross in the first century. In short, I can now only say what I have repeatedly uttered, viz. :—That the thirst for learning among the Japanese, is one instrument with which to meet them wisely, and be of service to them, for the great aim and end of establishing the Gospel among them. This is very different from *the missionary himself proposing education as a means to an end!* We can no more despise the oppor-

tunity afforded us in this way, than Christian families can afford to make light of the desirability of seeing in our high schools and seats of learning in England, fully consecrated men and women of God. I uphold no distinctive denomination, inasmuch as that which represents the primitive church, which God set in motion in the first century, has no *visible* corporate existence. But it exists, for all that!

6. Though educated as a Presbyterian, my experience abroad taught me to keep outside merely man-made organisations; for the thing of first importance to me, *as a labourer,* was the liberty which I needed in order to prosecute the work which God himself signally led me into, contrary to all my expectations, among the male sex, viz., sailors and Japanese students. Did God make a mistake in leading me into this *unsought, unlooked-for* work? Or was it because God had failed to find a man ready to His hand, *He* took up a woman? *Let Him be the Judge!* And let it be mine henceforth to keep in the attitude of Mary, saying, "*Behold, the handmaid of the Lord!*" There are a few, both at home and abroad, to whom I owe much for the sympathy and help they have given me in the prosecution of my work. I have so thoroughly acknowledged the Lord's own hand in it all, that I am afraid I may have ignored the human media too much. But let such remember that He (who is the Rewarder) is faithful; and will not forget their labour of love.

7. I often ask myself, "Why is it that missionary organisations have such a strong tendency of bringing a worker into bondage, when, on the contrary, they should be facilitating his efforts?" If it were only a question of settling down and making oneself comfortable under the ministry of some favourite pastor, or attaching himself to a body of Christians interested in the heathen, one would have no difficulty; but when, for example, a woman is told, in the face of what looks as clear as sunlight, that it is unscriptural to speak to men, then she has either to *sin* against light, or *walk* in the light given her, and bear the cross of being accused of "acting independently," and long for the day to come when once again labourers, together with God, shall by the Holy Ghost give the injunction, "*Help those women who laboured with me in the Gospel.*"

CHAPTER X.

Visit to Kobe and Osaka.

(*Extracts from my Journal.*)

"In all thy ways acknowledge Him, and He shall direct thy paths."—Proverbs iii. 6.

MY pupil I—— has gone home for his autumn holiday. I miss him intensely. He invites me to Osaka. Everything seems to fit in so seasonably, that I cannot help saying to myself, *This proceedeth from the Lord.* My sister has arrived from Shanghai, and she will look after the sailors who come in groups in the afternoon and evening for reading the Word, prayer, and praise. This and the ladies' Bible class at Mrs. Cargill's, will be what she will delight in.

AT KOBE,

After thirty-six hours' sail in a steamer I arrived at Kobé. True to promise, I—— and his father met me. I felt most unworthy of the cordial welcome given me. My pupil acted as interpreter, and the father's smiling face seemed to say, as he looked at his attendants and nodded, "Well, well, my little son has indeed been industrious; who would have believed that in so short a time he could have made such progress!" Some time after getting ashore we entered a small Japanese hotel. The neat hostess came forward and made her obeisance. We were next shown into an upper room decorated with neatness and simplicity. It had, however, a pretty European square rug on the floor, over the mats. I—— told me that we sat in his father's specially engaged room. On looking over a little railing, I saw, twenty feet below, what looked like a grotto, the wall of which was covered with ferns and lichen. They called it the garden, although the space could not have been more than twenty by fifteen feet. Smooth and sharp stones composed a cairn or rockery in the centre: a shaft of bamboo, which simulated a fountain at play, by some means or other reached the water, and with its delicate spray bathed everything within its reach. I perceived that the flourishing state of the ferns was solely due to this simple contrivance. "Why," said I to myself, "have not we, adult westerns, more of the child-like life of the inhabitants of this fairy land?" Ah! why not? Because we have not sat at the feet of Nature and imbibed those teachings which give perpetual youth. But I—— is more taken up with the men-of-war and other vessels from the western world, lying at anchor in the harbour immediately in front. After partaking of tea, and confections, my friends took me to a ship-builder's yard to see a midget man-o'-war, which was remodelled at a great cost. It was, in days gone by, used by their chief, but now that things have changed, the good old boat was to be converted into a passenger and cargo vessel. My pupil's great delight was to sketch his father's steamer during his recreation hours, but I little thought that I was to be favoured with a sight of it so soon. The "Shotan-Maru," for that was her name, gave great promise of a long and useful life. After spending an hour or so at the naval yard, we went to see a waterfall, a mile or so off. All who have visited Kobé know that it is among the prettiest spots on the coast, and that it well pays a visitor to take a walk to it, as it affords an opportunity of taking in at a glance what he can never again forget. The glassy harbour in front, with its splendid variety of ships of war from the different parts of the civilised world ; the steam ships, sailing vessels, native junks, and flotilla of fishing smacks, the European settlement, with its rows of well-built villas here and there, decorated with waving flags, afford the accomplished artist such scope for his imagination, that he can scarcely bear to leave it until he has sketched it in words, if not in colours. On reaching the waterfall, I was amazed to find that an English luncheon, good enough for H.M. the Mikado himself, was provided by my pupil's kind-hearted father. Hundreds of children were on the move to and from the centre of attraction (viz., the waterfall), many douching themselves under its dashing spray. The background of what I have so imperfectly described, consists of a stretch of irregularly shaped hills, the greater part of which is covered with grass, trees, and shrubs. Many of the latter impart a beauty and picturesqueness to the scene which is rarely enjoyed at seaside resorts.

The American missionaries at Kobé, as in all the treaty ports of Japan, have made a good impression on the native population. They have preaching halls in several directions, also excellent schools, where English is taught, and their crowded audiences every Sunday will never fail to refresh and cheer the Christian tourist who may feel disposed to break his journey *en route*.

In this unique, well-kept settlement, one finds representatives from nearly every part of the world. During this, my first visit, I saw several Coreans on the quay. This was to every one a novel sight.

After luncheon we proceeded by rail to Osaka— the most important *commercial* city in Japan. We then rode in Jinrikishas through miles of clean and crowded streets. The people seemed to drive a busy trade in rice, fish, isinglass, china, and lacquer ware. On arriving at Hommachi we soon got to my friend's home. The lower part of the house, in front, was full of clerks; at the back were pretty sitting rooms, and artistic little gardens. Flowers decorated the corners of the *boudoir* into which I was shown. The polished floor boards, as well as the curious devices some of the posts and panels had on them, greatly interested me. The lady of the house and her children came and saluted me in true Japanese fashion. I found that Mrs. N—— was very domesticated, and a most dutiful mother and wife; she knows how to "look well to the ways of her household." She and her maidens seemed to be on friendly terms; but never are the latter guilty of outstepping the boundary which she, as mistress, has assigned to them. She had a pleasant face, and an unusually fair complexion. Unlike most Japanese married women, her eyebrows were not shaven, nor her teeth stained black. The eldest girl is six years old, she has sweet dimples and winning ways, and has the cut of hair girls of her age cultivate. Her dress is of a soft rich Japanese crêpe, with some of the favourite flowers of Japan stamped in permanent dyes all over it. Everything I see speaks of the refined taste, blended with the simplicity which characterises the race. One would almost think that at some early date they must have had the fairies, or some sweet genii from another world, to teach them. But I must not indulge in *foolish talking* in order to give utterance to the impression I received in this sweet home. The next move was into the garden. Camellia trees, with their rich, deep green, form a contrast to the highly-coloured slippery elm tree in full bloom. To get to the garden, I ought to have said, we had to cross a pretty miniature bridge, which spanned what answered to a natural bed of smooth round stones; some of these had hollow tops, so that they served the purpose of small reservoirs. Such have always a bamboo ladle laid across them, so that if anyone wishes to cool or cleanse his hands, all he has to do

A COOPER AT WORK.

is to take a ladleful of the rain water, and pour it over them. The stones and ferns, as well as other plants, are none the worse for this extra contribution. At the rear of the first room we sat in, I saw that some partitions and slit bamboo blinds were being removed. Several servants were busily engaged laying out another English dinner. Soup, fish, and *entremets à la mode*, were brought on in turn. The provider was an enterprising hotel-keeper on the European principle, in Osaka, named Jiu-tei. This explained a great deal to me; for I wondered how they could have cooked European food so well, to say nothing of the excellent way in which two well-dressed young men waited on us. I need not say that I was tempted to look round the room to take note of its neatness, cleanliness, and the exquisite taste displayed in the ornamentation of arches, panels, and whatnots. Here and there were elaborate pieces of bronze, lacquer, and one silk scroll, or *Kakemono*. My surprise was very great to find that the head of the house had arranged them himself, for my dear pupil told me that they were brought out of the Kura expressly because I was on a visit to them. Here I learned for the first time that it is an old standing custom to put their valuables away in the fire-proof house, and only bring out a few of them when the absent head of the house and other members of the family are expected home, as well as when friends whom they wish to honour are under their roof. I was *touched* by this proof of their generosity and courteousness. I felt that God, in some way or other, was in it, and that they, without knowing it, were doing His pleasure, which made me all the more desirous that He would be the rewarder of such impartial kindness, bestowed upon me, an empty-handed stranger, sojourning among them. While drinking our beautifully made coffee, a big wrestler, who performed the duties of gardener, came into the grounds with two buckets of water, with which he filled his mouth till his cheeks looked so distended that it was impossible not to smile. He then aimed at the tops of the somewhat tall trees as well as lowly shrubs, and squirted the water dexterously on every leaf and flower. This was done to every tree, and two buckets failed to supply the *mouth-hose* with sufficient spray. They told me that this was done every day in the hot weather. No wonder the leaves and flowers looked glossy and free from dust! After dinner my friends opened the ponderous doors of the Kura, where the heir-looms of generations were stowed away. Without having seen it, I should have thought it incredible that at least a thousand separate boxes, each containing treasures, were piled one above the other, and only a few taken out occasionally to express love, respect, and a welcome, on the return of the husband, or the arrival of a friend. But, doubtless this is one of the ways which are adopted for banking their money—curios of value are often given in lieu of debt. . . . I must cut my story short by saying, that according to oriental custom, I was asked to take a present from them, a second article for my sister, and a third for my servant.

CHAPTER XI.

Self-Help.

"If ye continue in My word, then are ye My disciples indeed."—John viii. 31.

THERE is a mighty element of self-help in Japan; and this is, for the most part, to be found among the Samurai class. In former days they were the military force of the nation. The chief of each clan required that much time should be devoted to the arts of fencing, wrestling, and other tactics. There were those who attained to great excellence as swordsmen, and, according to their skill and moral qualities, they were promoted to positions of honour and trust. They also gave much attention to intellectual pursuits. Literature and the fine arts were subjects which were vigorously entered on, and while *we* were in a savage state, they were clothed with silks, satins, and crapes.

Immediately after the Tokugaawa rebellion (1868) many of them were reduced in circumstances. One of these proved to be a youth of great promise, named Neejima. His interest in Christianity was first awakened by coming in contact with the missionaries, and reading Christian books. The unsettled state of the country at that time (1867) led many youths to reflect seriously. Mr. Neejima had a strong desire to visit the West in order to study English. He asked permission of his liege lord, and parents, but was unsuccessful. He then boldly set out as a runaway, and concealed himself in the hold of a ship sailing for China. If discovered he would have been at that time beheaded. In China he became a servant; but this failed to satisfy his longings, so he secured a post in a ship about to sail for the United States. On board this ship he was "Jack of all trades." On one occasion he was asked to wash the captain's feet. This made his Samurai blood boil. He got very angry, but had to obey.* The captain introduced him on their arrival to the owner of the vessel he sailed in, the late Hon. A. Hardy, of Boston. He asked young Neejima what induced him to visit America. His answer was, "to get a good Christian education." Mr. Hardy felt greatly moved, and forthwith invited him to his house. He was sent to school, graduated at Amherst College, Mass., then went to Andover Theological Seminary, where he completed his course

---

* Mr. Neejima refers to this incident when preaching to his countrymen in connection with the condescension of the Saviour, who took upon him the form of a servant ; and gave his disciples a practical example of that humility which is, in the sight of God, of great price. He, the lowly JESUS, girded Himself, and washed his disciples' feet.

in the year 1874. At this date he was brought in contact with the special Japanese Embassy, visiting America and Europe for the first time. He was invited to accompany them in the capacity of interpreter, an offer which he accepted. At a later date he was offered a good position in the Government, but declined it. After this he returned to Japan, and selected the ancient capital, Kyoto, as his field of action. He appealed to the authorities for a site on which to erect a college for imparting to the ambitious youths of Japan a thorough knowledge of English, and specific branches of Western science. His Government was glad to accede to his wishes—doubtless, the friends whom he accompanied to Europe remembered that he had a right spirit in him, and that he had refused the lucrative position offered him. The site was immediately marked out, and the college was built at the expense of friends he had made in the United States. He next appealed to the Board of Foreign Missions for fully qualified professors of Christian zeal. They came with the understanding that they were to teach useful branches of knowledge, such as *medicine and natural philosophy;* and on giving five or six hours daily (Saturdays and Sundays excepted) to secular instruction, they were left free to teach anything else they wished. Of course this opened at once a wide door in the Gospel to the missionary-teachers, and God gave them and Mr. Neejima great success. Most of the students attended the Gospel services and Sunday-schools.

Many souls were saved. A flourishing theological seminary grew out of this almost immediately. When I first saw it, there were about fifty of the students who not only professed to be Christians, but took an active part in proclaiming the good news to their own people in and outside the city. This is all the more remarkable because Kyoto and environs are, according to the letter of the treaty, closed to missionary enterprise and to trade. I state this in order to show how ready the Japanese are to encourage all that will contribute to their country's benefit, when once they see its good effect. In addition to these secular and theological institutions, a young ladies' school was started. Many of the lads had been the means of winning their mothers and sisters to a saving knowledge of the truth, and so the need for opening this school was felt. Several well qualified, earnest young ladies arrived from America, and with their open hearts, and affable ways, won the affection of a large party of interesting Japanese girls. I visited this school in 1881, and saw it flourishing. Applications were coming from all parts, from the parents of well-to-do Japanese, asking for permission to send their daughters to them. They were greatly taken up with such novelties (to *them*) as our different varieties of useful fancy work. The Christian spirit that pervaded the place, and marked the behaviour of teachers and pupils towards each other, betokened that God was among them, as well as among the young men. I must not forget to say that I had the honour of being introduced to Mr. Neejima, the director of this religious and educational movement. It was heart-inspiring to see one of the first-fruits of saving grace, as well as a specimen of Christian courage in Japan. The truly patriotic and humble Mr. Neejima is a man who has won the esteem and confidence, not only of the Church of God in Japan, but of the Government, as well as of his large circle of friends in America, where he received such a warm welcome, and was so well treated for Jesus' sake. Mr. Neejima is a thorough believer in the revealed Word of God. He propagates its teaching far and wide, through the help of his large band of enthusiastic young evangelists —both men and women—as well as by his own abundant labours. But the Christians in Japan are nevertheless exposed to great danger. They need to be taught the importance of holding forth the Word of Life from Genesis to Revelation, without supplementing it, as many in this country are doing, with the untempered mortar of philosophy and vain deceit, after the tradition of men, and not after Christ. Our modern theories, or "*advanced thought*" so-called, will not make thriving Christians of the Japanese, nor will the soundest creed, and most evangelical method, be of any great value to them unless its representatives are themselves clothed with the mantle of that love which suffereth long, and is kind, and seeketh not her own.

An Instance of Maternal Devotion and Filial Faithfulness.

"He that loveth father or mother more than Me is not worthy of Me."—Matt. x. 37.

In the turbulent and disastrous years of 1867-8 the Samurai belonging to the Shogun were deprived of their hereditary allowances, and many of them hitherto unaccustomed to the money-making affairs of this world, were yet tossing upon the sea of hard and merciless competition. The newly-opened harbour of Yokohama was considered as giving the best opportunity for success. Among the Samurai who had come to Yokohama as the City of Refuge, was a small family consisting of parents and three sons; want of experience and discretion had often reduced them to extreme poverty. At last the father succeeded in getting a position in the municipal office, and though not enriched thereby, the family was by this means supplied with necessary food. The parents, thus relieved from the daily cares of bread and clothing, began to discuss as to the method of educating their children, especially the eldest, who was then in the twelfth year of his age. The father said to his wife, "The days of the Samurai are gone, we will send our eldest son to a merchant's as an apprentice;" but the mother, whose lofty spirit and ardent ambition were very remarkable, was strongly opposed to her husband's proposal.

To her the lowly calling of a mechanic or a tradesman seemed degrading. Not enlightened by the light of the Cross, which gives a new and fresh significance to everything, it was quite natural that she should be swayed by such a vain idea as this. Her chief desire was to give the highest education to her beloved son, so that he might be well fitted to occupy a splendid position as a statesman; her love for the son, and her yearning for the restoration, through him, of the estate which the father had lost in the revolution, were equally unbounded. The son, too, inspired by his mother, set his whole heart on his future career as the first statesman of Japan. He was opposed to the superstitious rites and worship of the common people, but the dreary prospect of struggling for success, and the arduous task of an ambitious career, aroused the religious sentiment, which lay dormant in the boy's heart, to a strange pathetic activity. Kata-Kyo-Masa, the valiant and virtuous general under Hideyoshi, at whose name even the Chinese and Coreans trembled, had long since been the child's hero. From a lowly and despised position, he had steadily fought his way into a prominent position, renowned for his matchless valour and shining virtue. The boy was often found reading and meditating on this hero. He went to the temple of Kata-Kyo-Masa, a distance of two miles, twice a day—morning and evening. Thus, three entire years were spent. In the year 1872 the influence of English literature predominated throughout the Empire. A new field was opened for the boy. The mother thought that her son ought to be sent to an English school. She sold her jewels and clothes to pay the cost of his tuition, which was considerable, as he had to purchase English books and dictionaries. The head teacher of the school was an American missionary, whose devotions and religious teaching attracted the attention of a number of his pupils. Their hearts were opened, and before long they became the followers of Christ. Many of them also determined to devote their lives to the ministry of the Gospel. One of the number was the boy of whom we have been speaking; it was only after a severe struggle and an almost heart-breaking effort that the decision was formed. When the announcement of the change was made to the mother, she was deeply grieved, for it seemed to her that all her hopes were gone—hopes for which she had so bravely endured hardships—and to her the son had all of a sudden become a lost child. She entreated him to change his strange views; her tears and tender exhortations were heart-rending, but the young man stood firm to his decision, constrained by the love of Christ. He patiently waited for two years to get the consent of his parents. God be praised, the virtuous mother, in spite of her strong antipathy, was gradually brought to Christ, and not only consented to her son's proposal to study for the ministry, but solemnly promised to share in his labours and efforts for the spreading of the Gospel. A God-given mother she was; and, but for her loving efforts, the boy would never have received an English education. She was, in the mysterious providence of God, the means of bringing salvation to her son, and through him to the family; and, moreover, true to her promise, she has nobly shared in her son's labours, both as an evangelist and pastor. Her courage and tenderness in the time of trouble and adversity have been a strong support to him. Memories of her service and gentle virtues are still inspiring him with courage and consolation. Full of weakness and mistakes, and sometimes pained by misgivings and shortcomings, it is his humble desire to behave like a soldier of Christ. May God, who has dealt so graciously with him in the past, make him strong in faith and ardent in love towards Him!

CHAPTER XII.

Social Life in Japan.

"Give her of the fruit of her hands; and let her own works praise her in the gates."—Prov. xxxi. 31.

I HAVE often noticed, with pleasure, what far happier lives the Japanese women and children lead than their neighbours in China. In Japan, cleanliness and quiet prevail in the home, whereas, in China, it is too often the reverse.

The education of woman has greater reference to the home-life than to the part she is likely to play in society. Obedience is insisted on from earliest childhood, not by threats and blows, but by gentle humouring and reasoning with the child while the mind is plastic. Filial piety is, here a little, and there a little, with precept upon precept, carefully explained and inculcated. A girl is sent to an elementary school in her fourth or fifth year. As soon as she has learnt to read and write, she is transferred to a tailoress's school, where she is taught to cut and sew her own garments. At home, she learns to play the *samisen* (banjo), and *koto* (guitar), having for her teacher either a resident or daily governess. All the patching, mending, and re-doing fall to her lot eventually. Thus she is taught to bear the yoke in her youth, so that at an early age she becomes proficient in this and other things likely to conduce to the comfort of her family—such as learning to cook rice and vegetables—and above all, how to arrange cut-flowers artistically, and make and pour out tea gracefully. Although the woman in Japan is not exactly on an equal footing with her husband, she is not considered as a mere drudge, as women are in China and India. As a wife, she is taught to attend to her household duties, and to submit to her husband in all things. If he treats her well, she says, "Heaven smiles"; but if he is displeased with her, "Heaven frowns." The obedient wife finds her reward in the kindness and indulgence which she receives from her husband. Yet, in Japan, the code of morals laid down and strictly enjoined on the wife can too often be broken with impunity by the husband. I confess I often felt amazed at the apparent indifference of many women, who were well aware that their husbands spent much of their time in the company of dissolute persons. Far different treatment would be dealt out to any wife against whom the least charge of infidelity could be brought. I do not say this unkindly, but state it as an instance of what appealed to me as detrimental to the true elevation of women.

DINNER PARTY.

A handsome Japanese lady called on me one day with two of her servants, who told me they were having a party that evening. I expressed my astonishment at seeing them when such was the case. The lady and her servants looked at one another; and then said, that had it not been for the party they would not have been able to pay me so long a visit. "Our customs are different from yours," they remarked; "when our husbands invite their gentleman-friends, they also invite public actresses to play on the guitar, sing, and perform pantomime." I replied, that I knew they did so, but that that did not explain their absence. "It is not the custom of our country," replied one of the maids (whose duty, at that moment, was to keep her mistress's pipe supplied with tobacco), "wives are not fit company for their husband's friends; for we women are *tsuchi* (earth), while they are *ten* (heaven)." She said this humorously. On becoming better acquainted with the home-life of the people, I learnt that the wife's absence was one of the ways which rather proved the esteem in which she was held by her husband. Besides, the old-established rules of society rigidly forbade ladies joining in their husbands' dissipations. The conversation with my visitor then turned on the nature of the entertainment; how the best dinner-service was brought out, and how the most delectable soups, and other dishes, were prepared by the mistress and servants.

"But, perhaps the teacher would like to partake of *cha-no-yu*," whispered my friend in her maid's ear. The invitation was at once given and ac-

JAPANESE NURSE AND BABY.

cepted; and as the house was close at hand, we started off. On entering the guest-chamber, I found the feast was over, and the guests had left;

judging from the display of lacquer bowls, china platters, and tempting dishes (many of them untouched), it must have been an imposing sight. Having examined their *salle-à-manger*, and watched the servants at their work of clearing up, I was shown into what is called the tea-room, where the Japanese make and drink their *hiki-cha* (lit. ground tea). There I found the urbane and courteous head of the house smoking his tobacco pipe. As usual in Japanese houses, there was little or no movable furniture in the room; but cleanliness and taste were everywhere conspicuous. In one corner of the room, in a small recess, I saw a bronze idol, before which were arranged, as offerings, daintily made dishes. We spoke of idols, and I told them that over 1,000 years ago, our nations in the West worshipped false gods, and that it was not civilisation, but Christianity that had led us to give them up. I spoke of the one true God, in communion with whom I found the sunshine of my life.

CHAPTER XIII.

Child=life in Japan.

"A child is known by his doings."—Prov. xx. 11.

ONE cannot speak of the condition of women in any country without mentioning the children. A certain writer said of Japan that she is a Paradise of children; alluding, of course, to the fact already referred to, that men and women of all ages join, at certain seasons, with their children, in their characteristic outings. Japanese mothers are tenderly attached to their little ones, and like Westerns, give greater honour to the son. Both father and mother are equally full of concern lest they should fail to become a credit to society and a comfort to themselves. The patience of Japanese mothers is remarkable. I have rarely seen them slap or cuff their children, hence their bright manner; plainly teaching European parents a lesson in the management of the rising generation. Infanticide, foot-binding, and other cruel practices, peculiar to Eastern countries, are unheard of in Japan. It is comparatively rare that a girl is transferred to her mother-in-law at betrothal. This prospect is the terror of a Chinese girl, for it is then that her life of misery begins. It is a great disappointment in Japan when a son and heir is not born to the parents. They feel it nearly as much as the Chinese do; and like them, endeavour to propitiate their idols, especially Jeezo and Kwanon (patrons of children). Unlike the Chinese, however, the Japanese do not regard their girls as a useless encumbrance, or as a sign that their gods are angry with them. The girl babies are much petted and indulged, and the parents are greatly congratulated on suitable days, and not commiserated, as in China, when the family circle is augmented by a little girl. The Japanese embrace the occasion of the birth of a girl as much as that of a boy for making visits of ceremony, and (according to the station and circumstances of those visiting and the visited), presenting gifts in the shape of webs of crèpe, silk, and dress materials; also cakes of rice boiled with red beans.

MIYA-MAIRI.

Thirty days after the birth of a boy, he is dressed in his finely prepared robes. The inner-garments are made of silk and other materials of fine texture and hues. The outer one is made of rich black crape (which is not considered mourning in Japan or China). This outer garment has the family crest embroidered, if not woven, on the right and left sleeve, and between the shoulders at the back. Thus decked and adorned, the boy is carried to the temple in a procession of grand-parents, aunts, friends, and servants. This turn-out is called "miya-mairi," *i.e.*, visit to the temple. The object is to invoke the sun-god's blessing and protection on behalf of the child during the rest of his life. The youngster receives his name on this occasion. The father writes three different names on three separate slips of paper, and sends them to the officiating priest, who throws them in the air. The one that touches the ground first bears the lucky name. The priest hands it to the child's sponsor when the party breaks up. A boy infant has the Chinese character, *dai* (great), associated with its name; while a girl has *sho* (little), associated with hers: these respectively showing that the boy is destined to attend to the greater and more responsible matters of daily life; while the smaller and more obscure affairs fall to the lot of the girl. On their return from the temple, presents are sent to all the relations and friends. These gifts are composed of the red-beaned and rice cake already referred to, and dried *bonito*, packed in lacquered lunch boxes, which are covered over with elaborately embroidered wrappers. I ought to have said, that on the seventh day after a birth, a costly feast is prepared for the relatives and friends, as well as on other lucky days, besides that of the actual day of birth. So it appears that both girls and boys are made much of in Japan! Children there always carry a charm; indeed, it is considered indispensable to the preservation of their life. This sacred relic is often a written sentence, to be got from any priest; or the model of a little dog, or fox, and is put into the richly ornamented charm bag, already tied round its waist. In addition to this, they carry what we in England might imitate, viz., a pretty embossed card with the child's name and address written in full, which, in case of its straying from its home, would enable the police, or any humane person, to gladden the heart of the distracted and distressed mother and child. Children, when they begin to walk, do not get their little pates *entirely* shaven, which is always the case during the first year; but the barber, at short intervals, shaves a round patch on the crown, leaving a band of hair to grow in a circle. This custom varies according to the sex and age, and the varying fashions of the different localities. Japanese juveniles are, like other children, fond of toys, and their parents rarely grudge the money spent on them. The frank and bright countenances of both boys and girls are, I feel sure, due to the pains parents take to make their children happy, and by their gentle and thoughtful ways avoid spoiling their tempers, a thing often done when childish mistakes are visited by hard words and cruel blows. The prettiest sight in child-life in Japan, to my mind, is that of the girls turning out on New Year's Day, in their best attire of richly coloured silks, on which are stamped decorations of cherry, plum, and other blossoms, as well as the bright red maple leaves. Their hair, on this day of days, is done up to perfection, each wearing in it an artificial sprig of some favourite flower. They stand for hours at the door of their respective homes, playing at battledore and shuttlecock. The streets, during the first week of January—now that they have adopted our calendar—are lined with children at play. The suspended huge lanterns, with the family crest prettily painted on them; the tub containing branches of pine, plum, and bamboo on either side of the entrance, and red-boiled lobsters laid on a few fronds of ferns turned inside out, placed over the doorway (as is the mistletoe with us), are in keeping with the glee and hopefulness of the rising generation. "*Omé-de-tau*" (I wish you happiness) is the salutation on every lip on this auspicious day. As a rule the weather is cold, but dry and clear. The notes of the oriole, first harbinger of Spring, are already heard, and branches of the plum blossom are gathered and put into large antique vases, covered with historic decoration: it being the first flower of the season, its beauty and sweet scent give universal satisfaction. The oriole and plum blossom are associated in the mind of the Japanese in general, as well as in that of artists who make it a favourite subject, whether for wood-carvings, bronze-castings, or silk wrappers.

A LITTLE SAMURAI.

I should like to tell you now of a little boy, only nine years old. He was the son of a Samurai, *i.e.*, a gentleman, and was brought to me during my earliest years in Japan. His father, shortly after the revolution of 1868, bought and re-fitted a small steamer at a great cost, and became a merchant. His boy was the light of his eyes; and when placing him under my care, he honoured me with boundless confidence. My pupil had a stock of all sorts of paper, and every variety of vegetable paints, brushes, gums, and paste. He had a way of producing a fac-simile of his father's steamboat in folded paper, which quite astonished me. One would almost think he had studied naval science, and had passed a successful examination. Funnels, masts, a flag with red ball on white ground, and lifeboats, occupied their respective places. He would attach a fine thread to the prow, and with one hand pull it along the table, imitating at the same time the noise of the engines, "choh! choh! choh!" Thus, this much-loved pupil passed hours happily and profitably. The expert manner in which he, for a child his age, used his paint-brush made me sometimes think that one day he would make his mark in the world as an artist; but he is now (1889) in a large commercial city of the West, a junior member of a firm. My pupil, at first, showed great aversion to learning; but having a tender conscience, he was soon led to see that it was right to apply himself and make the most of his time and opportunity; thus he made fair progress. He had special taste for drawing and sketching, and when allowed to have his pencil and colours, hours would soon pass rapidly.

Of this I was most thankful; for at first I could not speak Japanese, nor could he speak English. At this time, the husband of my servant was a printer in a newspaper office near to us. On his returning home, I gave my pupil leave to go to him for an hour every evening to learn the news of the day. Thus he was diverted between study, recreation, and social intercourse, and home-sickness was held in abeyance. During this time the Satsuma war was raging, startling things were reaching our ears day by day; but my little charge, instead of being alarmed by all he heard and learned from the printer, would seize the first opportunity he could to depict, most graphically, the impressions he had received of what was going on at the seat of war at Kagoshima. Imperialists and rebels were familiar scenes in those days; and the skill displayed in the description he gave of heads, arms, and legs, bestrewing the ground in a mass of frightful *débris*, was truly wonderful. His indulgent father then made him a present of a box of soldiers, made to order; also, some men-of-war and gunboats. These he would arrange in battle array; and, of course, his conservative spirit conceived of nothing but the rebels being beaten and put to rout by the imperialists. He always furnished himself with a good supply of foolscap paper, and as soon as he felt tired of reconnoitring and marshalling his troops, he would take to painting vessels letting off their formidable guns at one another. He would dip his paint-brush in vermilion, and blow hard on it, which caused the bespattered paint to look exactly like fire issuing from the cannon's mouth. All this displayed great originality, and it gave me much pleasure to see him prefer spending his leisure time in this way, than that he should be spending it unprofitably.

KINDER-GARTEN À LA JAPONAISE.

Another amusement of the healthy kind pursued by two of my boy pupils, arose from their love of gardening. They were provided with two separate wooden frames, one foot deep and seven by five feet long; these they filled with soil. A favourite natural scene was evidently in their minds; very often their own lovely country with its manifold islands. The peerless *Fuji-san* was reproduced by a piece of flint, pyramidically shaped, the top of which was white, representing the cap of perpetual snow, which this hoary mountain always wears. The liliputian maples, pines, bamboo, plum trees, bought for a few cents, are put deftly into the ground with their tiny trowel of Japanese make. In one nook, under a few shrubs, is what answers to a waterfall. "Whence this white stream?" is queried in thought. The gardeners have a way of supplying every fresh fancy of their young patrons. They actually grind white pebbles, or glass, for the purpose of strewing it on the *would-be* beds of waterfalls, seas, lakes, rivers, and thus the most perfect imitation of water is produced. But this is not all. The sea is alive with men-of-war and junks. The lakes are full of tiny steamers and small boats with sails hoisted! The rivers,

SNOWBALL.

(Japan is not a tropical country, as many suppose!)

which are, at regular intervals, spanned with perfect imitations of their own quaint bridges, are full of bamboo rafts and men propelling them.

This flotilla and series of bridges are all made of fine-baked china like all the rest. Terra firma has also its towns and villages, castles, mansions, and villas, each and all animated as it were with a variety of the human species plying their various crafts. There goes the blind am-ma (shampooer), trudging along the street, blowing his double-barrelled whistle so as to announce his arrival! Here comes the nurse, carrying her charge on her back.! Yonder, under the trees on the banks of the river, are the easy-going storks, taking it very leisurely! The scene would not be perfect without the modern policeman, carrying his shillelah under his arm— and all made of china, bear in mind! "After this, surely there cannot be more," do I hear you say? Pause a moment! . . . What! a Japanese so selfish, so irreligious as to forget to build a temple, or set up a shrine! Look at yonder hill-top to the left! All those broad-eaved structures are temples! pagodas!—the habitations of the gods! And do you not see the string of pilgrims, with broad-brimmed hats, wending their way in and out among them? And those bald-pated gentlemen with rosaries in their hands, are they not the Buddhist priests? It may seem a woful waste of time to spend a few minutes studying child-life in Japan, and again as many minutes to write it down; but I must confess that such ingenious, simple amusements, made me often wish I were a child again.

KINDER-GARTEN, No. 2.

Before leaving Osaka, in 1881, I visited a Normal School, when, with my teacher, we were shown into all the various class-rooms. The teachers ciphered on the black-boards with an air that left one satisfied as to how competent they were for the post they filled. The pupils stood as we entered each room, and bowed when we retired. On being introduced to the head-mistress of the infant department, she led us to a large garden. A more engaging sight could not be seen! The children were not older than seven, and not younger than four years. They were dressed in all the colours of the rainbow. The plat of ground where they played represented the islands of Japan, so this explained the unevenness and irregularity of the parterre. This offered a practical lesson to the infant mind of the geography of their own country, embracing land, seas, rivers, and lakes. The courteous school-mistress, who conducted us through the garden, said, "*We teach the infants on the Kinder-Garten principle.*" And well pleased we were to be eye-witnesses of its good effect. Little mites were asked to show us Fuji-san, and Lake Biwa. This was no sooner said than done. Fuji-san was represented by a stone, in the shape of a pyramid; Lake Biwa was minus water on this occasion, as the tiny hollow, which represented its bed, contained only a few pebbles. The Island of Awaji was guarded by a miniature bamboo fence.

It was there (says mythology), that Izana-gi and Izanami-no-mikoto began to create the Japanese empire; hence the fence, denoting sacredness. The head-mistress impressed us as being both mother and teacher. The little dots, with that grace peculiar to the Japanese generally, turned round and bowed as we retired, and said, "Sayonara." *We* also bowed and said "Good-bye."

THE CARP ASCENDING THE WATERFALL.

(SEE COVER.)

"Fight the good fight of faith, lay hold on eternal life."—1 Tim. vi. 12.

It is a common sight to see, on Japanese works of art, and in picture-books, a carp trying to swim against a strong current or waterfall. This allegorical picture has a very interesting history, and is derived from a Chinese story. In some part of China there is a strong current, called Rio-mon, or Dragon's Gate. This stream is looked upon as sacred; so that, if any fish succeeds in scaling it, it becomes a dragon.* The passage is very difficult, it being rocky and steep, and every fish except the carp fails in the attempt. Very often, at the birth of a son, a carp is sent to the parents as a present.

This emblem seems to me to illustrate the courage which, at the present moment, characterises Japan. She is facing what look like insurmountable

---

* The dragon is said to be the ruler of the vapoury elements.

difficulties; but, unless her people will embrace the truths of Christianity *(not a religious creed merely)*, and have the *love of God shed abroad in their hearts by the Holy Ghost*, they will find in the end that they have spent their labour on that *which satisfieth not*. The true Christian also may be compared with the carp. He has the motive power of love to God and his glory, and consequently leads, day by day, an overcoming life. "*This is the victory that overcometh the world, even our faith.*"

"BE STRONG, AND VERY COURAGEOUS."

Children's Festivals.

The fifth of May is the day of the boys' festival. Indoors an exhibit is made of the models of all sorts of weapons, such as swords, lances, bows and arrows, etc., and sometimes even of the heroes and heroines of reputation. The origin of this display can be traced to the warlike disposition of the ancient Japanese to familiarise their sons to the sight of implements of war, and thus foster up their brave spirits from infancy. Early in the morning, the young boys go to the nearest marshes, and cut down flags, which they trim in the shape of swords or sabres, and indulge themselves for the rest of the day in sham-fights, and are as happy as the day is long. It is for this reason that it is also known by the name of the Feast of Flags. In addition to these, there is a martial array of banners and pennons floating from the top of long bamboo poles rising high above the roofs. Many of these are made in the shape of a carp, often of immense size. They are simply bags of paper or silk, coloured in the natural hue; but when the breeze gets through the mouth and fills the sides, it produces a wriggling of the body extremely lifelike. The carp is considered as an emblem of perseverance, on account of its great dexterity in ascending rapids, and even cataracts.

The girls celebrate their festival on the third of March. They have also a complete display of dolls, representing high-life, with all appendages. This is called *Hinamatsuri*, or the Feast of Dolls.

CHAPTER XIV.

Fragments.

THE Rev. C. H. Spurgeon says, that "*If the Lord will arouse Christian workers to carry on vigorously the work of evangelisation amongst the wonderful people of Japan, she may ere long become the*
BRITAIN OF ASIA."

The position of Japan in Asia corresponds so greatly with that of England in Europe that her people seem to claim justly a special amount of attention from us. Like the British Isles, she has an insular position, and her maritime power is being rapidly and successfully developed, and is likely soon to make her the most important naval power in Asia. Already her coast is guarded by a navy of thirty-one men-of-war, some of which have been constructed for the Japanese Government in European dockyards, and some in their own naval yard at Yokosuka; and it is not only in war-ships that the Japanese have followed our example, they have also given great attention to their mercantile service, and have already several lines of British-built steam-ships which carry on a constantly increasing commerce with China, Corea, and Russian Asia.

Advancing.

The military force of Japan, which has always shown itself efficient and reliable, has lately been greatly reorganised on the German model; discipline is rigidly enforced, and the weapons used are all of the latest European types. The postal and telegraph arrangements are excellent: the promptitude and regularity of the deliveries are not excelled even in England. There are nearly six thousand miles of telegraph lines laid down, connecting places at home, and communicating with foreign places by means of a submarine cable. Education in Japan is carried on in a thorough and systematic manner; University, Colleges and Schools being arranged on the American and European systems.

Changing for the Better.

The Japanese are sometimes said to be too changeable; but it must be confessed that in these matters they have decidedly been changing for the better. The spirit of progress has awakened Japan from centuries of slumber, and called her to assume her place as the pioneer of liberal measures in Asia.

JINRIKISHA.

Travelling is rendered easy in Japan by the Jinrikisha, which can most conveniently be hailed at any moment of need, so that it is easy to travel by highways, byways, winding streets and alleys to the destination for which one is bound. If a long journey is to be made, the speed may be augmented by adding one or two more men. The sensation when the good natured pull-men choose to move at their fastest rate is most delightful. They will halt at the first tea-house they come to, and wringing in water the towel they wear round their heads, will wipe the perspiration from their faces, and after refreshing themselves with a sip of tea will start off again to the next halting-place. They can accomplish journeys of thirty or more miles in one day, and their charge is very moderate. They receive their fare with a series of bows.

RAILWAYS.

A network of railways for the whole country is projected, and already there are nearly 1,000 miles of rail along the coast and inland. In 1871, seventeen miles composed the first railroad. This makes travelling in Japan much more easy than in Corea and China, where locomotives are as yet scarcely known.

THE PRESS.

The Press has immense influence in Japan, and as in England, that influence is capable of being good or evil. Under Christian management, however, it may become a powerful instrument for winning the people to Christ.

SCENERY.

The country of Japan is extremely beautiful: nearly everywhere in the interior the traveller meets with cone-shaped hills clothed in verdure to their summits, and with rich foliage in the valleys below. In spring, the country is ablaze with azaleas and other flowers, and presents a most beautiful appearance.

The valleys are cultivated everywhere, and rice, millet, wheat, barley, maize, and sweet potatoes abound. The sound of mountain torrents and waterfalls mingling with the murmur of insects, and the songs of birds, fill the hilly fastnesses with music. Gigantic pines and cedars reign in many of the forests among a great variety of other trees.

The Japanese are intense admirers of Nature. They seem to be made for their country and their country for them. In the spring and autumn they sally forth in parties in boats and Jinrikishas to see the plum, cherry, and peach blossoms, the peonies, chrysanthemums, and a magical show of maple. The Japanese are always so impressed with the generosity of Nature, that they seem to feel that on certain days they must pay their respects to her. Like the fashionable world, they are alive to her presence when she holds court and gives receptions for all sorts in the *height of the season.* Such outings are called *nagame* (beholdings).

The favourite *plum blossom* is the emblem of undying love, because, in the early spring, and even in winter, it bursts open and flourishes in the atmosphere of frost and snow; hence the place it occupies as a decoration at marriage-feasts, reminding the affianced pair that the trials and difficulties of their future life must be overcome by love. Royalty, I am told, would regard it as a misfortune were circumstances to prevent them from sharing in these rural festivities. It is interesting to notice the boat-loads of young and old, and cavalcades of Jinrikishas that go and come by watercourses and highways at such seasons. The month of April is the most popular, for in it the cherry blossom flourishes. They fill their conventional lunch boxes with supplies for the day, which they spend in spots where they can feast their eyes on the beauty of the trees so gorgeously apparelled. The *chrysanthemum Beholding* comes off later; also that of the maple, when hill-sides look brilliant, as if dipped in vermilion, with the exception that the rich and luminous mass is here and there relieved with some evergreen, such as cedar, pine, and holly, and all is canopied by an exquisite azure sky. This, of all the floral *Beholdings* is the most magical, and worthy of the skill of the many occidental and native artists daily on the spot endeavouring to transfer it, if possible, to canvas. There is also the *Snow Beholding*, which has a special fascination for artists who visit plantations of pine and such evergreens—as on them the snow makes picturesque terraces, which they like to paint on silk.

THE MOON BEHOLDING

takes place in the autumn, when the gazers stand, if possible, on the bank of a river, or on a bridge, in order to see it reflected in the clear and still water. Pictures of real merit are often produced from the reflection of the moon in the waters. They also like to look at it through the trees.

THE CREATOR.

There are many in Japan now as well as in the past, who ascribe glory to their *ideal* Creator for the lavish way in which he has beautified their country with his good things.

THE BOOK OF BOOKS.

The Japanese are not only ready to move forward with the tide of European methods, but also for the reception and spread of the Gospel. The sacred Scriptures are printed whole and in parts, and freely circulated, as well as a large variety of other Christian literature. Many reverently regard the Bible as the "Book of Books," and it is touching to see a devout Japanese handle the sacred volume. He clasps it in both hands and then elevates it, in the meanwhile bowing reverently as if he realized that he owed his creation as well as his redemption to it; and yet it is only within the last fifteen years that this change has passed over the minds of thousands with regard to the Bible. Before that period it was regarded as a collection of fables and records of history touching outside nations, and by many, as a book full of deadly* teachings. I have often watched with interest some of my own pupils pore over its contents for hours together, and now and then raise their heads, exclaiming, "This is truly a wonderful book! but is it true? If true, why don't your people practise its precepts? So many of them drink, oppress, and lead immoral lives, and are imperious and rude in their manners." It was often difficult to give a satisfactory answer. Generally, I told them that "God meant everyone to know His mind and will as recorded in the Book, and then left them free to obey." Those to whom *much* is given, from them *much* will be required; and how heavy is our responsibility, who have so long enjoyed the priceless possession of an open Bible!

The Japanese do not smoke opium; but women as well as men are inveterate smokers of tobacco; spirit drinking used to be unheard of among the women, but I regret to say, on official authority, that such is not the case at present.

The income of the Japanese Government is 62,397,570 dollars, of which 13,697,723 dollars is the tax paid for Japanese saké (spirits). In 1886,

---
* The tares of discord sown by the Jesuits, who visited Japan in the 15th century, led to this misconception.

imported spirits amounted to 500,000 dollars. This iniquitous traffic is daily increasing. The enemy of souls is everywhere taking advantage of the apathy of the Church, he follows in the wake of civilisation, and provides the natives of newly-opened countries with all that the perverted appetite appreciates. Oh, what a privilege to be able to enter such a country as Japan, and carry the Gospel to stem the rising tide of sin!

The Japanese want to see us as we are in family life, and to adopt our customs. What a responsible and enviable opportunity is given to us to give *shape*, *tone*, and *stability* to a nation which, from the centre to the circumference, from the base to the summit, beats with a desire to be to Asia what England is to Europe!

IMPERIAL RACE.

The Japanese are an imperial race in a higher sense than the term is understood by us. They have none of the sad traces with which serfdom on the one side of them (Russia), and overbearing mandarins on the other (China) have branded millions of honest toilers.

RELIGIONS.

Strictly speaking, there are but two religions in Japan, viz., Shintoism and Buddhism. The first is peculiar to Japan, and means the law (or religion) of the gods. The second was introduced from

Corea in the third century, and, shortly afterwards, Confucianism, which originated in China; its founder was the patron saint or sage of that country.

The emblem of the Shinto religion is a polished mirror; its teaching is, "Be righteous," "Keep a clean conscience," "Your actions reflect your character."

Buddha promises his votaries *nirvana*, or state of eternal repose. To attain to this, many incarnations in the bodies, first of animals and subsequently of men, are necessary.

The Confucian philosophy enjoins obedience and devotion to parents, and promises the filially pious a long life of happiness, but leaves him in uncertainty as to the future.

A Bright Future.

A Japanese artist said to me, lately, " Teacher, I find that, since I have begun reading the New Testament, a *future* is linked with my life. I suppose the reason why Japanese, Chinese, and Indians do not put perspective into their drawings is because Buddha and Confucius have not given them a future ; and the reason why English artists, on the contrary, put so much perspective into their drawings is because Christianity reveals a *bright* future, and lifts the heart above the material gains of this life."

They respect Law.

The Japanese are a submissive, law-abiding people. Taught, as they have been for ages, to regard their emperor as a direct descendant of the creator of their charming country, and to regard it an honour to lay their lives down for him if need be, it can be easily imagined what reverence and submission they yield to the voice of the throne. One would be inclined to think that, among such a people, democracy would be a system of government which would be regarded as an exotic plant difficult of cultivation. It is to be hoped, however, that the Japanese Government will not hamper and oppress her people with taxes, and thus breed and foster the discontent from which we in England are, to a great extent, suffering.

SIMPLE HABITS.

The Japanese are, as a rule, exceedingly simple in their mode of living. There are times, however, when festivities are carried to excess. The more I saw of them, the more convinced I felt that I lived among a people of truly great minds, and that all they stand in need of is the Gospel. I remember how, time after time, pupils from a distance would drop in and say they would like to take lessons in English from me, acting as if they were under deep obligation to me, when, indeed, it was I who felt under obligation to them. Frequently, some of them would come a long distance to conduct me to their nice homes. The exquisite cleanliness of each was what first struck me, even the large stones that decked the grounds, and the tiles that covered the roof looked as if they received care and attention. Not an atom of anything but what added interest to the scene met my eye. These dwellings were not showy in the least—the architecture was very simple, the houses being built with wood. The sliding partitions were covered with pretty designs, flowers, birds, and crests. The grounds were laid out with curiously trained pines and maples; but there is nothing that answers to our unrivalled park lands and grass lawns in England. Such decorations, in nature and in art, blended, I thought, nicely with the sober but rich attire of the elderly dames, as well as the bright obi (sashes) of the younger ladies. And their almost solemn yet sweet manner, while we partook of a specially prepared repast, was in keeping with the surroundings. I often felt, as I bade them farewell, that an indissoluble heart-link had been formed between us; and, when my pupils after a while left me, my prayers followed them. God met them, and some of them have learned to call Him, "Abba, Father." Pray for them, and not for them only, but for the millions in Japan who do not know the glad tidings of a Saviour's love; and that the time may soon come when the Sun of Righteousness shall rise over that land with healing in His wings.

CHAPTER XV.

A Trip to the Haconé Hills.

"Come ye yourselves apart, and rest awhile."—Mark vi. 31.

THE Haconé Hills are about forty-five miles from Yokohama. The missionaries are glad of this cool resort in the month of August, when it is very hot in the plains.

After a five years' soul-winning campaign among the sailors, I felt a strong inclination to go there for change and rest, more especially as my little school was disbanded for the time being, and the lease of my cottage was out. I procured my passport, and hired a Jinrikisha and two men, and set off by way of the Tokaido, the famous King's highway of Japan.

The sky was as clear as a looking-glass, and reposeful Fuji-san* stood out in bold relief, only that he wore a girdle of mist.

---

* The Japanese compare this phenomenal mountain to Nirvana. It is nearly 13,000 feet above the level of the sea. Tradition says that it and Lake Biwa came into existence on one and the same day. Its apex resembles the corolla of a water-lily, a configuration to which the Japanese attach importance. In all the Buddhistic temples Buddha is seen seated on what represents a full-blown lotus. This snow-white flower is said to typify the soul that has passed through the purgatorial fires into Nirvana.

The tea-houses *en route* have declined from the flourishing state of bygone days, when the *daimios* and their retainers came and went with great pomp. But many of the *Ochayas*, as the tea-houses are called, are very pretty, and I think prosperous, especially one of those we halted at. The boards, mats, and screens were, as usual, clean and bright. Tea and cake were served in the usual way. The maids who waited on us were neatly dressed. My Jinrikisha men went at a splendid pace, evidently bent upon taking me as far as Odawara that day; but night was setting in, and we concluded it was safer for them and me to take rest and shelter at a second-rate hotel we had come to. The room placed at my disposal was enclosed with a net, which smelt "reeky," as we say in Scotland. Sleep, in spite of all the precautions against the audacious mosquitoes, was rendered impossible by the presence of another class of insect met with everywhere. Early in the morning, on taking a cup of tea and a little rice, I paid my bill and left. The air was cool, and Nature so still that it seemed almost a pity to disturb her! The absence of singing birds, where there is so much to associate with them, was conspicuous. Very soon, however, the croaking of frogs, and the discontented, complaining voices of a variety of insects, as well as the presence of butterflies, assured us that those beautiful slopes and bamboo groves were not altogether destitute of life. On coming to a river we saw a crowd of men and women waiting to be forded to the other side.

We got on board an unwieldy-looking boat. At one end were some small cattle, *kagos* (litters), and Jinrikishas; at the other end the passengers. Instead of going straight across to the pier on the opposite side, the boat was rowed along the bank against the stream, a distance of a hundred or more yards, when all of a sudden a signal was given to "hold on tight." My bearers, in consideration of my ignorance of what it all meant, asked me to sit down. The boat then darted like an arrow down the centre of the river, and in a second or two we struck against the pier, which threw the passengers into collision, and provoked a hearty laugh from one and all. The quadrupeds, however, stood unmoved. The banks of those mountain streams or rapids were lined with elongated wicker-work barricades, called snake-baskets, filled with large, round pebbles. The force of the current, without recourse to this primitive invention, would, in a short time, carry all before it. Another hour's ride and we reached Odawara. We turned into a large hotel patronised by farmers and pilgrims. Instead of being served with tea, they gave us a delicious drink made from roasted barley. I paid my men, and engaged a porter to carry my baggage to the top of the ascent, viz., Miyanoshita, where I intended to stay a few days at least. Irregularly shaped hills and ridges, covered with grass, met my eye constantly while I followed my guide through a thickly-shaded wood resonant with a variety of chirping birds and noisy *katy-dids*. After a slow trudge of two hours I reached the summit. The population of Miyanoshita proper is principally composed of a few hotel-keepers. I chose the place my porter conducted me to. The hotels are not so spacious as those on the Tokaido, but they are very airy and clean. The landlord and landlady came and welcomed me by bowing again and again on bended knee, and giving orders to the maids to bring tea and confectionery. Tea was served on a plain but uncommon wooden tray. The neatly piled contents of a curious shaped china dish were pink and white ground rice cakes—mere " mouthfuls "—cut in squares. The tea was poured out by the lady-like hostess in tiny cups, and the maid, kneeling at her right, passed it on to me with a solemn bow. They sat gracefully on their cushions, with feet tucked out of sight. I had to apologise for my awkward posture. The sound of the waterfall near by, and the rustling of the trees of the forest in which this unique village lay embedded, had the effect of sending me to sleep. All around this many-roomed, open dwelling, emerald cone-shaped hills greet the eye. On arriving at Miyanoshita I thought I had reached the summit ; but no, far from it ; there are yet heights on heights. As a foreigner, I was of course an object of interest, and several of the guests, male and female, felt they must come and greet me. I took with me a Gospel, several tracts, and a small romanised Japanese hymn book. Among the visitors were students from Tokyo. I asked one of them to be so good as to read a marked-out portion aloud, which he did, stopping now and then to express approval, and give opportunity to his audience to do the same, for they all seemed deeply interested. I then sang a hymn, reading it verse after verse as I went on. To some of them this was very novel, but not to the male visitors who had been to the Treaty Ports, and had attended the preaching places. They told me that a missionary from Yokohama had visited the place lately, and preached the doctrine in the villages and hamlets of the district. I found out eventually that the preacher was a gentleman who had learnt Japanese in London, and could preach in that tongue soon after his arrival in Japan. I visited some of the guests in their rooms, and found an interesting young man named Inosuké who persistently read a Chinese gospel I had given him. In this, as in every hotel of this village, hot spring baths covered the greater part of the ground floor. These are constantly availed of by the visitors from all parts. The simple contrivance by which these baths are supplied is noteworthy. Bamboo trees take the place of pipes. These are laid horizontally along the hill-sides, terminating, I presume, at the hot water springs, possibly miles away. On touching them one finds out that the temperature is not far from boiling point. The baths are not unlike a baptistry, lined with boards instead of zinc. At one end there are two small openings for admitting the hot and cold water; at the other end there is an outlet which gives the bath a chance of being perpetually clean and inviting. I walked one day across the hills to a village, where I found some acquaintances from different parts. The neatness, tastefulness, and superiority of the hotels over those of Miyanoshita and Aishi-Noyu was very striking. The missionaries and native Christians who come to these places have an enviable opportunity of speaking a word for the Master, by having little meetings among the Japanese visitors who are, summer and winter, to be found there. Here, treaty restrictions do not prevent the foreign missionary, any more than the native, from sowing the seed, and letting the light shine. Many a Japanese traces his conversion to having been spoken to by an evangelist at some of those summer resorts; and frequently on their return to Tokyo and Yokohama, the missionaries are visited by them at their own homes, or preaching places, just as if they had wakened up to realise that the missionary was not the "*bogie*" they were, by some means or other, given to understand. Having spent a somewhat restful few days at this hill-top, I paid my bill and proceeded to Haconé on foot, a porter carrying my luggage. We went along a gradual ascent, passed through Aishi-Noyu, where we halted to reconnoitre the vast environment of hills and hollows. This village is by no means so select as that of Miyanoshita. The people who patronise the baths are not of the well-to-do class exactly. Here, for the first time, I had an opportunity of seeing more than twenty people sitting to their necks in a sulphur bath. After an hour or more's trudge we reached the Tokaido, modernised by the presence of telegraph posts and wires. Two letter-carriers brushed by us, puffing and blowing, as if their lives depended on getting to their destination at an hour all but expired. Each carried two small packets, suspended at each end of a bamboo pole. They were girded with a loin cloth simply, and the perspiration was pouring off their sun-burnt bodies. How suggestive, I thought, they were of the words, "*Salute no man by the way*"! We now sighted the Haconé lake. Fuji-san seems to be looking down in her deep clear waters, and gratefully acknowledging that her placid surface contributes much to his comfort; for without stirring from his kingly throne, he can see his numerous progeny (the Haconé hills) reflected in it.

Next day I joined some of my American friends to the top of one of the highest peaks of this celebrated range. The grass reached to our shoulders. We went single file, holding on to a strong rope. We would fain have rested *en route;* but how did we know but the slimy snake might object to our making so free in a domain, where indeed we should not feel surprised were it proved to us it held sway? This seasoning of suspicion spurred us onwards, and thankful we were when we reached the summit, which was smoothly matted with what looked exactly like the cranberry shrub, so peculiar to the Scottish hills. In a remote corner we saw a fissure nearly overgrown with stunted shrubs and creepers, making it impossible to peer into its depths. Doubtless he it was who vomited forth the shower of black boulders, bestrewing the peak from summit to base, thus creating a picturesque devastation all around. Far away at the horizon, we saw clouds of smoke and ashes. "Ah!" we exclaimed, "it is the safety-valve of this circuit"—the active volcano called O-shima. Our next turn-out was along the full length of the Haconé lake. Our boat was a somewhat capacious one. Grass-covered hills and woods were on either side; and as we were near to the shore going, we had a good opportunity of inspecting the variegated foliage, which always means a great variety of trees. Conspicuous among them is the pink flower of the *saru-suberi*, as it is called (from *saru*, a monkey, and *suberi*, slippery), the supposition being that the monkeys, which abound in the Japanese forests, are always defeated when they attempt to climb it. It looks exactly like a tree off which the bark has been peeled. On landing, we walked along a well-beaten path till we reached (I am afraid to think of it) a honeycomb of danger. The Japanese call the place *O-ji-koku* (lit. Great-hell). As we wended our way up-hill through a romantic wood, we found that the temperature was very suggestive of a Turkish bath. We had at length reached the top of a gradual slope. Trees and shrubs were few and far between in this desolate, steamy place. The geyser was throwing its lava into mid air: its groans and moans, how suggestive of distress and inextricable difficulty! Ferns, moss, and other tiny plants abound here, but they are pale; and no wonder—the marvel is that they exist at all—for nature, instead of being attired in green, partakes of the colour of the sulphur which abounds in every direction. We have to follow our guide closely, otherwise the many tiny footpaths might prove a false step, to say the least. By leaning heavily upon our umbrellas we can break the crust of earth on which the uninitiated might step at any moment to his disadvantage by getting his feet scalded, if not exposing his life to greater peril. *Here* is what looks like the bed of a river; *there* a meandering streamlet of cold, clear water runs over the sulphur-washed pebbles; *yonder* rises a hot spring, nearly at boiling point, and joins partnership with its gurgling, rippling neighbour a little further down. Some Japanese are at work here every day. They fill straw bags with the only product of the place, viz., brimstone. This is used in cities and towns for providing invalids with sulphur baths. Surely this place would not be true to its name were it entirely without that unpopular reptile called a snake. Here and there we caught sight of it gliding silently out of our way. We retreated early, and thankful we were that no evil had befallen us. The most home-like sight in the forest-world my eye rested on, on that day, was the raspberry plant (I can scarcely call it a bush), a oot or so in height, bearing the well-known fruit.

Such, however, is without the rich flavour of that known in England. The hills, with the glorious sunset casting its golden reflections on them, attracted our attention as we wended our way by land and water to our respective hotels. We, at intervals, struck up a favourite hymn of praise. How could we help doing so, surrounded as we were with such a display of our Father's unsullied handiwork, to say nothing of His protecting care! All His works praise Him, and His saints do give Him thanks! Here, missionaries have opportunities, as at all inland places, for preaching the Gospel. Our passports, as British and American subjects, only entitle us to travel for health. But to get permission to hold meetings in a private house or hotel, all that has to be done is to ask leave of the civil officer of the place, and it is granted. And whether the European is forbidden to preach beyond treaty limits or not, it is gratifying to know that the Japanese are at liberty to do so. And, with and without the co-operation of the foriegn missionary, one hears of how such-and-such a place has been visited by the native evangelist, and how gladly the people have congregated to hear the glad tidings of salvation of the grace of God proclaimed by Him. I attended Gospel meetings in this place, when a crowd assembled each time. Ere many years shall have passed, the Japanese will be dispensing with the services of their western brethren, for the truly saved among them seem to feel that woe to them, also, if they do not preach the Gospel to their people. I hope that they will, in the meanwhile, be learning from the manner of life of all foreign missionaries, that they are men and women of God in *life*, in *doctrine*, and *charity*.

MISS G—— AND I LEAVE FOR YOKOHAMA.

The whole household came and bowed and wished us "Good-bye." We felt how little can be done by such weak tools as we are! Yet, in our hearts, we regretted to leave such interesting people in ignorance of God and His free and full salvation. We can but pray, however, that the day is not far distant when this nation shall bow down before Him who will have all men to be saved, and not before dumb idols, as heretofore. Our porters had no sooner shouldered our luggage than we followed them on foot through the village towards the Tokaido. The day was exquisitely fine; very soon we glided into one of the most beautiful passes or glens in the country. The gigantic cryptomeria are peers among all the trees of the forest, and there is a splendid variety, judging of the variegated display of foliage, which covers a vast area; our three hours' tramp was anything but tedious.

We passed enormous rock boulders, nearly as round as a cannon ball. The water oozed freely all over one of them, and the modest sweet-scented *Yu-bana* (a species of polyanthus) grew in thick tufts at irregular intervals. This flower is unknown in England. We asked our men to make a halt so as to reach us some few sprigs to take with us in memory of the superb gullies

TEA-HOUSE MAID.

and ravines of Haconé. On reaching Yumoto, at foot of the descent, we entered a beautiful, newly-built tea-house, called Fuku-sumi. I saw an old pupil of mine in this place; we were pleased to have met so unexpectedly. Our porter, on receiving his fare, returned to his home. We had great difficulty in procuring Jinrikisha men. They are more difficult to deal with inland than at Yokohama. They charge double fare, and take advantage of strangers. The day was beginning to wane, and we had a long way to go. At last, after much parleying, two men offered to take us to Odawara. But we found, to our sorrow, that they were very inefficient, so that we had often to alight and walk in the dark. On reaching Odawara, our next difficulty was to procure a place to put up in for the night. Finally, we enquired at the house of worthy people, who were friends of missionaries; they begged of us to enter. The head of the house lighted his lantern, and went to the local officer and told him that we had arrived late, and could not proceed further that night; what was to be done? Permission was given to him to shelter us, which he and his gentle wife did most cheerfully. Early next morning we left for Yokohama, feeling thankful to God for putting it into the hearts of strangers to show us kindness.

On my arrival I found that my tried faith was rewarded by a letter which contained a fresh proof of my Father's care. So I thanked God for putting me into the furnace and bringing me scathlessly out of it.

> "What more than others I deserve?
> Yet God hath given me more."

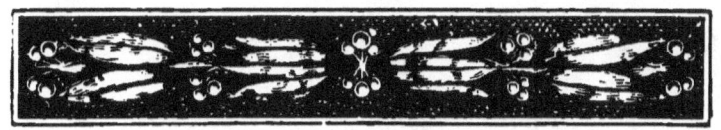

CHAPTER XVI.

How Orientals in London may be reached.

"I was a stranger, and ye took Me in."—Matt. xxv. 35.

IN addition to all that I have said, and will say, in reference to the facilities for evangelistic work in Japan, I should like to make a few suggestions, as to how we may become missionaries without having to leave England. At present there are more than one hundred Japanese in this country—the greater number being in London and its environs. Many of these are students at our Universities, public schools, and in connection with commercial houses in the City. There are also many representatives of other Eastern nations, more especially our Indian fellow-subjects. In no way can we more effectually help forward the cause of missions, and strengthen the hands of those who have already crossed the seas, and are bearing the burden in the heat of the day than by seeking out those strangers, and like true lovers of souls, prove to them—in spite of all they may see and hear to the contrary—that Christianity is, beyond doubt, a *Divine* reality. In England, they are, practically, set free from much that acts as trammels and hindrances to reaching them, and their embracing Christianity in their own lands.

How it Strikes a Stranger.

A Japanese student in London said lately, he thought his own people had hitherto over-valued the state of things called civilisation. Many years ago they had heard much about the blessings which resulted from it, and they were led to expect something much greater and better than what actually exists; not that he looked for perfection, for he frankly admitted that there were many excellent institutions, but the sad fact remained that there were many vicious elements which counteracted the good. He said this in accordance with his best reflection, or unbiased conclusion from observed facts, and not as the result of any national or race prejudice. "We can see," he added, "that Christianity is the religion of love, and its influence and efforts are certainly wonderful; but we cannot help asking why so much disunion exists among Christian people. Its benevolence extends to the utmost parts of the earth, and yet it seems powerless to make its votaries willing to worship their common Father at a common altar." But in spite of this inevitable suspicion, he concluded, "That Christianity had mitigated the evils and injustices of modern civilisation, and that if Christian people could forget minor differences and misunderstandings among themselves, and attest the true spirit of love before the whole world, their influence and confidence would be much enhanced." . . . .

My experience in dealing with strangers sojourning in London, has taught me that the above candid remark is but a sample of how we are regarded by all Orientals, while we and they are at a distance from each other, *i.e.*, while we Christians are neglecting to obey the injunction, "*Be not forgetful to entertain strangers.*" Those of them who have been brought nearer to us, admit that their first impressions were misty and mistaken. "I was a stranger, and ye took Me in," saith our Lord. TOOK ME IN! means personal and mutual intercourse! So that they cannot help *feeling* and *seeing* that God is among us.

By inviting them to luncheon, dinner, or to spend the Sunday with us, and taking them to bright Gospel services and Bible readings, where they can see heart and soul put into the teaching, preaching, and worship of the true God, great good may be done.

Indeed, many things will suggest themselves to soul-winners. Our love for the heathen in this age of progress (when Easterns come to our shores by thousands) may be gauged and tested by God, by the efforts we are making to win them to Him on the spot. We have already lost glorious opportunities. Numbers of Oriental students, who have spent years in our midst, have returned without having been spoken to once about *Jesus and His love*. As already stated, they cannot help seeing the efforts we are making in sending missionaries to their people, but our apathy towards those of them who are here is apt to be misunderstood. Who can estimate the numberless pit-falls and snares, waylaying the stranger, which may be obviated by

> "Little deeds of kindness,
> And little words of love"?

I have already proved how large-hearted English Christians are. In this respect they stand alone; for all that is needful in order to elicit sympathy and practical help in any worthy cause, is to have their attention drawn to it by accredited persons.

Many incidents could be cited to prove the blessed results of efforts of this sort in this great city. I pray God that His children may be more than ever on the look out, touching "*How Orientals in London may be reached.*" All that is wanted is a loving heart.

I feel profoundly thankful to God for the way He has made it, thus far, easy for me to introduce my foreign friends to His own children in this great city. This is a day when many are running to and fro. The Easterns, like the Queen of Sheba, are coming to see things for themselves. May they before their return to Japan, be brought into living contact with Jesus, and thus be forced to say, "It was a true report which I heard in mine own land of thine acts, and of thy wisdom: howbeit I believed not their words, until I came, and mine eyes had seen it: and, behold, the one half of the greatness of thy wisdom was not told me: for thou exceedest the fame that I heard." WHAT A TESTIMONY!

CHAPTER XVII.

Osaka Notes.

"I am the Lord thy God ... thou shalt have no other gods before me."—Ex. xx. 2, 3.

OSAKA is a city of 362,000 inhabitants. It is situate on the south-eastern part of the province of Settsu, and near the mouth of the Yodo river. It is divided into four *Ku* or divisions, viz., eastern division, western division, southern division, and northern division. It has nearly 400 bridges, so that travellers from the West have called it, the "Venice of Japan." Some of the streets run at right angles, and are kept very clean; each householder being responsible for the front of his own dwelling.

The famous castle of Osaka, built three hundred years ago, by Toyotomi, Hideyoshi—the Iron Duke of Japan—is in the eastern part of the city. The site on which it stands was, originally, called Ishiyama. Some of the hewn stones are so large that one wonders how they were carried there, considering the primitive appliances of the times. Our well-informed Japanese teacher told me that it is supposed that several rich daimios, living in distant provinces, presented them to the great soldier.

TEMPLES.

There are two large Buddhist temples in the middle of Osaka, called Mido. The one to the south, is called Minami-no-mido; the one to the north, Kita-no-mido—viz., southern temple and northern temple. They belong to the Nishi-Honguanji sect. Some of the carved works of the celebrated Hidari-Jingoro are to be seen here. There are, besides, paintings of Domonomatahei. The name given to the high-priests of the Honguanji is *Monzeki*. Their headquarters are at Kiyoto, and on paying Osaka an official visit, all the old people come up to them in order to obtain their benediction. Another name given to these ecclesiastics is Ikiniorai, or the living representatives of the gods. In this city there is a street entirely composed of temples, viz., *Teramachi* (temple street). The celebrated temple and pagoda of Tenoji is in the south-eastern part, and the original one, built by the famous prince, *Shotoku-taishi*, was the first Buddhist temple of Japan.

On visiting this place one day, I was struck by the tattered appearance of the interior of a cloister not far from the entrance. The clothes and playthings of children hung on the walls. The bell rope, which the priest at that moment held in his hand, was festooned with the charm bags and other personal relics of the children for whom he was offering up prayer in inimitable cantos. Young women, conducted by their mothers-in-law, came and went with their hearts crushed with sorrow. I entered into conversation with one of them, but her heart was too full to give me a verbal answer when I asked her if she had lost a little one. She had been to Shotoku-taishi's shrine to dedicate her departed treasure's playthings to him, thus propitiating his favour on its behalf.

"*How then shall my daughter, my winsome, wee child,
Find her way through the shadows so lonely and wild?*"

is a translated Japanese couplet showing how the yearning mother heart follows her child through the barren solitudes and cold, deep river of the Buddhistic purgatory. I need not say it was, at least, my privilege to shed a sympathising tear with this mourner. And when we think of how ready they are to receive the comfort which the Gospel alone can give, how can we have the heart to keep it from them any longer?

WHOLLY GIVEN TO IDOLATRY.

I feel it is not too much to say of Osaka that it is a city *wholly* given to idolatry. One uproarious, extravagant festival is followed up by another in quick succession. But, I always felt as I gazed on the frantic crowds at those *matsuris* (festivals), that such a condition of things was more to *our* discredit than it could possibly be to *theirs*, by having left them so long groping in the dark. This is their way for "*making the god happy*," or, of expelling *ill-luck*, whether in shape of disease, non-success in business, or otherwise. How can they know and do better, so long as we retain the key of knowledge of the only living and true God?

A DAIMIO'S CASTLE.

But, while I speak thus, I must bear testimony to the fact that the precious Gospel has been preached at Osaka for many years by a goodly number of American, and a few English missionaries. The net has not been let down in vain by them, as a few extracts on page 220 will show. I give God thanks for the presence of so many American and English missionaries. I feel specially thankful that Miss Tristram and Miss J. Holland are at work in that large city. And yet, with some thirty or more foreign workers, and an efficient staff of native evangelists, one cannot help exclaiming, " What are these among 362,000 souls ! "

The sketch on page 179 represents the interior of a place of worship, and passers-by looking curiously on the prostrate congregation during prayer. It is touching to watch the faces of a Japanese audience as they listen attentively to the preaching, and, like a cornfield bending to the passing wind, they, at intervals, bow assent *en masse* to what appeals to their sense of right.

AT OSAKA.

After spending five years at Yokohama my steps were directed to Osaka. The father of one of my pupils had long cherished the hope that his son would, one day, accompany me to England. But this was most unexpectedly put a stop to by a heavy commercial loss which he had just then sustained. My strength being a good deal exhausted when I left Yokohama, I felt that a visit to England would be beneficial, but the change to Osaka had so far restored me, that I made up my mind to accept an invitation to tarry among them for one year at least. The little sister of my dear resident boy pupil joined us. She was a most engaging child, and, like most Japanese girls of her station and age (nine years), she was never so happy as when in full dress. The day her mother and servant brought her to me she wore a crêpe garment stamped with cherry blossom, birds, spiders and spider's webs, in permanent colours. The thought of being separated from her mother for the first time in her life made her act very naturally by shedding a few tears, which she tried to hide. She was not only a good, but a clever girl.

In less than one year she could read " Peep of Day," " Line upon Line," and the Gospels, as well as any English girl her age. In her second year she could speak a little English, and understand the meaning of much that she read in the Royal Readers she used as school books.

This was proved to me accidentally, when on one day Tennyson's poem, the " May Queen," formed her reading lesson. I could see, as verse after verse was read, that her face grew pale, and her voice faltered ; she closed the book, put it into my lap, and sobbed as if her heart would break, while, with great effort, she said, "*I cannot read this lesson, it is too pitiful*"—*i.e.*, touching. Time after time, as we sat together reading a chapter in the English New Testament, and discoursing at intervals on the "LOVE OF GOD IN SENDING HIS SON," and the "Happy Home Above," my pupils would, one and all, say with emphasis,

JAPANESE BOWING DURING PRAYER, AT CHURCH. Those behind are passers-by.

"Ten-koku-iki-tai" (I should like to go to heaven). This may seem so small a matter, as to be scarcely worth relating. But to me, dim although it is, it is but the "Hosanna to the Son of David," reproduced in *smiles, gestures*, and unuttered prayers of "babes and sucklings."

Japanese Christians have but a child's grasp of things that are full of significance to us; and we are apt to force our meridian measure of light upon them when indeed the dim dawn of "line upon line; here a little, and there a little," would, at this stage, have a more telling effect.

In about one year five interesting boys, the sons of gentlemen, were brought to me; and as I was provided with a house, and the school fees of my Japanese, and a few European pupils being sufficient to meet current expenses, I felt all at once started on a fresh campaign. As at Yokohama, I endeavoured to make the access I had to them the means for reaching them, directly and indirectly, with the WORD OF GOD. I was not placed under any restrictions by the parents of my pupils as to what their children were to be taught. They had no settled prejudice against Christianity, but believed that a knowledge of English had a more practical bearing than anything else I could teach them. The boys were told in my presence by their parents that they were to obey me, and learn their lessons well. Every injunction was responded to by a profound bow. It was a pretty sight to see those well-dressed parents and children sitting, *vis-à-vis*, and at one and the same time *enjoining* and *assenting*.

A CORDIAL RESPONSE.

Another happy recollection of Osaka is the readiness with which some few of the Japanese students from the College came to me, on being invited for three nights weekly, to get assistance in English pronunciation and dictation. When they proposed some arrangement as to how I should be remunerated, I suggested that nothing could repay me like seeing them come on Sunday and read with me in the New Testament; for it was the book which gave us knowledge of God as revealed in His blessed Son Jesus Christ, as well as the knowledge of the Holy Spirit, manifested in the acts and lives of the apostles, etc. The proposal met with a most cordial response, far beyond my expectations.

The week evening text-books were the "Peep of Day" and "Line upon Line" series.

It was most gratifying to watch these bookworms, as ever and anon their faces brightened, and they would draw each other's attention when they read of some miracle, or a parable as related by our Lord. I give these simple instances of how they, even at this early stage (1872—1881), read the Scriptures, and the use that can be made of their thirst for learning to lead them to the Saviour.

IMPROMPTU MEETING.

One of the pupils who attended this class took me aside, one evening, and said, that if I would promise to be present, he would ask the guests in his hotel to come and listen to a Gospel story read to them, by himself, out of the HOLY BOOK. I was only too glad to answer in the affirmative, and fixed the evening for meeting with them. They hurried over their dinner, so as to be in time to hear the reading of the Scriptures. It was delightful to see their engrossed attention while a simple Gospel narrative was read without note or comment. This informal meeting may appear a trifling thing to relate; but I do so to show how much wayside seed may be sown through the introduction of a pupil, pupils' friends, or servant. For my object in writing this book is not to treat on great subjects, but on such as are apt to be overlooked by many who possess the talent for such service.

STORIES ABOUT THE TRUE GOD.

Another instance to show how ready the Japanese are to come to Gospel services and Bible-classes, I may state that on one occasion two of the C. M. S. missionaries took it in turn to come to our house in the city, to address a small meeting of men and women. All I had to do in order to bring them together was to hang a small paper lantern outside the door, with the announcement, written on it in Japanese :

"WE ARE TELLING STORIES ABOUT THE TRUE

GOD AT 8 O'CLOCK;

ALL ARE WELCOME TO ATTEND."

Again, in the same house, I invited little children to come to me every Sunday morning for half an hour to sing hymns and learn one passage of Scripture. It was astonishing how those little mites picked up the hymn and tune, and repeated after me such verses as " Suffer the little children to come unto Me," " God so loved the World," etc., until they were learned. This unpretending start was suddenly put a stop to by cholera having broken out in our neighbourhood. My seven charges were called, *pro tem.*, to their homes, and I was advised to take a house in the foreign settlement, where we resumed our operations after the desolating disease had subsided.

BRITISH BLUE-JACKETS.

Another pleasant recollection, is when a band of British blue-jackets, who had been at the time cruising at Kobé, twenty miles down the coast, paid me a visit. It was most refreshing to be thus visited by a party of *out-and-out* Christians—some of them old friends. A crowd of Japanese gathered round my door wondering, no doubt, what the singular invasion could mean. We spent about two hours in singing hymns, reading and prayer. After tea they left with the young Christian officer under whose charge they were permitted to come.

"*Thou dost refresh thine heritage when she is weary.*"

THE LATE LADY PARKES.

Another happy recollection is when the late Lady Parkes, who had been on a visit to Kobé, came and spent a day with me. Our subject of conversation was the only one, as she used to say, "WORTH TALKING OF." I have rarely met any who had the tact and power to lead off in a spiritual conversation at all times, and in all places, that she had. In speaking of things that related to Christ, she only yielded to her spiritual instincts, and desire to witness a good confession as she had opportunity ; just as if she felt that "*Time was short.*"

> " Faithful may we constant be,
> Called and chosen, Lord, by Thee,
> Till our earthly course be o'er,
> And we rest for evermore."

It is now some years since Lady Parkes and, latterly, her husband, Sir Harry, have passed off this scene. Yet little traits that adorned their characters come frequently before my mind. One of these is, when, on the last night of 1875, the blue-jackets and myself held a midnight prayer-meeting in the Church school-room at Yokohama. To our surprise, Sir Harry and Lady P. entered, and in their wonted genial way wished us a Happy New Year. They were the only members of the British community who, on that evening, favoured us with their presence. Much might be added to record the deep gratitude which my friends the sailors and I, then and since, felt for the hearty interest Sir Harry and Lady Parkes took in the good work going on, in those days, ashore and afloat.

A PASTORAL VISIT.

A pastoral visit, now and then, from a spiritual father in the faith would do a world of good to the missionaries. And if they and their native churches were in the habit of looking forward to receiving a pastoral visit, it would create a sense of the oneness of the Christian family, and react most healthfully on the Church both at HOME and ABROAD. One of the most striking features in mission work among the Christians of Japan is, their sense of responsibility for sending the Gospel to their own countrymen to places where they have emigrated. It can be truly said of them as of the Thessalonians—"*From you sounded out the Word of the Lord.*" For the Japanese Christians have sent native evangelists to their brethren in the Sandwich Islands, Corea, and to various parts of Japan. Moreover, we are in this great city, London, brought into contact with earnest Japanese, who tell us, in our own tongue, of the great things God has done among them. I have also grateful and happy recollections of the excellent opportunities I had of seeing and judging of the progress of the Lord's work, through the kindness of the American missionaries, who invited me to pay them visits, both at Kyoto and Kobé.

It is well-known that the American missionaries are systematic and hard workers, and have the talent of provoking others to good works.

The American missionaries seem also to realise the importance of a native agency; for no matter how well the missionary may speak the language, one learns more and more that the Japanese mind must be *handled by a Japanese mind.* They have been educated to reason things out, and there is less time wasted when combated by one from among themselves.

THE JAPANESE AT HOME.

I had frequent opportunities of visiting the homes of my pupils, and it was then that I un-learnt false ideas which I had imbibed about Japan from the reports of sensational writers.*

I saw how necessary it is to know them in their daily life before they can be rightly understood. Very often we see the lady of the house waiting on her visitors at meals. She takes to this work in a cheerful, matter-of-fact way.

---

* "A snail overturning the castle wall with its horns" is a Japanese proverb, expressive of *impossibility*. A Japanese scholar quoted it one day in my hearing, in reference to those who wrote books on the domestic life and moral condition of the Japanese, before they had learnt the language and the character of the people from personal observation. A thing which cannot be done in a day!

In my ignorance, I often remonstrated with her by saying it made me feel uncomfortable to be waited on. But my entreaty seemed as absurd, to her, as it would be to ask a chivalrous English gentleman to discontinue showing little attentions to his beloved wife, or lady friends in general. What I wish to impress on the reader is, that to wait on her visitors does not degrade her in the eyes of her people, any more than in her own.

This custom, with its advantages and disadvantages, is, in common with many of Japanese old usages, dying out. It is Christianity alone that can impart that chivalry towards the weaker sex which we, as a nation, love to encourage, and which we need to cultivate a little more than we do if we would come up to the Scriptural standard, viz., "BY LOVE, SERVE ONE ANOTHER." This is something higher and better than what the WORLD calls gallantry.

MORAL TRAINING.

The Japanese do not show their feelings by *kissing* and *terms* of *endearment*, as we do: but they love one another for all that! Their extreme reserve on this point is the outcome of their sense of delicacy and moral training.

Let those who say that the Japanese know nothing of love, go and stay in a family of the middle class, and they will soon see that the wife is kindly treated; though, of course, she is subordinate to her husband in every respect. The husband's devotion often shows itself in what we would call *pampering*. Look into her wardrobe, and see how her carefully put away silk and crêpe dresses proclaim attention from the husband! Watch his countenance when she is laid on a sick bed! All that money can procure is ungrudgingly provided, as well as the best medical aid. Does she wish to spend a whole day at the theatre? all that is necessary is that, for her own and husband's credit, she should be properly attired and chaperoned. If, however, she is inclined to be too much given to pleasure, he expresses his love in another way by sending her to a lonely country place, to stay with a poor relative, who is expected to give her " DISCIPLINE, DRILL, and DUTY; and when she wants a change, to give her DUTY, DRILL, and DISCIPLINE," and thus correct her in time! In a few months she is restored to her own home, and, doubtless, the first thing she does is to acknowledge, as she salutes her husband on bended knee, that the discipline, although humbling, was the best corrective that could be devised. Her lord listens meekly, looking as grave as a judge; but in his heart he loves her; it would, however, be contrary to etiquette to say how glad he is to see her, and how lonely the house has been without her. With an air of coolness and affected contempt he will tell her to be careful, and not repeat her folly, lest . . . . . ! She leaves his presence half crestfallen, and half inclined to smile; and the husband smiles too, but only *inwardly!*

ONE THING THOU LACKEST.

A Japanese gentleman has lately affirmed that, "*If we look into the relation between the parents and their children, and the mutual relation among brothers and sisters, he will not hesitate to declare that we shall find far deeper feelings of love in Japan than in other countries, where society consists entirely of individual units. If we take the whole community of Japan, he does not think that the people, as fellow-countrymen, love one another in less degree than those of other civilised states.*" Yet, with all these superior advantages which Japan holds over every other Eastern nation, and over many in this country, yet "ONE THING THOU LACKEST!" is written legibly on her walls. The only elevating and purifying influence is Christianity; and until she has this, she will not be truly stable, nor permanently happy.

ENTERTAINED BY MR. AND MRS. FUJITA DENZABURO.

Just as I was preparing to leave Osaka for England in 1881, the father and mother of one of my pupils honoured me with an invitation to stay with them for a week or two. They had no idea what a boon this was to be to one who wished to inspect the family life more closely than could be done by simply calling on them. Their curiously constructed dwelling, the best in Osaka, was a pleasant study. It was a pattern of neatness, to begin with, inside and out, indeed the tiles looked as clean as a new penny. The mistress and her train of servants devoted much of their time to needlework, and the various duties which necessarily devolve upon women everywhere. The home expenditure was carefully entered into a book, and balanced on the reckoning day by the mistress, and handed over to the head of the house.

The female hairdresser came twice a week to rearrange Mrs. Fujita's hair. Only an artist can put up a Japanese lady's hair properly! An hour, at least, is spent over it.

THE LOVE CUP.

No pains have been spared to make my visit at Mr. F.'s happy and profitable. I asked all sorts of questions about every thing I saw. On one evening, Mr. F. had a party of gentlemen to dine with him, female minstrels were invited to play and dance before them. Mrs. F. and my pupils sat for hours with me in my room, while the feasting and music went on below. They with characteristic good nature answered all my questions. When the guests retired, I was asked to join Mr. and Mrs. F. in the prettiest little room I saw in Japan. My presence at that unusually late hour (9 p.m.) gave surprise and pleasure; and my hostess smilingly told her husband of my astonishment at the account she gave me of his own and friends' carousals: the response met with consisted of a series of dignified bows. He then clapped his hands, instead of ringing a bell, and the sliding doors were pushed back, and a servant entered, and at once fell forward on hands and feet. Orders were given to bring in the apparatus for making tea (*hiki-cha*), and soon a large and rare-looking stove made its appearance, with a round black metal pot and ladle. The pot soon bubbled and boiled; and then the master of tea ceremonies entered with the queer-looking tea bowls, a box containing ground tea, teaspoon, a bamboo whisk, and tea cloth. The bowl in which the tea was made was handed to me. I did not like to drink alone, and said so; whereupon my host explained that only one bowl of tea was made at a time, and was passed round, each one taking a sip. He said that three hundred years ago the tea-soup, *or love-cup*, had been a very popular institution. Ri-kiu Hide-yoshi's, master of ceremonies, was not only an adept at the making of tea, but had also brought the manufacture of tea-bowls to a high degree of perfection. I ventured to say that it seemed to me to be a pity that so much money should be spent on a custom which was a mere relic of an effeminate age. "I believe," he replied, "that if the custom were revived amongst us, it would tend to counteract the increasing love for wine and spirit drinking."

Our host kept a man constantly employed to ransack all the old art shops in the place, and buy up any old tea-vessels he could find. He has a wonderful collection of them, and showed me some of the oldest and most valuable. Some of them were worth one hundred to one thousand dollars each. An old man comes at regular intervals to make bags of silk and satin, for holding and preserving these valuable relics.

Were I to relate all that I saw at Osaka alone, and which my friends took great pains and pleasure in explaining to me, I should have to write much more than I have space for. I owe special thanks to my pupils, and Mr. Nakamura, our teacher, for their untiring efforts in contributing to my notes on Japan. I am, day by day, seeking to requite the debt of gratitude which I owe them, by asking God my Father to *bless, preserve*, and *prosper* them. Nothing delights me more than hearing from them, which I do occasionally.

Mr. and Mrs. Nishikawa, Mr.* and Mrs. Fujita Denzaburo, Mr. and Mrs. Munakata, are prominent among those in Osaka who had throughout acted most considerately and kindly towards me. I also owe special thanks to Professor Summers, who at different times carefully and efficiently examined my pupils, and encouraged them and me in our studies.

MINO

is a place about ten miles outside Osaka. Here are glens and a waterfall. Mino must be seen in order to be appreciated, especially in October, when a brilliant show of maple tints predominates. A rainbow spans the cascade always when the sun shines. Here, monkeys are often seen perching on the boughs of trees, looking morosely at all who come and go. Small Shinto shrines are at the entrance of this gorgeous ravine.

---

* Mr. Fujita Denzaburo is the merchant prince of Japan, and is represented in the City of London.

CHAPTER XVIII.

A Trip to Arima (*August*, 1880).

. . . "The strength of the hills is His also."—Psalm xcv. 4.

ARIMA is a pleasant summer resort, consisting of a community of straggling villages and hamlets, in the prefecture of Hiogo, about eighteen miles inland from the open port of Kobé.

Missionaries and others residing at the treaty ports go to this cool retreat during the months of July and August. Amah and I left Osaka at 12 o'clock noon, and went by rail as far as Kobé, where we hired our Jinrikisha and two pull-men, and thus pursued our journey. The further we got inland, the more romantic the scenery became. The running streams—rippling and gurgling as we wended our way, seemed to salute us like old friends, for the wooded glen through which we passed, bore a striking resemblance to familiar places in Scotland. The villages and scattered hamlets are half hidden amongst a profusion of rich vegetation. The houses are built simply of wood and clay, and are not always so suggestive of comfort as our experience of the Japanese domicile would lead us to expect. The cots are, however, compactly covered with a thick thatch of coarse grass, and here, as at other places, one sees the iris growing in irregular tufts all over the roof.

The soil of this district is fertile; and, judging from the square patches of millet, rice, wheat, barley, cotton, Indian corn, and sweet potatoes, which frequently meet the eye, it is also very productive. One longs for the plough of civilisation to visit these inland places, if only to elevate the condition of the thrifty farming population, who seem not to have the comforts their toil and steady going habits deserve.

We arrived at Arima at 6 o'clock. We stayed at a second-class Japanese hotel, which was not all that we could have wished, but of which we made the best for the time being.

Arima is imbedded among a community of hills. The people are thrifty, steady, and independent. They have few needs, and live contentedly amidst the beautiful scenery which surrounds them.

The trade of the place seemed to be freely and equally divided among the inhabitants; and this, I think—with the absence of drink, which destroys the happiness and contentment of so many homes in England—is the cause of the look of independence and satisfaction, which the visitor cannot fail to perceive. Monopolists, it appeared to me, could neither flourish, nor be tolerated in such a place as this.

I saw but few children playing about, the reason being, as I presumed, that they (like East End match box and envelope makers) were busily at work all day with their nimble fingers: for every alternate house seemed to be a factory on a small scale.

It is in the bamboo basket shops that we see the taste and skill of the villagers, running in a different direction to that of agriculture. Many of the things in these shops are exact imitations of what English and Americans use. The manufacture of articles made from bamboo and straw, seems to go together. Heaps upon heaps are to be seen in tasteful variety, and the makers are at one and the same time retail and wholesale dealers. The trade carried on in this class of goods, both with the Europeans and native traders, contributes much to the flourishing condition of the locality.

NATURE'S WATERPIPES.

As a rule, the houses here are surrounded with plots of ground, shut in by rude dykes, or bamboo fences. The water is conveyed to the village from a distance, by means of wooden aqueducts of immense length. Bamboo trees, when cut down, very frequently, supply the place of waterpipes. The water itself is most wholesome, clear, and tempting. There are two public baths to which the natives resort. These are supplied in much the same way they are elsewhere in Japan.

The Japanese are in the habit of bathing *en famille* at their homes, especially the mother and children, the husband alone taking the precedence in this, as in everything else, by having the bath all to himself. The labouring classes, however, are not fastidious, for it is a common sight to see a group of at most ten availing themselves of the accommodated space of fifteen feet square. They do not swim about, but sit to their necks in the water. This is to the Japanese not a luxury merely, but a necessity. It is very puzzling to them how Europeans can dispense with such an inexpensive advantage, as a warm bath, at any rate, once a day.

One thing struck me at Arima as being most homelike, viz., flocks of chickens and ducks. I saw no horses, except those passing to and fro as beasts of burden.

Here, as elsewhere in Japan, the people are as happy as they are industrious. At the back of the village there is a temple; in front of which are two flights of steps. One would suppose that they led to a more magnificent edifice than is the case; but, in common with many other buildings of the sort, the glory has departed from it, for the worshippers are losing confidence in their idols; and as they are flourishing in temporal affairs, are, like the Westerns, becoming engrossed in amassing wealth, and are to all intents and purposes saying: "Let us eat, drink, and be merry." In a wing of the temple I found a number of children congregated, humming their lessons.

The deserted look of the whole place, absence of fuming incense, lighted candles, the forlorn and impoverished appearance of the priests, all indicated that there is a decline from the state of affluence which once obtained among them. The presence of certain idols proved, also, that in times past many had recourse to this temple in order to do them homage.

As I turn away from this depressing scene, and revel with delight in the glorious panorama before me, the unsullied work of God's divine finger, I am forced to say that "Every prospect pleases, and only man is vile." But let us proceed to the waterfall (Tsu-dzu-mi-no-taki). The pathway winds in a zigzag direction, until it ends at the edge of an almost dried up mountain stream. No doubt at one time it could boast of a bridge, or something of that description, but the storms and furious waterfloods, issuing at times from boundless sources, far above us, in common with much else, have carried it away. But for such uprootings of trees, by the force of wind and torrents, the enjoyable devastation, which contrasts so beautifully with the richly covered hills all around us, would not exist.

The hill to our right is well nigh perpendicular, and, gazing at it from its base, we see nature capping it with a canopy of white cloud, as if intelligently doing honour to so august and majestic a scene. Pines and fir trees crown these cone-shaped heights, and at the base are to be seen scrub-oak, chestnut, and bamboo. There is nothing here that represents our fully-developed English oak.

Another shrub, peculiar to the Arima hills, is the san-sho. Its blossom and leaves resemble those of the mountain ash; its leaves are used for flavouring soups; its fruit is a pungent peppercorn. This plant is also often seen in flower pots, and sold by market gardeners for a few cents.

BLAE-BERRY.

In the course of my rambles I alighted on a spot where abounded our well-known Scottish "blae-berry." The sight brought to my recollection early associations. It was a veritable *blae-berry* bed, bearing sparsely its own fruit. Yet the Japanese poet could not, with the Scottish bard, sing, "Where the blae-berries grow 'mang the bonnie blooming heather," for the only thing of a Scottish origin that kept it company was a soft bed of golden moss.

The waterfall itself can scarcely lay claim to the name, as it is only about 10 or 12 feet in height, diverging into two and living a twin life, flowing on in endless song—a spring of water that never runs dry.

This cascade is much resorted to by the natives, who stand under its dashing foam as one of their summer luxuries. At the base of the precipice it disappears, as it enters a deep cavern, screened in front by a neck of rock, alongside of which is a bridge of planks. An old man, who is evidently tollkeeper, expects to receive a few cents from all who make use of it. From this platform a good view of the waterfall is obtained. A little lower down the stream appears again, and flows meandering over a pebbly bed for a considerable distance. The flora of the place are about the same as at

Miyanoshita. The azalea, wild camellia, and other flowering shrubs, abound here ; but now, in the autumn, all look sere, and flowerless. The honeysuckle, with a variety of the vine tribe, each in beautiful blossom, trailing over the trees and shrubs abound in every direction.

YU-BANA.

In visiting a grotto, on the western side of the village, I lighted on an enormous boulder, covered with moss ; and here and there on the summit I saw sweet tufts of the yu-bana. This flower is as rare as it is delicate, the gardeners only are acquainted with it. It richly deserves a place among the honourable company of hot-house plants, though I have strong suspicion that it will not flourish in any other than the place assigned to it by Nature. Its colour is violet, and not unlike the potato flower in its formation, but most delicate and sweet scented. Its leaf is long and thick, something like that of the primrose.

I saw nothing of the tsuta-mamé, or pea ivy, which is so frequently seen at other places, festooning and clasping itself around cedars and stately pines, until their branches look picturesquely entangled in it. The juniper seems to be quite a native of the soil, for each shrub was crowned with a crop of its own berries. Whether or not the Japanese have discovered the use it is put to in the manufacture of gin, I cannot say ; though doubtless the herbalist and the apothecary have, in common with a thousand other rare roots, barks, leaves, and fruits, turned it to a good account. I am glad, however, to bear testimony to the fact that Japanese women are not drinkers, and in keeping with much that I discovered as praiseworthy in their character, I have not once, during my sojourn of nine years among them, seen a woman under the influence of strong drink. I regret to say, however, that drunkenness is on the increase.

The hills at Arima range more widely apart than they do at Mino (a place outside Osaka, celebrated for its autumn tints). A few are conical in shape, rugged and steep. Immediately above the village there is a clear mineral spring, which the natives call "Tan-san-sui." It strikes me that the inhabitants are, as yet, but little aware of its medicinal qualities and virtues, for such a spring in Europe or America would be shut in with an elaborately built pump-room, and, resorted to by thousands. As to the bird tribe, I observed the lark, and the oriole. The mellow notes of the latter being at this time subdued by the humming and querulous hissing of the thousands of insects, which congregate in trees and bushes, especially the cicada.

BUTTERFLIES.

Butterflies, of uncommon size and beauty, flit about in every direction. At night our light attracts, through our open windows and verandahs, rare and beautiful moths. The walls and ceilings of our rooms afford ample scope for entomological research; but beyond expressing admiration for their magnificently painted wings, we had no inclination to deprive them of life and liberty by

CARPENTER AT WORK.

carrying them off as trophies, leaving this to naturalists from the western world, already to be seen on the spot, embracing the land of the " Rising

Sun," as a wide field for the cultivation of their taste and talents. On my return home to Osaka, I went across the mountains; not so much because of its being a shorter route, but that I might get a better view of the glorious sweep of hills, valleys, plains, and streams, under the dominion of the "King of Day," careering in strength, and dispersing blessings everywhere in this realm from which it sprang and had its birth. Japan means " Spring of Day," or " Sun's Source."

Arima certainly looks blessed and grateful for the lines having fallen to her in pleasant places. In the ascent, the journey was rendered easy and pleasant by a winding pathway, newly made from base to summit. The mist fell insensibly, and soon it penetrated to the skin.

The soil is very rich, and much finer grass carpets the ground than one generally sees in Japan. Some cows, employed in carrying loads of merchandise, were met by us. Here, to all appearance, landslips are things of frequent occurrence in rainy weather. As we drew near to the top, we passed under a curiously constructed tunnel-shaped arch. The water oozed out overhead, and stalactites were formed. The current of air passing through it at that moment was too fresh to be pleasant. Quite at the top of this continuation of hills, we found the temporary abode of the man, with his wife and children, who served us in passing, with tea, cake, and watermelon. Now, on surveying this vast scene in all directions, silence took possession of us, as if in recognition of the mute, and yet eloquent, presence of Nature. And notwithstanding the respective charms of what we beheld and admired on the plains below, yet we had had practical proof that "Distance lends enchantment to the view!" After this, we commenced to descend in the direction of Sumiyoshi, the scene changing as we moved onwards, but continuing in panoramic beauty and effect. As we pursued our course in the winding pathway, the hues of green grass, wherewith the sugar-loaf shaped hills were clothed, became varied. The sun, already above the horizon, was casting up darts of gold, and, like a gigantic sunflower, was compassing the vast tract of sky, land, and water. One felt constrained to halt for a moment, and endorse the language and feelings of the poet king: "*The sun . . . rejoiceth as a strong man to run a race*"; the snow-white clouds are scattered by its appearance, and between its golden corona lies the blue, calm sea. For some time I mistook it for the sky, until suddenly a prettily rigged barque began to flit and float in gleeful play on the placid main. Oh! how we deplored the want of talent to reproduce this enchanting scene with pencil or pen, and so let less privileged friends at a distance, possessed of capacities for appreciating the "Beautiful," far beyond what we could lay claim to, luxuriate, in a measure, in this never-to-be-forgotten "Beholding."

As we approached the plain, the scene became less captivating, our winding pathway leading us alongside undulating ravines and murmuring brooklets, and the clematis, morning-glory, and common pink, profusely illuminated the green carpet on both sides. "*O Lord, how manifold are thy works! in wisdom hast thou made them all: the earth is full of thy riches.*" Psa. civ. 24.

The American missionaries, and their efficient native evangelists, manage to bring many of the villagers together on Sunday evenings, and they listen most attentively to the preaching. Even in this out-of-the-way place—Arima—there are a few who have embraced the precious promises, and laid hold on eternal life. May God's saving health and way of salvation become increasingly known here, as in the many towns and villages all over the land! "*Then shall the earth yield her increase; and God, even our own God, shall bless us.*" Psa. lxvii. 6.

N.B.—More than thirty years ago, a bed-ridden child of God, in Scotland, on my having given her a bunch of spring flowers, pressed them to her breast, closed her eyes, and looked as if wrapt in adoration. Suddenly the silence was broken by herself, saying: "Oh! ——, I often say to myself, *What must the beauty be that is in Himself when He has put such beauty on the flowers.*" I have never forgotten the remark, and I have often felt its truth and force when spending a few days at a summer resort in different parts of Japan.

CHAPTER XIX.

Hotel Life at Osaka.

"Ho, every one that thirsteth, come ye to the waters."—Isa. lv. 1.

NOW that my happy visit at Mr. Fujita's is at an end, and my cases are packed, and sent to the shipping office in readiness for leaving for England soon, I cannot do better than spend the remainder of my time among the Japanese, and see them as they are in hotels. The landlord and his wife are old friends of one of my pupils, and, for his sake, they have given me a hearty welcome.

As a rule, the hotel-keepers in Osaka do not care to entertain foreigners, as they soil their mats. On conducting me to my room, my host clapped his hands; this was at once responded to by an audible *hoi-i-i*. Immediately a maid pushed aside the sliding door, and knelt to receive her orders, and was told to bring the *hyi-bachi* (fire-box), tea, and cake. "Hé," was the reply, and off she went. They apologised for the poor room placed at my disposal, as well as for the noisiness of the servants. Orders were given to spread the coverlets, and to bring txe *kotatsu*. Of these, there are different kinds; mine consisted of a large earthenware bowl full of ashes, with a ball of ignited charcoal buried in it: this was covered with a square wooden frame, with cross bars at side and top to let out the hot air. It was placed on what represents a mattress, and over it were laid the upper coverings. In a very short time this shake-down was warm enough to be enjoyable, especially in the first week in March, when, as with ourselves, the weather is rather sharp.

The *kotatsu* is not only of use at night, but also in the daytime. Ladies, very often, while at needlework, sit in a circle round it, with a pretty silk coverlet placed over it, so as to get the full benefit of the warm air. To us this might seem a luxury; but, as the servants, as well as their masters and mistresses, avail themselves of it, we may look upon it as one of the common necessities of life in Japan. At five o'clock a.m., the servants of this hotel are expected to be up, and at work. The cook seems to be a very religious man; the first thing done by him is to go outside, and turn his face towards the East or *Isé*, where the shrine *par excellence* of the "Sun Goddess" is situate. He claps his hands, raising them reverently to his bowed head, and then he rubs and claps them again, praying audibly the whole time. On entering the house, he goes through the some performance in front of the *Kami-dana* or shelves, on which are placed the tiny tablets, as well as offerings of food and flowers. He then begins to light his fire. I told him one day that his heart yearned for happiness, and that the gods he worshipped would never give it; that there was a true God who loved him, and that He longed to bless him, and make him happy. "*Hé, hé, naru-hodo!*" (Yes, yes, really!) was all the reply I got. Shortly afterwards I gave him and the maids tracts in their own language. They looked at them with astonishment, and bowed, thanking me, and at once sat down and read them in a sing-song way, now and then exclaiming, "Really! How good!" They returned the tracts as soon as they had done reading them, but I told them to keep them, whereupon they skedaddled to their mistress's room to show what I had given them. How deeply I regretted at this moment, my run-down health, and being obliged to leave such interesting people! The maids enjoyed waiting on me; my questions amused them. The clerk of the hotel sat behind a grating casting his accounts, with the abacus before him, and piles of thick account-books around him.

Domestic Sorrow, and my Trip to Nara.
(From my Diary.)

I have been in this hotel nearly a month. The swallows are actually building their nests inside the entrance, a circumstance which the people of the house consider lucky. The only child in the family, a girl of four, is frantic with excitement. Is it the boldness of the swallows, brushing by her as tamely as if she and they had been nurtured together, and therefore understood each other, that makes her so jubilant? It is difficult to say. Everyone who enters is struck by her bright chirping manner as she hops about, while with a salaam and an *O-hairi* (please enter), she salutes all the guests who cross the threshold. In the evening a dark cloud hovers over the household; the maids look pale and sad, and the mother is out of sight. "Where is your mistress?" I inquired. "She is with O-Haru-san, who is dangerously ill." "What is the matter?" I asked. "She has had a fit, and the doctor thinks she cannot live," was the altogether unlooked-for reply. "I trust the pet of the parents is not to be taken from them," I inwardly prayed as I returned to my room. The doctor had paid the little sufferer his second visit, but no hope was given that she would see another day. The parents looked the picture of misery, the grandmother none the less so. I was a sufferer too, and all the more because I could render no assistance. The mother, as if taking advantage of all the guests being asleep, gave way to weeping aloud: "You have not said 'good night' to your mother; *say, good night! say, good night!*" I heard her say to her lambkin who was sinking fast. The servant went and fetched the grandmother, who was asleep near by; she came directly, and, like Hagar, sat at a distance from where the child lay, as if she had not the courage to see it depart: her grief was not wild, but deep. The doctor paid them a third visit, his servant accompanying him, carrying a lantern, on which were prettily painted the name and crest of his master. On entering the sick room, the mother's disconsolate sobs were for the time being suppressed. He felt the child's pulse, and in a moment our wistful ears heard him say, "She is dead!" The grandmother, burying her face in her hands, would at intervals take a sheet of paper (pocket handkerchief) out of her sleeve, and wipe her eyes, and mutter to herself "Dead! Impossible!" It was only yesterday that she played about the place, and said "*Ohayo*" (Good morning) to all who entered. The mother's wild grief was most affecting. "*Domo!*" (exclamation) was uttered by one and all, as they poured in to express their sympathy. I, at last, about 3 a.m., felt strengthened to go and join the mourners. On entering the room, I found it full of relations and friends, and the little body of the departed child was lying on its pallet, looking as rosy and sweet as if sleeping; and so it was. I assured the mother that it was well with the child; that if she trusted in Jesus as her Saviour, she would meet O-Haru again; she bowed and thanked me, but I felt that all present regarded my words as an expression of condolence merely. "Do not grieve too much, or you will make yourself ill! O-Haru-san has gone on a long journey," her relations kept saying to her. Fresh friends came and went at intervals, showing their sympathy more by expressive bows than by words. The nearest relations were busy writing letters to friends at a distance, inviting them to the funeral. This scene was a very harrowing one, and I sometimes wondered whether, like the Chinese, they would not attribute the death of their little one to their having a foreigner under their roof; but it made not a shadow of difference, they were as kind and as attentive as ever. Oh, that I could bear this burden with them, or what would be infinitely better, teach them to cast it on the "Burden-Bearer"! There were no superstitious observances that I could see; at any rate, for six hours after the death. They sat in the stooping attitude of desolated hearts around the body of the living, and I believe, happy departed spirit. I intended to leave that morning for Nara, in the company of a party of missionaries who were going there for the day, but I felt the impropriety of so doing, while the whole house was mourning. I told them this, but they entreated me to go, saying, "Your remaining with us will not bring her back." As I felt that if I were out of the way, they might feel at greater liberty to attend to the obsequies of their dead treasure, I took my leave of them sadly. The day was very fine; my two Jinrikisha men trotted fairly the long distance of twenty miles, stopping for rest at the different tea-houses *en route.* Villages, temples and shrines appeared at short intervals all along the journey. The fields were beginning to look green, especially the wheat patches. The nearer we came to Nara, the more we realised how much attention was given to the cultivation of tea. I found my friends enjoying their pic-nic under the shade of a spreading cedar. We went through some of the temples and exhibitions of antiquities of this ancient capital; but I felt too tired to enjoy all the sights and to ask questions, so I made up my mind to stop at the largest hotel in the town and take a survey next day. All my friends left for their homes.

"COME UNTO ME . . . . I WILL GIVE YOU REST."

The place is alive with pilgrims—what a sight! They are seeking their Creator, and He is seeking them. They look weary and disappointed; some of them have been to the head-quarters of Shintoism, and others are going there; this they have done for ages. Oh, mystery of mysteries! How much longer will those who are entrusted with the Gospel leave them seeking rest where it cannot be found?

The constant inflow of pilgrims, with their tinkling bells, gives the place a peculiar, and, to my mind, a monotonous character. I met a group of interesting women, to whom I gave a few tracts. They were looking towards the western mountains, behind which, at that moment, was sinking the setting sun, which had a peculiar magenta appearance. One of the women said, with a solemn face, that *Ten-shoko-dai-jing* (Sun-goddess) was ill, thus accounting for the peculiar tinge!

The hotel where I am is evidently constructed with the view of accommodating the long processions of pilgrims, which arrive at certain seasons of the year. This, it seems, is an auspicious time, for no fewer than 500 are at this moment (March 31st,

8 o'clock p.m.) in the lower story, washing their feet. And what a Babel! Of course, all have something to say to the maids who wait on them. What with the clapping of hands, and other noises, to say nothing of the clatter of dishes, the marvel is that the human brain can stand it. One would think that, as I was not a pilgrim with a broad-brimmed hat, gourd, and tucked-up garment I should not be one of the number who required to have their feet washed. But yes; a smiling maid came to me with a wooden footbath and towel, and asked me to let her wash my feet. I assented, and in five minutes I was, in common with 500 of my fellow creatures, enjoying the comfort which feet-washing after a journey always gives. The maid, instead of shrinking from me, a stranger, seemed to take to me, and begged of me not to feel lonely. She told me that European gentlemen had lodged with them before, but not ladies. She then served me with rice and a few nick-nacks, and, on saying *O-yasumi* (Good night!), I gave her some tracts to give to the other maids.

Suddenly the hum of voices ceased, and the contrast was so great that to break the intense lull would be a relief. A lady in the room next to mine opened the sliding door between us, and said, "*Good night, foreign lady, we are near you, so don't feel lonely.*" I thanked God for this little ripple or *touch of nature*, in the midst of what seemed an unbearable stillness. I did not rest well that night; whether my sleeplessness was caused by the strain of the previous evening at my hotel in Osaka, or by the depressing effect of seeing so many pilgrims trudging on foot for hundreds of miles seeking rest for their immortal souls, I cannot say. At dawn, about five a.m., the maids were up, and, soon after, the perpetual jargon of 500 voices prevailed. After that, the clatter of dishes, and sliding partitions being pushed into their receptacles for the day. "If to sleep was impossible before," I say to myself, "there is far less chance for it now"; so I made up my mind to have a quiet nap after the pilgrims had departed. As soon as they had done breakfast, the maid brought me a basinful of hot water and a towel. I dipped the latter in the water, and then wrung it out—according to the custom of the country—and wiped my face. Another good wring, and I wiped it dry. In a minute, several persons stood outside, peeping through the creaks and crannies to catch a glimpse of the first European some of the pilgrims had ever seen. In about ten minutes, the hubbub of many voices died away, as one after another took their leave of host and hostess. I craved for a little sleep, but the maid told me it was their custom to clear the room of all bed clothes, and then dust everything. Thus my request to be left alone for another hour was unheeded. The day was exquisite. I found my way to the *Dai-butzu-do*, or temple of Buddha, where I sat for half-an-hour on the steps in front of this idol. A few curious lookers-on gathered around me, among them a man who professed to be a guide to any visitors who cared to employ him. He gave me a printed statement of the date of the casting, as well as the component parts and dimensions of this enormous statue, viz :—

THE DAI-BUTZU OF NARA.

Height 53 feet, or 7 feet more than that of the Kamakura Dai-butzu.

Length of face	16-ft. 0-in.
Breadth of face	9-ft. 5-in.
Lehgth of eyes	3-ft. 9-in.
Length of ears	8-ft. 5-in.

Its face is said to express supreme indifference to all that is going on in the lower world, or having reached the nirvana. We then proceeded to the Ni-gatsu-do. Lighted candles abounded, and the hum of voices, as the priests and people intoned and bowed in the presence of their respective idols, was very painful. Binzuru, the god-of-healing, had his face and other parts of his body nearly rubbed off by the frequent rubbings of devotees. Whatever portion of the body is afflicted, they rub the corresponding part of the idol's person, and, by such means, they expect healing. Stalls and shops abound here, where there are charms and every variety of priestly invention calculated to appeal to the religious sentiment of the worshippers who go and come by thousands. The loftiness of the cedar trees is very remarkable ; the temples, of which there are many, are shaded by them. Here, as in many parts of Great Britain, " The deer across the greensward bounds." Along a well-beaten pathway are old women with stalls, on which are laid dry bean-curd cakes. They press the sale of them upon every passer-by, so as to perform the

BUDDHA.

meritorious deed of ministering to the servant of Kasuga (a Shinto god), with whom the deer is always associated in art, if not in fact, according to the belief of the superstitious. The tame creatures, forced by hunger to wander about these traps, come quite close to one, and eat the cake out of his hands. Familiar terms with the human species have not improved their appearance, I think. They seemed to me to have lost their native dignity. The park or wood in which they roam is a very wide one, and, doubtless, in many respects, superior to Richmond and Bushey parks; but well-kept walks, fine grass, primroses, and birds that sing vigorously, like the thrush and blackbird, are always to me a great want. I paid my guide for his help; and my two Jinrikisha men, who chose to wait to take me back to Osaka, said it was time to start. They took me by a different route, across the hills, on the return journey. In less than an hour we got into a beautiful glen, where Nature gave us fresh insight into her vast realm.

On reaching Osaka, I went straight to my hotel, and found that preparations were being made to give a great feast to all the relations and friends, and thus "make the spirit of O-Haru-san happy." Would that they could find their chief joy in being able to say, " The *Lord* gave, and the *Lord* hath taken away; *Blessed* be the name of the *Lord*"! The funeral had taken place on the previous evening, and already the father and mother had paid the resting-place of their darling a visit. " Why did you go to the grave so soon?" I asked. " Lest she should find it lonely," was the reply.

CHAPTER XX.

Secular Education in the Mission Field.

"Whatsoever ye do, do all to the glory of God."—1 Cor. x. 31.

MUCH has been said lately, in England, *for* and *against* secular education as a means for prosecuting missionary work. From the little experience I have had in this departure, I may, perhaps, be allowed to say a few words.

It is not secular education, it seems to me, that hinders or promotes missionary work, *but* the teacher. For example, if the teacher's motive and aim is to get at the class of people who can only be reached by his becoming *their servant for Jesus' sake*, he will be sure to meet with success. And on the other hand, if his motive and aim is to promote education for its own sake, or earn a living—good and right in its place, although this is—he is, so far as fitness for the Lord's work is concerned, but a dead man.

I am sure that God will use every legitimate means that comes in one's way in order to honour His great name, on those to whom *He* sends His servants.

A gentleman who has lived for many years in

India, writes :—" Having been saved by grace, and freed from Satan's power by that same grace, we are free to love and serve Him, and not as any school of Theology may dictate, but as He, oh, praise His name! may lead. In India, I found an unspeakable advantage, particularly among Europeans, for they could see that I was living among them, earning my living as they were. So when I spoke to them, it was not as a "professional," as they were pleased to call the ministers, but for the desire of the glory of God, and their salvation. Indeed, I, many a time, got a hearing when a minister, *as such*, would not. Oh, my heart bleeds for many of those dear devoted souls, because of the treatment they sometimes get, and from professedly Christian people too!"

It is one thing to engage in secular work, in order to live for *oneself*, but quite another to *work* with hands and brain, in order to *live for God!* The former is earthly and lawful; but the latter, apostolic and heavenly. "FOR ME TO LIVE IS CHRIST!" may become the motto of the mechanic who is a man *of God*, as well as that of the most consecrated and scholarly theologian.

AMERICAN PROFESSORS

and teachers, in colleges and schools, in Japan have had the honour of commending the Bible and its Author to their pupils, long before the missionaries could see their way to engage directly in working for their Master.

Prominent among many names which might be mentioned are Captain James, Mr. W. Clark, and Mr. J. Ballagh. The field has since been reinforced with many such workers in common with missionaries, and they are to-day reaping a golden harvest as the result of the patient, unassuming toil of those Christian teachers.

IN HARMONY

with what Mr. Eugene Stock says in his excellent remarks on Christian educators (in the *Christian,* of May 24, 1889), I should like to say that I met, and now hear from, lay workers in Japan, who went there with no other object than that they should bring the Japanese to the feet of Jesus. A gentleman from Edinburgh, who arrived in Japan in 1880, has been engaged as a teacher of English in different parts of the country; and directly, and indirectly, he planted the Word of God as the source of that knowledge so all-important in all lands—even the knowledge of the living and true God and Jesus Christ, whom He hath sent. This young Christian teacher reached Japan with absolutely nothing but the living God and His unfailing promise to lean on. And surely this was enough! "It is enough for the servant that he be as his Lord."

He was nurtured in a refined home. He left it and all that he held dear in life for Jesus' sake, and is willing to be counted a fool if only he can honour and serve his MASTER in a field where labourers are few and far between. His faith at first was severely tested. He was not connected with a society or any party of Christians, though bound up in the bundle of life with all who call on the Lord out of a pure heart. He received nothing from the Gentiles, nor from the Church of God, but accepted from the Japanese a salary far below what they were willing to offer him. He thus convinced the natives that gain was not his object in coming among them. He sought not *theirs* but *them*. He is, in a peculiar sense, a man of God and a servant of Christ.

I state this to show that God has diversities of operations in His vast field, and a variety of tools in His laboratory.

EXTRACTS FROM AN AMERICAN MISSIONARY REPORT.

"THE past year has been one of steady expansion in the evangelistic department of work in this field, and of remarkable growth in the educational department.

"The Membership of the churches has advanced from 623 to 818, being an increase of 30 per cent. The larger portion of this increase has been in the City of Osaka and in Sakai, a town of about 40,000 inhabitants, seven miles to the south of Osaka.

"At this latter place, 36 have been received on profession of faith, thus tripling the little band of believers that had been gathered there a year ago, and the first of April brings a further addition of ten Members. This rapid development is due to the faithful efforts of the native evangelist, with the co-operation of the Osaka Church, and specially to the presence and labours of Miss COLBY, who has lived in Sakai the greater part of the year.

"With reference to the four Osaka churches, we have to report in general that each church is crowded every Sunday.

"Even Temma, which opened its new building only one year ago, has not one seat vacant. Two of the other three are exerting themselves to the utmost to erect new buildings on new sites and the third to enlarge before the end of this year. Each is blessed with an earnest and intelligent English-speaking pastor, as well as a strong force of capable and devoted labourers. But the second church (the Naniwa) has met with a sad loss in the death of their beloved Paul Sawayama. Although for a year past he has been lost to the community, his death has stricken the hearts of us all, and especially of his faithful church. He lived just long enough to pass the tenth anniversary of the church and of his ordination as their pastor. He was the first ordained pastor in Japan, and perhaps it is not too much to say that he was the most widely beloved pastor in Japan. Over one thousand Christians of all denominations attended his funeral.

"In the Treasurer's report of Naniwa church at its tenth anniversary, it appeared that the contributions of this church alone for all purposes have averaged 800 *en* (dollar) for the past three years.

"The preaching meetings in and around the city, sustained by the four churches, have, in all cases, shown a steady increase in interest and numbers, four new places have been opened. The Members of the Naniwa church (among whom are some of the older scholars of the Girls' School), have for months been making regular visits to a town named Amagasaki, five miles from Osaka. The meetings were small for some time; but, after a special effort to move the people to attend the services, things took a sudden turn in favour of Christianity. A former student of the Doshisha is now labouring there, and is entirely supported by the congregation. He is able to secure a regular audience of sixty or seventy, a large number of whom are of the better class; six of this number are to be baptized in June.

"Another school enterprise is the Women's Industrial

School opened last January. This school has about 150 Members, mostly from the merchant and professional classes. Already it has been instrumental in bringing some women into the churches, while many others are studying the Bible, and thus learning things which will be of more lasting benefit than the knowledge of foreign ways.

" In this connection we must also mention a Boys' School for English which has been opened in Nara, during the past three months, under Christian influences. It has sixty scholars who attend at different hours of the day. In the evening class there are six priests connected with the Dai-butzu temple in Nara.

" These institutions in the country especially are proving themselves to be very valuable agencies in spreading the knowledge of Christianity among classes not hitherto reached. Within two years there has been a vast increase in the enthusiasm and intensity with which the study of the English language has been pursued ; and, within a few months, under the inspiration of the Empress and the larger emulation of the Capital, there has arisen a great desire for European styles of dress, for ladies as well as gentlemen, and for a knowledge of Western etiquette, table manners, etc.

" With this there has, of course, sprung up an increased desire for a knowledge of Western sewing, knitting, cooking, dressmaking, and other household arts. The leaders of the people have determined to adopt Western civilization *en masse* ; and we may add that, with this determination, there has come a disposition to look favourably upon Christianity ; especially as the moral basis for the new fabric of society."

CONSECRATED EUROPEAN EVANGELISTS

who desire to give their whole time to Gospel work among the masses, will find a wide and effectual door open before them in Japan. But a thorough knowledge of the native tongue and of the character of the people will be absolutely necessary in seeking to labour efficiently and abundantly. "WHO WILL GO?"

I do not hesitate to say, on the authority of Japanese Christian gentlemen now in England, as well as on that of carefully weighed conclusions I have come to, that the present moment is the golden one if loyalty to Christ, and sound instruction in the truth are to be set in motion through the instrumentality of men and women of God from the West. This enviable chance for serving Christ may elude our grasp if we are not careful. The influx of Western ideas has profoundly modified the life and thought of the country. The old religious systems are rapidly losing their hold on the people, and the barriers of prejudice and superstition, which formerly obstructed the spread of the Gospel are, in a large measure, broken down.

In political and social life the last twenty-five years have produced undreamt-of changes in Japan, and unless the restraining influence of Christianity is brought to bear upon them, the progress of the country may become too rapid and lead to dangerous consequences. "WHO WILL GO?" It is noteworthy that God "Shut to the door" in Japan three hundred years ago. The Jesuits had then bid fair to bring Japan into the same bondage Spain is yoked with now. Had they succeeded, we should to-day find it more difficult to convert them from Romanism than from Paganism. God's set time to rid them out of the hand of the oppressor of souls has evidently come. Her hermetically closed doors are thrown wide open and *no* man can shut them! "WHO WILL GO?"

GLEANINGS FROM LETTERS LATELY TO HAND, ETC.

"MY object in work, you know, is to bring the knowledge of the Gospel to souls, not to make converts to a church. I have already begun a school for men, at the request of the Japanese themselves, in a heathen house. The house belongs to a Company, and the managing partner lends one room. About twenty men have joined. I and a friend teach them English, from eight to nine, and from nine to nine thirty, they have Bible instruction.

"I am holding, also, in the same room, a Sunday-school of boys and girls. Twenty came last Sunday, and all behaved well and attentive. I am beginning with the "Peep of Day." The landlord, although a heathen, allows his wife and children to attend: it is very interesting. I take pictures with me each Sunday, and my little organ on a Jinrikisha. A young Japanese Christian, who knows a few words of English only, having studied the lesson previously, gives the Japanese colloquial to the children. The class is supposed to consist of children about fifteen years of age. They all know a very little English, so that we sing hymns in English and the translations in Japanese. I consider you gave me a very good impression of the country and people. I am so very glad God in his love has brought me here. I was never happier. . . . .—J. M. HOLLAND, OSAKA."

"I MUST write to thank you for your earnest and kind words for Japan,* every word of which I can confirm as being true. I long for England to do more for this land. I can, from experience, testify that there is much to be done, and a kind and loving heart will always find a welcome from a Japanese. Yokosuka, as you know, is the naval dockyard of Japan. Two men-of-war are launched every year. I teach the officers' wives English.

---

* In my "Open Doors in Japan."

"I am teaching the younger pupils to sing hymns, and am much needing a helper. I am the only foreigner in the place. I have had many difficulties since I came to Japan, but the Lord has been tenderly caring for me, and I am thankful to have been brought to this sunny land. I am sure the dear Lord is working in the hearts of many, and what is needed is the teaching of His Holy Word. I had a Bible class at the Tokyo Charity Hospital, composed of fifty members. I often wish I were younger—it is difficult to acquire the language. I send you this short line to encourage you to help Japan all you can in England.—A. M. Swift, YOKOSUKA, NEAR YOKOHAMA."

"SOME people regard the institutions of the *European model* as the best thing to be relied upon. Others insist on the wide diffusion of Western science among the people, as the only hope of regenerating the nation. When the people are so hotly disputing these problems, we consider that this is a golden opportunity for giving to the *Christian Church of Japan* the supreme importance, thus making her the instrument of promoting the evangelization, not only of Japan, but of the whole Eastern world. We want to convince our rulers that Christianity forms one of the historic bases of European civilization, and that the Christians constitute the PURIFYING BODY OF CITIZENS in money worshipping and power-intoxicated nations of the West. Once this is proved to the conviction of *leading minds of Japan*, the evangelization of the land will be quickened, and the efforts of evangelists and missionaries will tell on the people with greater force. Now, it is part of our business to collect facts and books which might be useful for this purpose; and I am sure that nothing can help us better than to come in close contact with Christians of this country; and if you will kindly give us opportunities of seeing *good Christian people* and Christian institutions, you will place both us and our country under great obligations to you."—M.U.

N.B.—Should friends feel disposed to send me such books as will help to counteract the deadly influence of infidelity in Japan, or any useful, nicely bound Christian works, I shall be glad to forward them.

The Gospel in a Mountain Village.

Yokohama.

Rev. E. Loomis:—A young Christian from Kumamoto recently went to a distant mountain village to become a teacher in the local school. There was living in the same place a young man of about the same age, who had been adopted by the most wealthy person in that region. When he learned that the teacher was a Christian, he would not associate with him at all, and for a considerable time tried to make it as unpleasant for him as he could.

But the teacher was not deterred from the path of duty, and in time won the confidence and esteem of the one who had hated and opposed him. Then a warm friendship sprang up between them, and the teacher was able to lead his friend to a belief in and acceptance of Christianity.

When the father of the young man heard of what had happened, he threatened to disown and cast him out if he did not give up this new and hated religion; but these threats were of no avail, as the son said that the presence of Christ in his heart was of more value than either gold, houses, or lands.

When the time came for the young man to be baptized, the father was present. Both returned to their home, and by neither word nor act was there any manifestation of opposition. On the contrary, the father seemed to be convinced of his former error, and allowed his son to do as he chose.

This young man has been chosen to be the head man of the village; and when he goes to the Christian services every Sabbath, he takes all his associates and officials with him. In this way the triumph of Christianity in that place is fully attested.

Preaching on Ship-Board.

Rev. Mr. Brandram, C.M.S., was recently going from Oita to Osaka on a small Japanese steamer, and, for some reason, there was a delay in the course of the passage. There were about forty persons in the cabin with himself, and one of them asked him if he would not preach to them. Mr. Brandram replied that he had come to Japan for that purpose, and it would give him great pleasure to speak to them; but, as there were a large number of passengers, he did not wish to compel anyone to hear him speak, and so he would first like to know if there was any objection to a Christian service being held then and there.

Then a judge, who was among the passengers, asked if there was anyone who was opposed to having a missionary preach to them. Not an objection was raised, but, on the contrary, all seemed quite desirous to hear what this foreigner had to say.

Mr. Brandram was much pleased, and gave them a plain and simple gospel sermon. There was close attention on the part of all, and much interest and pleasure was shown by the hearers. As there was quite a diversity in the capacity of his auditors, Mr. Brandram feared that his discourse might not be acceptable to some who were men of superior learning and position.

But to his great pleasure and surprise, the next day the judge repeated the illustrations and points that he had given them, and said that they were very good: and then he added "Preach just like that all the time. We all like to hear such good and plain doctrine as that." Another service of a similar character followed.

Among the passengers was a young man of wealth from near Tokyo, who was travelling for pleasure. He was so much interested and pleased with what he had heard that he came to Mr. Brandram, and said that he would like to become a Christian. This led to a most pleasant conversation with him; and, on reaching Osaka, he was introduced to some of the Christians living at that place.

The result was, that he decided to postpone his return to his home, and stay a while in Osaka in order to hear more of the precious doctrine. He then sent a telegram to his father informing him of his plans, and said to his new-found friends, "This is so good that I want to learn all that I can, and then go home and tell my parents and friends."

A few days later he sent a letter to Mr. Brandram, saying that he had given his heart to the Lord, and was happy in his love. And now he has gone to his home to tell others what great things the Lord has done for him.

CLIMATE OF JAPAN.

A glance at the position of Japan on the map bespeaks the similarity of climate with that of the British Isles.

Japan is 24° 6'——50° 56', N.
„   122° 45'——156° 32', E. of Greenwich.

The northernmost islands, Hokkaido and Hondo (main part), are very much what Scotland and England are respecting cold and heat. In Shikoku and Kiushiu the summer and autumn are much warmer and longer.

In 1887 the annual record of Japanese estimates reported 86 centenarians, of which 68 are women. 7,330 lived to the age of 90, of which 4,955 are women. 414,727 lived to 85. 145,942 lived to 80; 1,738,505 died at 50, of these 853,587 were women.

TIME.

There are 8 hours 38 minutes 20 seconds difference between the time in London and Tokyo.

POPULATION.

The population of Japan is nearly 40,000,000.
„   „   Tokyo (the Capital), 1,122,000
„   „   Osaka, 362,000.
„   „   Kyoto, 246,000.
„   „   Yokohama, 90,000.

British subjects in Japan, 1,200.
German and French about 600.
Americans about 600.

More Gleanings from "American Foreign Mission Letters."

Rev. H. Loomis writes:—"About twelve miles from the great city of Nagoya is a beautiful valley, in which lies the little village of Midzuno. It is one of the oldest settled portions of Japan, and in the hills near by are some caves in which people dwelt before the modern style of constructing houses was introduced. The whole village contains about five hundred inhabitants." . . . Here the people are idolaters: in times of trouble they appeal to the false gods. . . . On hearing of the new religion they concluded it must be better than that in which they had been taught, so inquired of a native pastor, Mr. Yamamoto, who preached Jesus to them, and immediately they lost all confidence in the false religion and accepted the true. Mr. Loomis visited this place, and thus writes:—" In the meantime the number of believers increased, and the good work extended to other places. A church has been formed, consisting of about forty members, and a suitable house of worship was recently completed." They are like the Bereans in this village, giving great attention to the reading of the WORD. . . . Some of the women could not attend the services at this time, as they had to watch the rice crops, but a special service was held for them in the afternoon, and the men took their turn in watching the grain.

"We were invited to one of the most neat and comfortable houses in all that region. We were told that the owner was one of ten Christians, and I afterwards met him at Osaka as the elder and representative of his church in the meeting of the General Assembly. We were provided with refreshments, and returned with grateful hearts for what we are continually permitted to witness of God's gracious blessing upon the Christian work in this land."

Rev. J. B., of Osaka, writes:—"The total number of communicants reported (at the meeting of the Presbytery, 1888) was 1,178, being a gain in six months of 128 persons.

The gain in membership during the past year was 282. The money contributed (by the Japanese) during the past year was 1,357 silver dollars 80 cents."

One of the most interesting features in the history of the Christian Church in Japan is that revivals have sprung up through very simple, unpretending means originating among the Japanese themselves. The above extract, related by Mr. Loomis, is only a sample of many that might be cited but for limited space.

THE SCRIPTURE UNION

is mightily at work. This most promising association was formed within the last few years, and now its membership exceeds thirteen thousand.

KYOTO (OR MIACO).

I regret to say that space will not admit of my dwelling on the ancient capital Kyoto, and its beautiful natural scenery. I have already referred to it as an educational and evangelistic centre. One cannot feel too thankful for the way in which God is honouring His great name through the instrumentality of Mr. Neejima, his co-workers from America, and an efficient staff of native evangelists, among the 246,000 souls of this city. The tentative thriving work of Mr. Neejima is much to be commended, and, through God's goodness, its success is due to the wisdom and care displayed in handling the Japanese mind at a difficult moment ; *i.e.*, shortly after the grim edict, which appeared on all the notice boards throughout the land, had been revoked, viz., "*So long as the sun shall warm the earth, let no Christian be so bold as to come to Japan, and let all know that the King of Spain himself, or the Christians' God, or the great God of all, if he violate this command, shall pay for it with his head.*" The wolf must have committed great havoc among the Japanese, or surely such words would never have been penned. . . . . "With God all things are possible." "Who can set thorns and briers before me, that I should not go through them?" are words which may be aptly quoted as we look back on the career of Protestant missionaries in Japan. "God has indeed set before *them* an open door." "Praise His name!"

THE NEW CONSTITUTION IN JAPAN.

In February, 1889, Japan, with much anticipation and splendour, proclaimed her intention of becoming forthwith wholly assimilated with the civilised nations of the West, by the promulgation of the New Constitution; and now she is again preparing to have it enforced on a much grander scale, in February, 1890. It is then that the elected peer and members of Parliament will sit for the first time. A national exhibition will be opened at Tokyo in April or May. This would be such a nice time for Christian tourists to visit Japan, in order to join their Japanese brethren in celebrating the event.

EXTRACT FROM THE "CHURCH MISSIONARY GLEANER."

TOKYO, *February* 15*th*, 1889.

Your readers will, I am sure, be interested and thankful to hear that religious liberty has at last been officially proclaimed in this country. February 11th will henceforth be more than ever a red-letter day in the calendar of Japan. It is the day annually observed in honour of Jimmu Tenno, who is regarded as the first emperor of the country, and from whom the Japanese claim an unbroken line of descent for their emperors down to the present time, and from whose reign they also date their era; this year being, according to Japanese chronology, 2549. And this was the day selected for the promulgation of the new *Constitution*, an event looked forward to with the greatest eagerness by the whole nation. It must suffice to say here very briefly that this Constitution is framed somewhat on the lines of that of our own land, provides for a House of Peers and a House of Representatives, confers many civil liberties on the people which they have not enjoyed hitherto, and—what your readers will be specially interested to hear—contains a clause granting to all subjects of Japan freedom of religious belief. Practically, there has been no interference on the part of the Government, in late years, with the religious belief of individuals, no obstacle placed in the way of Christian teaching; but this is the first official proclamation of full liberty in this respect, so that Christianity will now stand on a different footing in the eyes of the people generally, many of whom have, no doubt, hesitated to lay aside their old suspicions of the religion of Western lands, because there has hitherto been no recognition of it on the part of their rulers.

The day was a grand one in Tokyo, and all over the country; according to native newspapers, the grandest day Japan has ever seen. It would take a long time to give any adequate idea of the impressive ceremony at the palace, where the Emperor, in the presence of the Empress, princes, princesses, noblemen, cabinet ministers, the Foreign Diplomatic Corps, and other officials, Japanese and foreign, and last, but not least, several editors of leading Japanese journals, delivered a speech, and formally handed the draft of the Constitution to the Prime Minister, Count Kuroda; or of the Royal Procession through the streets, the Empress riding with the Emperor, in the same carriage, a thing unheard of before; the splendid state carriages, specially built in Europe; the gorgeous liveries; the crowds of orderly, merry people, dressed in their best, lining the route; the processions of schools, large and small; the wonderful decorations; monster ornamental cars drawn by strings of oxen and towering above the heads of the people; triumphal arches lit up at night with scores of electric lights, flags, and lanterns innumerable. The people all through the country had been roused to an extraordinary pitch of enthusiasm over the promulgation of this new Constitution. They feel that Japan now, more than ever, stands foremost in the matter of civilisation amongst the nations of the East, the only kingdom in Asia that possesses a constitutional government, the only one that enjoys perfect religious liberty.

The Christians have not been behind, but rather before, their fellow-countrymen in the interest taken in this great event. Our own little band of converts of their own accord arranged for a service in church to seek God's blessing on the day, and in the evening a general meeting for praise and thanksgiving was held by Christians of all denominations in the large public hall, originally built for the purpose of delivering lectures to combat Christianity. One of the speakers said that the promulgation of the new Constitution, which had taken place that morning, was sure to give a great impetus to the spread of Christianity, for that there were many Nicodemuses in different parts of the country who would now come forward.

FROM "A SABBATH IN OSAKA," IN THE "MISSIONARY HERALD" FOR JANUARY, 1888.

The writer, Rev. C. P. Blanchard, is describing a visit to the Congregational Churches in that city. "The usual attendance is about two hundred; to-day it is only twenty-five less. The large number of adult classes and their attentive earnestness in the study of the Word are pleasant features. Each late comer, as he takes his place in the class, first reverently bows his head in silent prayer. Two hundred or more little wooden tablets, each about eight inches in length by two in width, covering a large space on the wall, attract our attention and awaken our curiosity. Each tablet hangs on a separate pin, and native characters are written upon it. This is the roll of the church. Each member's name thus hangs conspicuously on the sacred walls of the house of God. This is the general custom among the churches. It certainly has much to recommend it. It would seem well calculated to develop the sense of individual responsibility for each member thus to see, every time he enters the church, his tablet bearing his name. Certainly he will not wish to be unnecessarily absent, for a silent witness against him is hanging on the walls.

There is little in the exercises of the school to distinguish it from schools at home. The pastor makes a brief closing address, evidently applying the truths of the lesson with earnestness and directness. A hymn is sung. How strange yet sweetly familiar "Rock of Ages" sounds sung in a tongue no syllable of which you can understand! It was refreshing to notice, as the closing prayer was offered, that every head was reverently bowed, and to hear, at its close, a fervent amen uttered, not by the pastor, but by the entire congregation. * * * * * The pastor chooses his text and shapes his discourse to meet his evening audience, which is largely composed of those who have not accepted the claims of the gospel. Some are interested in Christianity, some are indifferent ; probably few are hostile. His theme to-night is "the man without a wedding garment." The preacher has a manly bearing, an unusually intelligent, attractive face, and is exceedingly easy and graceful in his address. He speaks with great fluency, without manuscript, gestures freely, and not unfrequently turns to his Bible to illustrate or clinch an argument. His fervour increases as he proceeds, and a glance at his interested audience assures us that he is a popular orator of no mean ability. Our regret that he spoke in an unknown tongue was increased by a sketch of the sermon afterwards given us. It was full of gospel truth, and abounded in happy illustration. Here is a single example of its felicity. The presumption of the man who presented himself without the prescribed dress, and of the class he represents, was made vivid to his audience by a fitting allusion to the royal reception given by the Emperor during a recent visit to the city, when the only condition attaching to the invitation was that each guest appear in full foreign costume, the newly prescribed court-dress. It is easy to see what effective use he could make of such a timely illustration.

So closed a day of rare privilege. It left the conviction

that the churches of Japan, if these of Osaka are fair representatives, are very fortunate in their ministry and the ministry equally happy in their churches. With such churches and such a ministry the future of the kingdom is full of hope. As illustrative of the rapid growth of these churches, take as an example the last one visited. Formed eight years ago with nine members, it added to its membership three the first year, seven the second, fourteen the third, fourteen the fourth, twenty-one the fifth, forty the sixth, fifty the seventh, and fifty-two the eighth. Multiply these figures by four and you have the approximate growth and membership of the four churches. All but one of these are compelled either to rebuild or enlarge their house this year. This, with the necessary enlargement of the Girls' School, which they unitedly sustain, lays a burden upon them that would appal a less courageous people.

Those who met the Christian philanthropist, Mr. Shimada, in England, may be interested to hear that he is elected to represent his party at the next (and first) parliament in Tokyo next year. He not only needs, but would value our prayers. He and his friend, Mr. Uemura, are anxious to develop the girls' and boys' Christian schools under their management. A self-supporting lady helper would be invaluable to them at this stage, as well as other help. I state this for the convenience of those who might desire to correspond with them.

Address—

Mei-ji Jogakko Kudan Park,

Tokyo, Japan.

CHAPTER XXI.

Moral Condition.

"The whole head is sick, and the whole heart faint."—Isa. i. 5.

1. HUMAN nature is exactly the same in Japan as it is in any other country, so that her people cannot be said to be highly moral. Yet I think that, without the counteracting influence of Christianity, the drunkenness and all its attendant evils would have dragged us as a nation far below the example Japan sets before us to-day—though, let it be understood, I am far from seeking to prove Japan to be a model in this respect. It is the purifying influence of Christianity that has given the British people that unrivalled energy, vein of benevolence, and excellence of character peculiar to them—despite their many drawbacks. Immorality, crime, and poverty are prevalent in Japan, but not nearly as conspicuous as in England, unless it is at the treaty ports, where many of the money-making and demoralised Westerns are a snare to women weak enough to be ensnared by them. But it would be unfair to judge of the morality of the Japanese by what we see at the treaty ports, and just as wrong to condemn wholesale our own country people who

live there because there are base characters among them.

2. God forbid that the streets of Japanese towns should ever be disgraced with the presence of public-houses and sottish men and women as in Great Britain. We have, indeed, cause to bow our heads in this respect, and there is much besides that is detrimental to our far-famed reputation as a Christian nation. I feel forced to make this remark in passing; otherwise I would far rather not allude to a subject which is not in my line, but leave it to those who have a morbid pleasure in parading the vices of a people who are so ready to learn from us all that is worthy of being imitated. "*For what have we that we have not received?*" The only thing that can elevate an individual and a nation *permanently* is vital (not nominal) Christianity. England's government, civil laws, and home-life are based on Biblical principles; hence England's greatness! The British people, *as such*, enjoy liberty of conscience, and believe in the Sacred WORD which God's love and mercy brought down; and in the measure its counsels are heeded, in that measure are they free and happy.

If Japan will train up her children to search the Scriptures with as much ardour as she has in the past trained them to observe the moral injunctions of heathen sages, God will set her on high; she will become the "head, and not the tail," among the nations.

"*Seek ye out of the Book of the Lord, and read:*

no one of these shall fail, none shall want her mate: for my mouth it hath commanded, and his spirit it hath gathered them." This is the royal road to prosperity and bliss! May God move our hearts with compassion towards the lost and perishing, and give them the Bread of Life, that they may live.

SHARE THE BLESSING.

"Keep none of it till the morning."

" Here is a story from Japan which should do us all good.

"A poor man who is a Christian has to work all day away from home. He has put up the following notice on the door of his house—

"'*I am a Christian, and if any one likes to go in and read my Good Book while I am out they may. The Buddhist Priests need not come here. I do not want them any more.*'

"People go into his house and read his Bible.

"Would that *we* had more of that natural child-like desire to have others share in the blessings which we enjoy that this poor Japanese has!"—*Extract from* "*C. M. S. Gleaner.*"

CHAPTER XXII.

"The Eleventh Hour."

(APPEAL.)

"We do not well: this day is a day of good tidings, and we hold our peace."—2 Kings vii. 9.

IF we cannot see in a crucified and risen Saviour sufficient motive to tempt us out of England, we have as yet but a feeble apprehension of his love to us. We look at the Cross of Shame, and see, at one and the same time, God's eternal abhorrence of sin and love to the sinner laid perfectly bare. We believe that the middle wall of partition is broken down, and the flaming sword of justice quenched, and that our Great High Priest has entered into the presence of God for us, and has come out to bless us in the divine person of the Holy Ghost; and yet many, in this age of enlightenment and facilities for going into *all* the world on His errands, seem to be complaining that no man hath hired them. The Lord of the harvest says to such, even at this ELEVENTH HOUR, "Go ye also into my vineyard." How intensely one longs to convince consecrated men and women in England and everywhere, of the glorious openings there are in Japan at this moment for living among her people, and proving by their manner of life and conversation that they seek not *theirs* but *them!*

WHO WILL GO?

I would also fain prevail on Christians who are set free from home claims, and who are in possession of a large or small income, to take a higher and more influential ground than those who are held in by the bit and bridle of man-made rules, to go to Japan, and be AT HOME daily to receive all who come unto them. The Japanese are beginning to find out that England's far-famed home-life is worthy of imitation, so that an opportunity offers in this direction to show how God can be honoured with our substance, as well as personal influence. Gold and silver *truly* dedicated *to God* can *never* hinder, but help. Oh, that grace may be given to Christians who own lands, gold, silver, gifts, &c., to glory in their possession, because it gives them multiplied facilities for going right among those who are so ready to judge of our love to the Shepherd that died for his sheep, by seeing that we give *ourselves* as well as our means. Jesus Christ is appealing to you, who are His consecrated stewards, on behalf of millions over whom His heart yearns with intense pity and love.

In Japan, for example, your presence as self-supporting workers, whether as individuals or families, will be a greater testimony (to a *certain* class) to the reality of the Gospel than it can possibly be by going under the care of a mission. The latter has its place, and God forbid that I should level shafts at missions, for we have every reason to feel encouraged with the success which has attended the efforts already made by the missionaries. But as we are apt to forget the "*diversity of operation*" already referred to, I draw the reader's attention to this open door in passing.

Oh, for grace in us to imitate the Queen of Sheba's act of self-surrender, by going to the uttermost parts of the earth to proclaim the love and wisdom of a greater than Solomon! Thus, rising to the occasion and pressing need, we should be able to convince Easterns of the vital difference there is between *nominal* and *real* Christianity. "WHO WILL GO?"

There are excellent men and women of God who are daily splitting hairs by endeavouring to prove "apostolic methods, Scriptural ground, fitness for service," and various departures; but they fail to see that the most effectual and practical way for attesting what they teach, is that the "Call from Macedonia" should be responded to by themselves and go and carry the carefully winnowed and garnered grain, and sow it broadcast among the spiritually famine-stricken nations. Prompt action of this sort would soon disabuse our minds from all difficulty as to WHO IS WHO, and WHAT IS WHAT. I am persuaded that nothing else will do it

God has entrusted us with much treasure :—time, health, learning, reason, eyesight, hearing, temporal and spiritual endowments, friends and relations, and many facilities for proving our devotion to Him. We should not forget, moreover, that in addition to all our accountabilities, it is a stewardship or trust to be enjoying the protection and peace by which the illustrious reign of our beloved Queen is characterized, both at home and abroad.

May we, then, in the light of the Coming Day, on which the counsels of the heart are to be made manifest by Jesus Christ, ask Him to enable us to become " good stewards of the *manifold* grace of God."

I feel more and more that we must ask God to arouse us and help us to realize what an honour and responsibility it is to be put in trust with the Gospel, and say with King David, "*Both riches and honour come of Thee, and Thou reignest over all; and in Thine hand is power and might, and in Thine hand it is to make great, and to give strength unto all. But who am I, and what is my people, that we should be able to offer so willingly after this sort? for all things come of Thee, and of Thine own have we given Thee.*" May God, in his mercy, remove the nightmare we are under, and turn every *church*, *chapel*, and *meeting-room* in the land into wailing resorts, because we have failed to carry the Gospel to this prepared people! Nothing can clear us for having withheld it so long but making haste and *giving* it to them *now*. And nothing can more effectually enforce the undeviating teachings of the Book of books, like the "*living epistle*," filled with the Spirit. "WHO WILL GO?"

"*The day is breaking everywhere, and God deliver us from dawdling at the dawn of such a day.*"

"Oh, that dying, yet undying love!"

"And Jesus went about all the villages and cities, teaching in their synagogues, and preaching the gospel of the kingdom, healing every sickness and every disease among the people. But when He saw the multitudes, *He was moved with compassion on them, because they fainted, and were scattered abroad, as sheep having no shepherd.*"

The ten thousand villages, to say nothing of towns, all over Japan, will give a hearty welcome to those who are controlled by that love which always flowed from the heart of Jesus, when brought in contact with his untended sheep. WHO WILL GO? The Japanese are creating a literature of their own type, and, in 1887, 85,000 English books were imported. Educational works are much in demand, and so are philosophical writings of the *deadly-nightshade* order. What have Ingersoll and Bradlaugh done for the *true* elevation of Westerns? Are they likely to elevate Japan? "Doth a fountain send forth at the same place sweet water and bitter?"

I often wonder how true Christians, entrusted with means, can afford to deprive themselves of the blessing it would bring to their own souls, by failing to go where they are so much needed NOW, instead of being tethered, muzzled, and hampered with Saul's armour at home. But I must not indulge in riddles ; my meaning is plain, viz., I long for God's servants to be very simple, and having received their call to service, to look to Him and His Word for guidance—this would lead them to see the unwisdom of giving Easterns cumbersome observances. "*The letter killeth, but the Spirit giveth life.*" But unless the simplicity referred to is the outcome of the direct teaching of the Holy Spirit, and not that which suits one's own fancy or national taste, it is as deserving of censure as tawdry ritualism, or "mass in masquerade." Whatever brings a soul into bondage, or fails to prove edifying to it—let it be at "Friends'," "Brethren's," or Baptists' meetings—is as offensive to God as that described in Isaiah i. 13.

HEAR THE WORD OF THE LORD!

... "BRING NO MORE VAIN OBLATIONS!" ...

"God is a Spirit: and they that worship Him must worship Him in spirit and in truth." May God, in compassion to Easterns, send those to them who are under training at the "BACKSIDE OF THE DESERT"; those who will, in the power of the Holy Ghost, play skilfully on the Gospel bells by repeating the "COMES,"—"FEAR NOTS,"— "BLESSEDS ARE YE" of Jesus. I am sure that the *best* and *soundest* of teachers, are those who, by word and example, lead souls to crop for themselves in the green pastures of truth. A friend of mine said one day, " I find that what I listen to at some meetings is very comforting at the time, but it soon vanishes; while what I dig out of my Bible, abides."

A Bible-reading Brahmin once wrote to a missionary as follows :—

" We are beginning to see through you. You are not so good as your Book. If you were as good as your Book you could convert India in five years."

HOME MISSIONS.

The Japanese Christians are doing all they can to manage their own home missions. But at this critical moment our assistance will be of greater value to them than at a later date. Hundreds of Christian students often go to distant towns and villages to preach Jesus to their people.

"NIPPON DEN DO KAISHA" is the name of the lately organized society for promoting missionary work in Japan. Professor Wadagaki, Imperial College, Tokyo; Professor Bunji Mano, Engineering College, Tokyo; and Professor T. Watasé, Agricultural and Colonisation Department, Tokyo, are personally known to many in this country. They have the spiritual need of Japan much at heart. Mr. Neejima Doshisha Kyoto would, with them, give a hearty welcome to Christian tourists who wish for information about this Christian work, and would turn to excellent account donations sent by their brethren and fellow-labourers in England, towards the spread of the Gospel.

The MASTER will soon be here! We shall hear him say, "*Give an account of thy stewardship.*" He will then gird Himself, and make *us* to sit down at meat. He will remind us of how we visited Him in prison, clothed Him, fed Him, and the joy it gave Him that we saw *Him* in His members. Oh, let not Satan out-manœuvre us of our privilege! Now is *our* time for witness-bearing, our *only* opportunity for proving our loyalty to Him!

POSTSCRIPT.

In order to make this book the pure and simple expression of personal observation in Japan, I have endeavoured to confine myself almost exclusively to my jottings and to what has left an indelible impression upon my memory. I feel under deep obligation to my Japanese friends in London and in Japan for the valuable help they have given me by permitting me to take extracts from their letters, and for informing me on points—up to date—altogether new to myself, and which, I trust, will be of interest to the reader.

There are, besides, a few extracts from American and English Missionary Reports, viz., "The Church at Home and Abroad," "C. M. S. Gleaner," clippings and re-quoted extracts, &c., altogether unknown to me as to their authorship; but for which, in common with other help, I offer hearty thanks. I must also express gratitude to the many friends, and others, whom I only know by name, for ordering "Echoes from Japan" in advance, a circumstance which has greatly encouraged me.

The book makes no pretension whatsoever to being a complete and organised account of Japan and her people, but is simply what it professes to be, *echoes* from that country, or the substance of notes taken in the intervals of a busy life. I feel that, from a literary standpoint, it contains much that will be trying to the critical reader, but since the good of

Japan is my only motive in casting these seedcorns on the flowing tide of abounding literature, I bespeak forbearance and charity, and ask the reader rather to entreat Him (who so graciously condescends to choose the "*foolish things of the world to confound the wise; and the weak things to confound the things which are mighty*"), to use the feeble echoes which hereby reach His ear by leading many earnest workers to go and live among the Japanese. Were the writer, moreover, in possession of those gifts which are so necessary in order to write in a popular and telling style she would feel equally inadequate to undertake the work in hand, as in transcribing one's thoughts for God's glory we must say of all we have by nature and by education, &c., "*I cannot go with these; for I have not proved them.*" It behoves us to act thus in every engagement entered on in Christ's Name; otherwise failure will be the result.

The extracts from the letters of our true-hearted and loyal men-of-war's-men, and likewise from those of my sister (who laboured happily among them at Shanghai, China), are so closely linked with the work given me at Yokohama, both ashore and afloat, that I offer no apology for appending them. Besides, I feel that they are necessary in order to show out the blessed fruit of the great grace which was upon them. It is a good thing to give thanks unto God at the remembrance of those Pentecostal days.

A learned friend has favoured me with a paper on the Japanese language, but limited space prevents my introducing it here. I need not remind the reader that, although I am able to continue in constant happy intercourse with Japanese visiting our Metropolis, I contemplate returning to Japan as soon as I receive my MARCHING ORDERS. The Master says, "*Be not ye the servants of men.*" An advanced Christian once asked me, "Would you be willing to go to Japan as *our* missionary?" "*I would rather go as God's sent one,*" was my reply. "There are diversities of operations, but One is our Master, even Christ."

JAPANESE.

ケダシ カミ セケン ヲ カノ
ホド アイシテ ソノ ヒトリ
ウマラス ノ ムスコ ヲ スラ
アタヘテ オヨソ コレ ヲ シ
ンズル モノ ホロパズ シテ
カギリ ナキ イノチ ヲ ヱ
セシム ガタメ 。

JOHN iii. 16.

APPENDIX I.

Jottings from my Note-book.

"Call unto me, and I will answer thee, and shew thee great and mighty things, which thou knowest not."—Jer. xxxiii. 3.

IN a month after my arrival, I was enabled, by the good hand of my God upon me, to rent a small bungalow of three rooms, the largest not more than eighteen feet by ten; for which I pay sixty dollars per quarter. When it became known that I was prepared to receive a few pupils, several of the English and American residents sent their children to me.

The variety of evergreens, trees near, and at a distance, make Yokohama such a contrast to Shanghai, at this late season (December).

I am feeling quite at home in my little cot. A man, his wife, and baby, live in the outhouse, next to the liliputian kitchen. The man goes out early to work at his trade, and comes back late. The baby is strapped on his mother's back while she sweeps my rooms, cooks, etc.

God has satisfied my longings, with His own presence, far beyond my expectations. The half cannot be told.

I teach my European pupils in the morning. The Japanese come in the afternoon. Their determination to learn is unexampled. History and Natural Philosophy are studied by some. They are wearing European hats for the first time in their lives, evidently, for frequently on going away they forget to take them with them, and think nothing of leaving them in my charge till next day.

H.M.S. *Cadmus* has arrived. Some of the Christian sailors belonging to her called on me, bringing with them a note of introduction from my sister. They began to sing and pray at once, and were like "giants filled with new wine." Some of our English neighbours raised a storm, objecting to our unconventional worship. They sent out their servants with tin kettles and gongs, but "God stopped the mouth of the Lion," and gave us rest.

My little bungalow is full of melody, and my health is much improved. I can see clearly that God meant me to come to this favoured land, to give the blue-jackets a welcome. Would that all Englishmen were such a credit to the British flag as they are! True Christianity makes them contented, loyal subjects. They pray for the Captain, officers, and ship's company; thus fulfilling the

Divine command—1 Tim., chap. ii., verses 1, 2 and 3.

When out this morning, I saw a battalion of three hundred marines march along the Bluff. The thought flashed through my mind, "Why not tend these as well as the blue-jackets?" The index finger of Faith was ever and anon referring me to the walls of Jericho, and to weak instruments, gaining victories. But at last the Master Himself seemed to draw near and say, "Go with the Name of Jesus to the dying!" and with these words I felt my marching orders were distinct and clear. The set time had come. Oh, how beautifully everything fitted in! the gates of brass, and bars of iron, melted away. The sense of God's presence was overpowering, and gave me the conviction that "He was making bare His holy arm, and that the shout of a King was among us." This fresh expression of God's favour was no small encouragement to one who only a few months previously felt ready to halt. It was not a work of which the "Church" would make anything, as our method was very simple, and outside the ruts and grooves of human formula.

The red-coated marines join the blue-jackets nightly, to get comfort for their sin-sick souls: and others declare, with their sunlit faces, that the darkness has passed, and the day-star has arisen in their hearts. I have not a doubt now, that the burdened feeling I had about visiting the camp was a guiding voice.

New Year's Eve, 1874.—We gave a tea and watch meeting in the Church schoolroom. The Captain of H.M.S. *Thistle* has lent us the Flags of all nations. We only asked for two—the English and American. He also sent a detachment of men to put them up. A petty officer on board is an earnest Christian, and helps on the work. Several of the Missionaries came and addressed the meeting. We had a good time. The Chaplain, Rev. E. W. Syle, was so encouraged by eight marines recently converted, applying to him for admittance to the "Lord's Table," that he sent me a truly kind Christian epistle, and three five dollar notes, saying that my visit to Japan was a venture of faith which God had evidently owned. *See R. M.'s letter on page* 298.

My hands are full of truly spiritual and happy work among the sailors and marines. My pupil, Hirano-san, is a great help and comfort to me. He grows in grace. The sailors love him. He visits the ships with me, carrying books and tracts, and enjoys our meetings on board as well as those on shore. As I have the means and opportunity, I send a note to one or more ships, inviting a small party of sailors to tea. The Christians on each vessel are glad to pilot the unsaved ones to my house. The fifteen dollars enabled me to give many small treats. This social pastime gives such a nice opportunity for passing on the words of Jesus to the weary and heavy laden, far away from Him, as well as from kith and kin. As a rule the unconverted sailors are public-house resorters, when allowed ashore on "leave days," so that inviting them to one's house and showing them little deeds of kindness, and speaking words of love for Jesus' sake, often avert much harm to body and soul.

The *Thalia* has arrived straight from Hong Kong, and not *viâ* Shanghai, like the other vessels. There are three very spiritually minded men on board. I asked them "who directed them to me?" "The Lord directed us, Miss," was their reply. It was my privilege to welcome them in "His blessed Name." They are true men of God: the right sort of visitors to heathen shores; they are praying missionaries, and true fellow labourers with me in the Gospel.

The ship *Thalia* has gone on a cruise: she may be away for one or two weeks. We have agreed to pray for a greater blessing on the ship's company as well as on the battalion ashore till we next meet.

Lady Parkes has called to see me. I did not expect to find her such an advanced Christian. She spoke feelingly of God's wisdom and love, and of how she had learnt in the furnace, that which could never have been learnt out of it. I had a fresh sense of God's presence, while we sat together, and spoke of Him. When I returned her call, I found out that she was as ready as ever to show her colours as a Christian.

March.—Another happy chat at the British Legation. After luncheon, we talked for hours of God's goodness and ways of dealing with us. Lady P—— entered heartily into all I had to say about the work on board the ships and in the camp. She used her influence with captains and officers from the vessels to give me a welcome on board ; so that, through God's goodness, I attribute my access to the sailors to her. Happy the country whose ambassador's wife takes such a pronounced stand against the recklessness and scepticism which generally characterise Europeans in Eastern lands !

Another truly profitable evening amongst the marines. God is blessing us.

Nice letters from the *Cadmus* men, *en route* for Hong Kong, *viâ* Shanghai. They are " sowing beside all waters." They visit the missionaries at the different ports, viz., Kobé and Nagasaki, and attend their prayer meetings.

My friends, the sailors, seem overflowing with joy, but they are perfectly free from excitement. Oh, for many such men ! They remind me of David's three mighties. They know how to keep rank ; their eye is ever on their Great Captain, and they only move at his bidding. We are meeting daily to pour out our hearts for more blessing on the British and American fleets on the coasts of Japan and China. Prayer in the Holy Ghost is a rare thing, it seems to me, but these men know how to deal with God; and so they bring down blessing.

We are arranging to give a large tea, and have already invited sailors from the vessels to meet the marines. God has given us faith to believe that there will be showers of blessings. Captain Woolcomb, of the *Thalia*, lends me all the help in his power. It is the Lord's doing. Praise His Name!

The more I have to do with the sailors, the more I see how completely self has been cast out, and Christ is showing himself through the lattice (or thin veil of flesh and blood). Oh, that this state of things might obtain everywhere amongst Christians! Satan knows that a God-wrought unity is the most powerful preaching in the world; everything short of this is religion in the flesh.

Some of the Thalians were asked to accept promotion in their different departments, but they begged to be permitted to decline it. The captain, however, after a while insisted on it, and, as servants, they felt that they must obey their master. The lowest rung on the naval ladder was, to them, a more enviable arena for displaying the grace that wrought so mightily in them than the highest could possibly be. O GRACE of God, how lowly thou art!

My room barely holds all the men who come from the *Thalia* and camp alone; most of them the fruit of our last Gospel meeting. " Praise God from whom all blessings flow!"

Day by day the sailors retire to the gully below my cottage, and there pour out their hearts in prayer: when they come in their faces look radiant. They are active workers, they dole out "the bread of life" to the hungry on board, and in the hospital and prison.

A dear sailor said to me to-day, "We see from the Word that the early Christians came together to remember the Lord's death, and it is laid on our hearts to do the same." This somewhat novel idea did not take me by surprise, for I had often wished that all Christians met more simply than they do. It was my privilege to offer them my sitting-room, whenever they wished to make use of it.

One Sunday evening, after the Lord's Supper, I discovered a packet of dollars had been left on a chair in the room where we worshipped. Thinking it had been mislaid by one of the men, I kept it until next day, when I questioned one of the greatest (because grace had made him one of the least). His only reply was, "*We have given it to the Lord, Miss,*" and then slipped out of my way. Of course I concluded that the sacred offering was to be spent in the blessed work, to which we were one and all called. Teas, etc., were seasonably provided by it, as a means of gathering together their unsaved shipmates to hear the Gospel, and by several such unlooked-for, voluntary offerings, from time to time. Never had money been offered in a more princely fashion! It was the King's current coin! They gave unto the Lord, and not to the cause. It is a grand thing to be filled with the Spirit! We are misers until we are! The dew of Pentecost is on everything the Church afloat does.

The *Thalia* has a large band of faithful witnesses now; they show a bold front to the enemy on board their ship. They are men wondered at by the whole crew.

The Word of God is full of point and power to our hungry souls. Some of the young Christians say that they have lost all longing to return to England. The Golden Gates of the home above seem so near, that they only want to be used, no matter where or how, " Until He come."

A Worker among the Sailors at Shanghai attacked by Chinese Rioters.

(Extract.)

I am very much afraid that the news of my disaster will have reached you before this, and no doubt frightened you. I was most miraculously taken through it all. I could not have been in greater danger of my life; and yet, I am now so far recovered that I can scarcely realise that I was at all in it. For hours my place was mobbed, but I could not anticipate danger to myself. I felt that a few Chinese, who were having a bad feeling out on the landlord, were creating the mob. Had I known that it was a feeling against the French generally, I should have got away, but I had no fear from beginning to end. Even when the rioters came upstairs I could not believe that they would strike me, until they did it, and then I left them. I had no idea that I should be thrown down in the street: I was not "dragged down" by my hair (as stated in the local papers), but tripped up by a Chinaman, who put his foot on mine; and though I received a great many blows, they did not seem to hurt me, only my wrist was much mutilated, and deep scars made in my forehead, but both are nearly healed up now. It was a clear case of being in the lions' den and not devoured. Though the natives of Shanghai enjoyed seeing the French get beaten, a few Ningpo men, who knew me, thronged round me in the tea-shop to save me. The rioters were composed of all sorts of wheel-barrow men, boatmen, and opium smokers. I was in a state of perfect calm, and when, as at one moment, death seemed inevitable, I resigned myself. I knew that it must be instant death, or instant deliverance; and so it proved. They were crying out, "*She is French, and she must be killed.*" At this moment I recovered consciousness, and with a last, lingering breath, as it were, God enabled me to shout out, "I am not French, but English!" On having declared myself a British subject, a great calm pervaded the crowd. . . . I have not, through God's grace, shed one tear, nor have I had a single emotion of regret, since I have been thus dealt with. I know that it is God's hand, in love, that has permitted it all; and I have no doubt that it will be to the furtherance of His cause and glory. It was a great blessing that Mr. W—— and Mr. C—— called then. We were having a Bible reading and prayer meeting in the upper room, before the sailors' meeting came on, and were paying no attention to what was going on below. My friends, in trying to save me, got severely injured about the head, and were carried off to the hospital, in a state of unconsciousness. The wreck of nearly all my things was brought to me. I am asked by the British Consul to put in claims; but I feel I cannot, for I heartily rejoice in suffering thus for Christ's sake.

This is a fiery trial to my faith, but I do not think it strange, for God's gold must go through the fire. "And when He hath tried me, I shall come forth as gold." This passage has been much in my mind of late: "He shall sit as a refiner and purifier of silver: and He shall purify the sons of Levi" (*i.e.*, God's dedicated ones for holy service). He shall purge them as gold and silver, "that they may offer unto the Lord an offering in righteousness." God's offerings must be made to Him, in His own prepared vessels. . . . I do not know yet what God means me to do. At present I am full of work again among the sailors. . . .

I hope you will get this before any other news. I do not feel very strong yet, so must stop.

J. McL.

There is a great deal of the parade of Good Templarism cropping up lately, and many of the sailors and marines, who seemed to take delight in reading the Scriptures, and joining in prayer, have grown quite cold, which is a grief of soul to the more spiritual on board the ships, and myself.

Lady P—— has invited me to conduct a young ladies' Bible reading at the Legation every Wednesday afternoon; and Mrs. C—— invites me to have a Bible reading for adult ladies at her house, every Monday. "There is a running spring in our Bibles; but, alas! we often fail to dig deep enough, and so come short of being refreshed."

Dr. H——, and his successor, Dr. L——, are

more than willing that I should visit the English naval hospital ; this proves to be a wide door, and effectual.

'Too full of blessed soul-winning, and soul-tending work to take notes.

Mr. Robertson, the Consul, is quite willing that I should visit the British gaol, on Tuesdays, Fridays, and Sundays. This is another door which seems to open of its own accord; and it affords opportunity for sowing and reaping.

It is rumoured that H.M.S. *Thalia* will be leaving shortly for England, *viâ* Shanghai and Hong Kong. This is a sore trial to us all, for the Lord has made us so united.

A large band of the *Thalia's* sailors comes ashore, nowadays, earlier than usual. Amah and they are busy at coffee and tea making for one hour in the afternoon. Half their number sing hymns in the open air, while the other half are taking their tea in my little schoolroom. They enjoy this picnic style of refreshing themselves before our evening meeting commences. It is such a treat to have a room which one can offer them. They bring their own bread and butter, and coffee and tea, with them. Amah delights to cater for them.

We went to the front of the British Legation to

sing hymns, by way of saying farewell to the friends whom God had raised for us on this foreign shore. The Thalians are leaving soon, and Sir H. and Lady P., and family, are going to their newly-built house in Tokyo. After coming away from the Legation we called at Mr. C.'s, to serenade them also. We knew that they would be glad to hear those sweet songs of Zion. We were urged to come into the dining-room. It was a pretty and novel sight to see a few of the *pride of the British Navy* occupying some nineteen or twenty seats, and with uplifted faces, singing heartily. The spirit of prayer and praise rested upon them! Before coming away the young ladies handed them tea, out of their best china. These noble men looked as if they were on God's errand; and so they were. Any amount of attention, when on His business will not elate. All that the world could bestow could not promote them; its contempt could not degrade them, its passing glory is as dross to those who tread the King's courts. They wished their kind friends, and mine, farewell, for their ship was under sailing orders.

The *Thalia* and her band of witnesses have left. Our parting meeting seemed a repetition of that referred to in Acts xx. 38. The ship's company, according to the inflexible rules of the Royal Navy, were soon to be disbanded, so that they had sorrow upon sorrow. Some were to be transferred to other ships, in different parts of the world; and those who had served their time were going home for good. It pays to become so united, so as to learn what a rock the cementing love of Christ can produce, out of what would, otherwise, be poor, fragile clay. We praise him for giving us such a unique sample of Pentecostal times.

Dear Hickey is in the Royal Naval Hospital. When the anchor of the *Thalia* was being weighed, the chain struck against his leg, and broke it in two, so that he could not join his brethren. He wept over his separation from them much more than over his broken leg; but in the hospital he grew in grace, and witnessed a good confession.

The *Cadmus* most unexpectedly pays Yokohama another visit. The noble band of Gospel heralds called on me about 6 p.m. They said that "the Lord sent the *Cadmus* to Yokohama again, and *not* the Admiral"; we say so too.

We went to the camp. Some seventy or eighty met for Bible reading and prayer, and we had a time of blessed refreshment.

The Lord makes himself increasingly precious to us as time goes on. Some marines called in the evening. The sacrifice of praise and prayer never grows stale or tedious.

THE PARSONAGE.
(A temporary abode.)

Nearly all the large and small vessels of the flying squadron are in the harbour. My sitting-room, at present a large one, is full of blue-jackets and marines every afternoon and evening. R. B., from H.M.S. *Frolic* is "out-and-out." He brings the unsaved here in large numbers. He, like the Thalians, is a "true fisher of men." Such helpmeets are invaluable to a solitary, but happy, labourer like myself. Human learning could not produce such workers; nor could all the gold in the world purchase such. We rarely have money hitches; our wants are easily supplied. The field is open before us, and God says, "Go forward! slack not thy pace unless I bid thee."

God has so abundantly owned our little social teas that he makes provision for such efforts, and sends the money, before we ask Him for it.

My sister has arrived from Shanghai. The vessel she sailed in got aground in a fog, but she and her fellow passengers met in the cabin to plead with God; and while in prayer word came to them that all was right. How great is His goodness!

A friend in England, from whom I have not heard for several years, has sent me a kind letter and a gift of money, which is a very timely help.

It being holiday season, and my pupils absent for six weeks, there is no *human* prospect of making the two ends meet. But the "*Mighty Man of Wealth*" is above such extremities, and to-day he says :—"*Blessed be thou of the Lord, my daughter.*" He seems to be educating me into a life of trust, sometimes through trial, and sometimes through glad surprises—"handfuls of purpose," which he lets fall by the way. Few know the heavenly art of giving "*as unto the Lord Himself*," consequently, the giver and the receiver come short of blessing.

I have not been writing home at all about the glorious work, nor even speaking of it, lest Heaven's sweet bloom should get rubbed off. But there is a time to *speak*, and a time to keep *silence*, for all that.

Cheering letters from the Thalians; they are at Shanghai. They say that Mr. S. D. C. Douglas is sent of God to that place, he is preaching Jesus, in the power of the Holy Ghost, in the cathedral and theatre. The Lord laid it on my heart to invite Mr. Douglas to visit the ports of Japan. We are praying daily that he may be brought to us, full of the only power and qualification which God can own and bless.

H.M.S. *Audacious* and *Charybdis* are fresh in. There are a few earnest Christians on each; but they do not make the same effort in bringing the unsaved to our Gospel tea meetings the other sailors have done. They say that a woman ought not to speak to men. This surely is the device of the tempter. There is no place in Scripture where a command is given to women to confine themselves to women in Gospel work; it is the human judgment that has so regulated it. I only aim at getting souls into the lifeboat. . The *Charybdis* men are holy men of God for all that, and are full of the love of Christ. I honour them for acting up to the light they have ; but there is danger of misapplying it.

The sailors visit the Hospital, and help their sick brethren. Surely this state of things is but a sample of the Pentecostal blessing of early date, when saved souls went "everywhere preaching the Word."

Every day is a time of refreshing to our souls ; whether we meet in my house, in the hospitals, ships or prison, our searching of Scripture is a business that pays.

My sister is returning to Shanghai ; the sailors there are longing for her return, and I must not detain her any longer. (See sailors' letters.)

September.—Mr. S. D. C. Douglas has written to me from Kobé; the Lord is sending him. I have invited all the missionaries, and Mr. Robertson, the British Consul, to meet Mr. Douglas as soon as he arrives, so as to arrange about the mission. Mr. Fishe, of C.I.M., has helped me to get posters ready, announcing the week of mission services, to be conducted by Mr. Douglas.

Went on board the U.S. flagship, and had a bright meeting. Thirty men attended. The captain and officers of this, and all the American men-o'-war, are always very courteous.

Went to General Hospital; several convalescents present. They seem harder and more difficult to make an impression on than the blue-jackets in Royal Naval Hospital.

Sunday.—Went to several vessels; the day being rather rough, the men did not expect me, and 'turned in;' but as soon as they were told that I was on board they 'turned out' directly, looking rather sleepy, but not put out in the least. This made me feel that they appreciate the Word of God.

My pupil I—— and myself went on board H.M.S. *Vigilant* to-day. The captain gave us a hearty welcome, and placed his cabin at our disposal. It was soon filled with men dressed in their best Sunday uniform. The wind and waves got up before we had finished our meeting. The captain ordered the ship's gig to take us ashore. He said it would not be safe to go in a sampan; besides, there was none to be had, as all the boatmen had made for the shore as soon as they saw the storm coming on. The ship's doctor sat at the helm, and in a few minutes we were being rowed by ten men, who pulled hard against the majestic waves.

Wrote to Captain Ryder, of H.M.S. *Vigilant*, for special leave to be given to several of his men. Truly nothing cheers me like seeing the unsaved come to my house.

Eight men have come, and we had a Gospel address after tea.

Mr. S. D. C. Douglas has arrived. Mr. and Mrs. Cargill have invited him to stay with them. Our meeting of conference passed off beautifully. Everything fitted in to a T. The Bible readings at Temperance Hall, as well as the Gospel services held nightly in the church, are much resorted to, and by many greatly appreciated. . . . . . Even the enemies of the truth crowd to hear the missioner: such gnash their teeth at him. The press hurls its missiles also, but he is impervious to them all; he sticks to the simple word of testimony, and appeals to the consciences of the people, and not to their brains. The missionaries have been greatly cheered and refreshed, and so have other Christians. Mr. Douglas visited the U.S.S. *Saco* with me; we had a nice little meeting on deck; and we sang "Gates ajar."

Several Bible readings have grown out of this movement; but the world has such a deep hold on people here, and such blessed exercises soon languish.

Lady Parkes has invited Mr. Douglas to the Legation, at Tokyo, and there he has fresh opportunities for preaching Jesus and the Resurrection. The foreign residents here need to be often visited by non-compromising servants of God, like Mr. D. If the privilege of serving such a Master is not enough to tempt holy men and women of God out of England, what can?

> Oh, let thy life be given, thy years for Him be spent.

MOVED INTO A NEW HOUSE.

No notes taken lately. Mr. Douglas's meetings have been so engrossing that all my spare moments have been taken up.

Have had much happy time with the dear blue-jackets lately. The sailors have indeed received Jesus into their ships. The officers are struck with the change in some of the men. "Thou makest the outgoings of the morning and evening to rejoice. Thou visitest the earth, and waterest it: thou greatly enrichest it with the river of God, which is full of water." . . . . . He has been all this to us! Praise His Name!

I visited the *Charybdis* to-day, and found she was coaling; the ladders were all drawn up, but I managed to get on board somehow. The Christian sailors wept for joy to see me. They have given up trying to discourage me from speaking to men. . . . . . They acknowledge the power of the Spirit at our meetings, but are at a loss where to draw the line. . . . . . . Some of the officers and the doctor spoke highly of them : they see that they are men of God.

New Year's Eve, 1876.—The *Charybdis* Christians have brought a few men ashore to tea. As they had special leave given them, we tarried in prayer and praise, before God, until midnight. We had a most profitable time. . . . . . .

New Year's Day.—" Faint yet pursuing." I see in the sailors what I find is lacking in myself, and in most Christians, viz., a Christlike tenderness, they " weep with those who weep." Went for an hour to the gaol, had a nice time with the sad-looking prisoners. There were seven men present, one of whom has passed from death to life, through reading a Bible, lately given him.

All my pupils are back, and my young friend Miss H—— helps me greatly.

Faith severely tested. My quarter's rent of seventy-five dollars due to-morrow, and I have not anything in hand towards it; pupils' fees not due until next week. I feel intensely the dishonour of not paying it on the very day, as usual; but "Truly my soul waiteth upon God: from Him cometh my salvation."—Psalm lxii. 1.

It was a bright and sunny day. I went as usual to the ships and hospital. Called, on my way, at British Post Office, to enquire about the next departure for England. The Postmaster handed me a letter which had lain there a whole week—I had no communication, in those days of blessing, with any but God Himself; so never called for letters. I recognised the handwriting of a succourer of many, and of me also. I opened it, and found a cheque enclosed. I took it straight to the bank, and found that, to a cent, it was enough to cover my rental; and I went home, and spent the evening praising and blessing God. .... This, however, is but one of several such God-given surprises; and I only relate this instance of His tender care, that the reader may see and learn that God is as good as His word, and that, "Blessed are all they that put their trust in Him." The only thing that should concern the Lord's servant is to be filled with the Spirit. "Our wants shall be *His* care."

Sunday.—My resident Japanese pupil I—— slipped out of the schoolroom on to the verandah, while we were having our Sunday class for English children, and began to cry in an uncontrollable manner. At last we discovered, that putting the "innocent boy"—Joseph—"into the pit," was what proved too much for his tender heart. I am so glad the sailors pray for my dear charges.

One of the *Charybdis* sailors weeps like a child when I speak of life's lessons. He is most Christlike, and I accept him, and the other brethren as sent of God to me at this time. W—— and P—— called, and sat some hours with me; spent most of the time in prayer. They are leaving for Shanghai, and have come to wish me "Good bye."

Heard from the *Charybdis* brethren: they are at Shanghai. They sent me a most tender epistle, and a small offering. "A sweet savour of Christ" truly. Nothing could be more unlooked for, and nothing more timely.

A touchingly kind letter from Lady P——; she invites me to spend the day with her at Tokyo, so as to talk of the "*only* subject worth speaking about."

Sunday.—Went to several vessels. Very wet. The Captain and Officers of H.M.S. *Vigilant* were surprised to see me. They were hesitating about going ashore to Church. The Captain said, in a pleasant, cheery way, "If *you* have ventured out on such a day as this, *we* too may venture ashore."

Went on board H.M.S. *Audacious*. What a monster vessel! A truly enviable field for anointed workers. This ship carries a chaplain. He has written me a kind letter, thanking me for kindness shown to his men.

Went early in the morning to U.S. *Alert*. Had a full meeting. . . . . Very rough on the water. Visited other vessels also.

Went on board the *Egeria*; she, like the *Frolic*, is favoured with a Christian captain, who heartily appreciates the interest taken in his men.

> " Call them in," the broken-hearted,
>   Cowering 'neath the brand of shame ;
> Speak love's message low and tender—
>   'Twas for sinners Jesus came.

APPENDIX II.

Preface to the Letters of Blue-Jackets.

SOME few weeks before setting sail for England, I undid my bundle of sailors' letters (already well thumbed by me and other readers), and began to ask myself, "Is it really the thing for me to cling to these treasures any longer, by making room for them in my circumscribed travelling cases?" While thus turning the matter over in my mind, I was carefully packing articles of intrinsic value, given to me by my dear Japanese friends, as tokens of love and gratitude. Much as I prized the articles of valuable china, lacquer and drawings, I could not say of them as I could of the sailors' letters, "Ye are unto God a sweet savour of Christ." Thus my scruples fled, and the letters found for themselves a place in my box, as well as retaining one in my affections. Since my return to England, a dear friend copied them neatly and legibly, which made it a pleasure to hand them for perusal to many of God's people, who felt interested in this gracious movement of the Holy Spirit among the sailors.

From time to time the opinion has been ventilated as to whether it was right to withhold

Echoes from Japan. 275

from the Church so interesting and remarkable a testimony to God's grace and power among our Blue-Jackets. These opinions, in connection with carefully weighed and matured conclusion, indicates to my mind, that to declare *His* and not *our* doings, is our privilege as labourers together with Him. M. McL.

THE CHURCH OF GOD AFLOAT.

*Extracts from the letters of sailors, addressed to my sister, who, with the late Mrs. John, laboured among the Chinese and sailors at Shanghai.**

H.M.S. Thalia, at Yokohama.

"We cannot but speak the things which we have seen and heard."—Acts iv. 20.

" How true the words, ' He openeth, and no man shutteth': He speaks, and who can resist His voice?" He opens the heavens, and showers blessings which exceed our farthest thoughts. So it is with us. Now, dear sister, Jesus of Nazareth is passing by. Yon 'lovely man,' now in glory, is knocking at the door of many hearts and demanding entrance. His still small voice is saying ' Come!' His saints

---

* Feeling that the story of the blessed revival among the blue-jackets and marines is better told by themselves than it can possibly be by me, is my only reason for submitting these extracts to the reader. I find it impossible to leave out allusions to the human instruments—who have learned, in the secret of God's presence, to say, "To us belongeth confusion of face," etc.—without robbing the simple narrative of its full force.

take up the strain with tearful eyes, re-echoing
'Come, oh, come!'

"This is, indeed, a happy time for us, for it is as though the gentle tread of His footsteps is heard in our midst, advancing quietly to *one* here and one there, and taking up his abode with Him. Souls are born to Jesus; oh, what a happy time! He has our heart's praise. Join us, dear sister, in our note of thanks for the wonderful manifestation of His love and presence at this time to us.

"Although never having seen your face in the flesh, I make bold to write to you in your sister's name. Her hands are so full of work just now, that she can scarcely find time for writing, so she grants me the pleasure. Perhaps you know of her intentions of giving a tea to the men of the *Ringdove, Thalia*, and British camp, for the purpose of getting a number together to tell them of Jesus. On Monday last, her desires were realised. Oh, how beautifully the Lord brought it about! It was such pleasure to see more than two hundred in the room together taking tea. After tea we had a gospel meeting; and oh the joy in hearing loving, truthful hearts pleading with the lost and dying, pointing them to Him, the sinners' Friend, the sinners' Saviour! And Jesus was there, dear sister—the tearful eye and bending head told that. The gentle rustle of His garment was heard, whilst loving, pleading words declared, 'Touch but the hem.' Not with any desire to set up the creature, but the rather to glorify the Master, I must confess the joy I felt in hearing their loving words to the unconverted. They seemed so full of Him and His love, that words failed to convey to others the depths of joy they had in their inmost soul to Him. Yet, as with a mother's heart of love, and as those standing between the living and the dead, they pleaded, 'Why will ye die?' Why turn from you this cup of blessing, when it is at your very lips? Drink, oh drink, and live! It was not a word of fear that was spoken, but a word of love. 'Yet there is room,' was re-echoed, for *you*, O sinner! for *you*, 'O lost one!' For *you* with drooping head and sorrowful heart! Yes! *for you*. 'O taste and see that the Lord is good: blessed is the man that trusteth in Him.'

"On the following evening we had our Tuesday night meeting at 57, Bluff. The brethren brought as many as they could, especially those whose hearts were moved on the previous night. They had a happy time. There are eight of our men from the *Thalia* who feel deeply concerned about their souls. We cannot limit the Spirit's power; therefore, we cannot define who are really His. Yet, time alone will tell, for the new life must show itself. Some men from camp, also, are deeply concerned. Oh, pray with us, dear sister, that the Spirit's power may clinch the words spoken upon the fleshy tables of their hearts. We are co-workers with Him, and with one another, and feel the necessity of being faithful witnesses to our *once* dead, but our *now* living and exalted

Lord. 'The night cometh, when no man can work.' May we think of this. To-day may be our last. Our barque may drop anchor to-day on that beautiful shore. Then there will be no time for work. Oh, let us remember this! Here, we labour; in the glory over yonder, only over yonder, we rest. But as we labour, may we learn to stoop and kiss the feet, as it were, of our dying shipmates or friends. His message of love is put into our hands to take to them, not to keep to ourselves. Then, as we go, may we scatter the good seed of the kingdom, fully expecting to see it spring up, some thirty, some sixty, and some a hundred-fold.

"Dear sister, please remember us much in prayer. God has put the wheel in motion; ask for strength in us to keep it revolving. The Spirit greet you all in love. Please remember us to the brothers with you, especially the young ones of *Modeste.**

"Tell them the Lord has answered prayer. We mentally prayed for her, as she steamed out of Nagasaki, without one follower or lover of Jesus in her, but He took her to the right place. To Him be all praise! Your dear sister is quite well in health; her only desire is to spend and be spent in the service of her Lord.

"Excuse this hasty note, and accept the love of the brethren."

---

* This vessel left Shanghai in a few months afterwards with a large party of saved sailors and a few officers.

H.M.S. ——,
Yokohama.

ADDRESSED TO MY SISTER AT SHANGHAI, WHO SOMETIMES
WROTE HELPFUL LETTERS TO US.

DEAR SISTER IN CHRIST,—Many thanks for your words of exhortation to the lambs of the flock. Would to God that not the lambs only, but also those older and stronger in the faith, would heed God's voice, when speaking to them through His revealed Word! Why so many uncertain sounds falling upon the ear? Is it not because God's Word is so little understood, or acted upon? What is to hinder a child of God in this dispensation from attaining to a similar experience to that of Paul or Peter? There is nothing, I think, on God's part, but we are "straitened in our own bowels." I prove, dear sister, that God's truth is very often known in the head, but not acted upon in the life. Many, I fear, stop at *knowing* what they ought to do, but they never *do* it; therefore they prove that the truth has only entered the mind, and never gone home to its place in the soul. I get no deep manifestations of Jesus, by simply *knowing* what I ought to do, it is in the *keeping* of the commandment of love that I get blessed (although in His rich grace He blesses "exceeding abundantly above all that we ask or think"); and I think it is clearly taught in the Scriptures, that the believer may not expect any blessing, apart from the continual "Fight" or "Work" or "Watch." God is a rewarder of those who diligently seek Him, and I feel that every believer upon every stage of experience, is called to put forth daily, hourly, his strongest efforts in digging deeper into God's heart of love, if his desires are "to grow in grace and in the knowledge of our Lord and Saviour, Jesus Christ."

Dear Sister, you can sympathize with me, when you know how I am placed here, in the ship. The seed of God's Word, which has, by some honoured sower, been sown broadcast amongst the men of this ship has, by the Spirit's power, been quickened into life, and springing up, bears fruit; some thirty, some sixty-fold. I seem to realise myself as a servant, to whom is committed the care of those tender plants. Upon the early training of a child depends, to a great extent, the position or character of that child in after-life. So with these young ones. "If" (as you said) "the milk given them is diluted, they are deprived of the nourishment requisite for their development into manhood"; therefore, their growth is but little, and slow. There is great responsibility, therefore, upon us older ones, that we, by example and word, train up those young ones in the way God would have them take (not in a way after us), giving them for their good, the sincere milk of His Word, coupled with the Living Bread. But what makes me happy, is to know that Jesus has the reins. He tenderly watches over His weak ones. He takes all care from me, if I willingly give it to Him. But I want your prayers, dear sister. Pray much, that as a body we may grow up bright reflectors of Him who loves us. We much prize the meetings at your sister's house. We thankfully take such good provision by the way; feeling that, He who spared not His own Son for us, has also given us a "Bethel" in a strange land. Please remember us to the sailor brothers with you. We are placed in peculiar circumstances, but we are called to honour *Him*. Oh, may we learn how to value aright the Father's greatest gift, that our lives may testify to the love in our hearts!

It is rumoured that the *Thalia* will relieve the *Modeste*; if so, I hope to see you. Pray for us, dear sister. With Christian love.

I rejoice to know your work is prospering. How sweet to do some little thing for *Him*, and to realise His approving smile and cheering "well done"! This is a joy the world knows nothing of. They scorn the work, they scorn the workers, but eternity will unfold who is really wise. We do not want *their* approval, it contents us to know that *He* knows.

H.M.S. ——,
Kobé.

DEPARTURE FROM YOKOHAMA.

DEAR SISTER IN CHRIST.—Knowing you are anxious to get a line or two from some of us, I embrace this quiet opportunity of writing, according to promise.

The parting cloud is gradually passing away, and the clear sunshine of God's eternal love is shining upon us in stronger beams than ever. To me, the parting was a happy one, because the dear presence of our loving Jesus was realised, speaking words of consolation, and pointing onwards to blessings yet in store for us. He seemed to say to me, "All thy wellsprings are in ME"; sit lowly at my feet, and learn to die to yourself, your friends, or your relations, and you will find in me that unspeakable peace and consolation that wealth, life, meetings or partings can never disturb. He says to us: "Your place is up with me in the heavenly places; for I delight in the sons of men. At my table, feasting upon the riches of my grace, is the place I set apart for my little flock, because your sin-stained garment is gone for ever, and the spotless robe of righteousness has taken its place." Oh, may we learn to walk in deep humility with the Father, and with His Son, to take our place as those redeemed by blood within the veil, doing the will of God! He says: "Draw near; why hesitate or fear? The wrath is gone, the cup is drained to the very dregs, the avenging sword of justice is satisfied, and your greatest foe is conquered." Let us draw near, then, in full assurance of faith, daily rejoicing in the grace which has saved us, and comforting our hearts by knowing that the crown of glory, which fadeth not away, will be placed upon our heads by Him who loved us, and who gave Himself for us. His "little while" falls sweetly upon our ears. But in His absence, dear sister, let us be of those who take our place without the camp, lamp in hand, *and burning*, waiting for and hastening unto the coming of our Lord.

Some of the brothers felt it much in parting, but you will rejoice to know that they look through the gloom, and see Him who is invisible. As a body, we feel that it is amongst the "all things" that are to work together for our good : therefore we say, " Go before us, Lord, and we will follow," experience teaching us how sweet it is to be "anywhere with Jesus." The world around us still frowns, longing for a God that will please the desire of their reprobate minds. They set themselves up against the Lord, and against His Christ. " But He that sitteth in the heavens shall laugh : the Lord shall have them in derision." He has set up Jesus as Lord and Christ, before whom every knee shall bow ; and sad it is to know that, in the face of all this matchless love, wicked man, by his daring impiety and open rebellion, covered by the cloak of profession, tries to usurp the authority of God's dear Son. Yet he declares, "Yet have I set my king upon my holy hill of Zion." Can frail humanity overturn this? It cannot; for He must reign until every power is brought under His rule and survey. "God is not in all their thoughts," is still the solemn verdict, pronounced now as of old, by Him who cannot lie ; yet vain, boasting worms of a day glory in their improvements, and shout, with one universal cry, "Not this man, but Barabbas!" But soon will this be brought low, for the wrath of God will be poured forth upon this doomed world, because they heed not His invitations of grace, but tread under foot the Son of God, and put Him to open shame. But in his own accepted time, "*now*," He pleads with sinners. He says: "Be wise, be instructed," "Kiss the Son, lest He be angry, and ye perish by the way, when his wrath is kindled"; but he delays his judgment, "for the longsuffering of God worketh salvation." He withholds His hand, for there is yet a wandering prodigal in the far-off land feeding upon the husks, there is yet another who must hear those gracious words, "Son, or daughter, be of good cheer; thy sins, which are many, are forgiven thee, *go in peace.*" Oh that every child of Adam could hear that cry, and prove by experience the deep reality of being a Christian, not in name only, but in deed, and in truth!

Hoping to hear from you soon, we remain,

Yours in Christian love,

Christians of *Thalia*.

P.S.—Pray for us.

"HE WILL NEVER LEAVE US."

Some of the brothers, if not all, felt the parting at Yokohama, and some shed tears of sorrow mingled with joy, on leaving the birthplace of their precious souls. They said that they had parted with friends in England on several occasions, but never felt it so much as parting with those beloved ones at 57, Bluff, Yokohama. I am thankful to say that the Lord has carefully led us thus far on our journey, according to His own blessed promise; and His promise is: He will never leave us nor forsake us, neither shall any man pluck us out of His hand. You must be much in prayer with us, dear sister, that the Lord may keep us near to Himself, and make us to continue in one heart and one mind. I thank the Lord that He is keeping us, as yet, and all the brothers seem to be trying to enter into deeper knowledge of our Lord Jesus, and the love of God seems to be knitting us closer together every day, and that gives us much joy and encouragement to go on; but still we are encamped with deadly enemies, those who are trampling God's love under their feet, and putting Christ to an open shame; but still our cry must be, "Arise, O Lord, arise! gird on Thy mighty sword, and scatter them before us," and let us not be discouraged; for we are under His command, and He has promised us that we shall come off, more than conquerors, through Him that loved us.

H.M.S. ——,
Hong Kong.

DEAR SISTER IN OUR RISEN LORD,—I received your kind letter of the 11th inst. on Tuesday last. I have not yet read it to all the brothers, I am waiting until the stores are disembarked, when we hope to get our quiet corner on the lower deck again; then there will be a fair opportunity of seeing all together. We arrived here on the

16th inst., but having Mr. Blackett down with small-pox, we were put in quarantine for three days. The disorder is not amongst any of the seamen, and his is the only case with the officers. He is recovering rapidly. Do you see anything of our dear brother H——— now, at the Naval Hospital? We received such a comforting letter from him the day we received yours, but as neither of you mentioned anything of each other, we thought, perhaps, you had discontinued visiting and so missed seeing him.

We could gather from his letter, *who* was his constant companion in his sufferings, and the joy and delight of his soul. It was Jesus only. No other love came in between theirs, consequently, Faith's eye pierced through things seen, and saw in Him the chiefest among ten thousand and the altogether lovely.

Oh, for power *to fix* our gaze on Thee, Thou spotless Lamb of God: to give Thee the highest place in our affections, that *Thy* will and desires may be *our* will and desires also! Then shall we be in the position to receive honour and blessing from Thine own hand; and beholding Thee, who art invisible, our souls will be so captivated with the glory there is in Thyself, that casting aside our garments, we will forsake *all*, and follow Thee. As Christians, we find many things are apt to cleave to us, which retard our progress Zionward. "But thanks be to God, who giveth us the victory through our LORD JESUS CHRIST."

Runners in the Race.

We are runners in the great race to glory; but hear the instruction given, "let us lay aside every weight, and the sin which doth so easily beset us, and let us run with patience." This is our practice as Christians. All things else should be as dross; things behind forgotten, and things before earnestly pressed forward to. He knows if this is the one desire of our hearts, dear sister. He knows if our hearts are continually singing,

> "O worldly pomp and glory,
> Your charms are spread in vain;
> I've heard a sweeter story,
> I've found a truer gain.
>
> "Where Christ a place prepareth,
> *There* is my loved abode;
> *There* shall I gaze on Jesus,
> *There* shall I dwell with God."

May it be so for His own dear name's sake! You are anxious, I know, to know of the little flock. In His own words, "He feedeth His flock like a shepherd." "He preserveth the feet of His saints, and takes them beside the still waters of His love." The Lord is indeed good to us, dear sister. The same little band that you knew at Yokohama are still quietly pressing toward the mark. There are things that occur amongst us which must characterise *any* body of Christians; as, for instance, some living beyond this confusion and bearing fruit a hundred-fold. Others learning the lesson that self cannot be trusted, others requiring a word of exhortation, or, perhaps, reproof, etc. Thus we go on, but as a body coming out from Egypt, and embracing the pilgrim's character. We are anxiously waiting to get our little corner again. He will give it us in His own time. I will, if possible, go on shore before finishing this, and, perhaps, you will get more news,

H.M.S. ——,
Shanghai.

ADDRESSED TO MY SISTER WHEN ON A VISIT TO ME AT YOKOHAMA.

DEAR MISS ——.—Feeling how deeply you are interested in us, I make bold to send a little note with Brother T———'s letter. On our arrival from Ching-Kiang, on the 3rd inst, we were somewhat surprised to know of your visit to Yokohama. We thought something of importance had called you away, in the way of sickness or pressure of circumstances happening to your sister; we are still in suspense, as no intelligence has reached us concerning you. I look at it as God's time for making this long-wished-for visit, and I hope, in a week or two, to see you here again, bringing your dear sister with you.

We feel truly thankful for the use of the little room; it was very kind and thoughtful of you. We had been asking the Lord to open a way for us to come together to remember His dear Son's dying love; therefore, when the note came, we took it as from the Lord. We have been there several times; last Lord's day we spent a happy time there, breaking bread together according to his command. I felt the blessed Lord was really in our midst to bless: it is a glorious privilege to meet around His presence, and talk to Him face to face. May we prize it more and more! Shanghai is all astir just now—Christ crucified, the sinner's only hope, is proclaimed in simplicity to any who may trouble to hear. A gentleman, making a tour, has arrived (I think, by the last English boat), and he seems to be turning the place upside down; he preached twice in the large cathedral on Lord's-day; and he also delivers gospel addresses in the theatre every night of the week, besides special meetings for prayer held in other places. I do not know his name, or anything of him; but it appears Christ has touched his *heart* not his *head*, so he is constrained to testify of Him. Time is short; I cannot say more. Hoping soon to see you here again,

I remain, in Christian love,

———

H.M.S. ——,
Shanghai.

ADDRESSED TO MY SISTER WHEN ON A VISIT TO ME AT YOKOHAMA.

DEAR MISS ——.—Many thanks for your kind letter of July 31st. We were truly glad to hear from you, and to know of your proposed return to

Shanghai in a fortnight, D.V. I should have written before, but as I understood your intentions were to remain away only one month, we all expected you back again by this, bringing your sister with you. I feel the brothers will be glad when you return, for more reasons than one. They often remark, " Shanghai is not like Yokohama." We have often been to your little room, up to last Sunday week, but from that time we have not felt free to go there any more. The alterations in the building, and extension of the large house, have completely closed up your little room. The house the coolie lived in is pulled down, and another erected in connection with the little room, so there is no passage between: the only way of entrance is by passing through the new house, or the house on the other side, which is now occupied, I suppose, by the former resident. We all feel desirous of getting another house for you; but as we do not know the locality which is best suited for you, we are content to wait until you come. However, we will invite you back *; the Lord will provide a house and home. I was at the Hall last Sunday; the meeting was purely a gospel meeting; several persons took part, but it was all in a simple strain. Christ Jesus our Lord was upraised as the sinner's

---

* Surely this is a fresh proof that the Holy Ghost, who filled the Christians of earliest date, filled these men also! They "were of one heart and of one soul: neither said any of them that ought of the things which he possessed was his own; but they had all things common."—Acts iv. 32.

Saviour, and the speakers besought the hearers to be reconciled to God. It is the best meeting I have attended there. It spoke to me of better things to come.

* * * * *

Oh, for that nothingness that would keep self always in the shade; not caring to move, or speak, or act, unless in accordance with the divine mind; and from the constraining love of Jesus to sit thus as nothing at His feet, and to be content to sit still and let Him bless me, is, I feel, my hardest task! May He, in His rich grace, turn my captivity, and fill my mouth with laughter, and my tongue with singing! The Lord knows I ask for nothing here; my ambition, Jesus, nailed to His cross, my greatest concern now is to be like Him in character as I wend my way, amongst this wicked and crooked generation, towards the glory in store for me. My ignorance and self-will He graciously bears with, causing me to prove daily my emptiness as a man; but, at the same time, revealing Himself to my soul in richest grace as the chiefest amongst ten thousand, and the altogether lovely.

There is a decided change in the weather here, it is much cooler now than it was three weeks ago, but it is still very warm, during the day, in the sun. The *Mosquito* arrived here yesterday. She is to relieve the *Swinger* at Hankow. We hear that the *Frolic* is coming here as our tender; if so, we hope to see Brother B——.

Marching Forth Singly.

The Lord is tenderly leading his little flock here beside the still waters; it appears as if we are come into port (on purpose to get a time of quietness and refreshment), to get the younger ones for the trial they will experience in the parting the one from the other. I suppose if things go on in their regular course, twelve months from this will find us scattered in many different places. The ship being paid off, the brothers will have to march forth singly, with perhaps difficulties surrounding them; and confess the dear name of Jesus, either amongst their unconverted friends, or in the company of new shipmates they will have to sail with, for perhaps four years; this will require much grace. The brothers feel this, therefore they cleave to the strong One for strength.

Please give my Christian love to your sister. Many thanks for her kind letter we received the mail before last; we hope to see her to bid her farewell before we take our final departure for England; the brothers send their Christian love. Accept the same from yours in Jesus.

H.M.S. ——,
Shanghai.

. . . . . "I cannot wonder at your surprise in not getting a line or two from me for such a length of time; but my delay was caused chiefly through the expectation of seeing you here with your sister. Knowing, also, that several of the brothers had written (thus letting you understand that the LORD is a wall of fire around us) it gave me rest. Many thanks for your letter, written on your return from Kobé. We were thankful to know that you were well, and also to see by it, your sister's intention of coming (D.V.) by the next mail. We were anxiously expecting her on Saturday last, but on receiving the letter, we saw that His ways are not as our ways. However, we are looking forward to next Saturday. I am glad to know you get some men from the *Charybdis* to come to your house."

* * * * *

Perfection.

" I hear and read of those who have attained to a degree of perfection far above many, in fact, above most Christians; but it cannot be perfection in themselves, for their carnal mind is as little likely to be tamed as my own; these must, in a measure, experience seasons of emptiness and depression as others, for it is only as their faith remains unshaken, and their confidence firm in Him who never changes, that victory can be gained—the victory that overcometh the world is our faith. This is clear in my own short experience, for there have been times when I have been *driven* to trust, as it were, and I always proved the Lord to be far, very far beyond my expectation. Unbelief has limited His powers and brought depression; whilst, on the other hand, faith has settled the matter by saying, '*God is able,*' and the result has been a settled peace and deep conviction that *all* is well. I am thankful to say the Lord has taught me many things since I last saw you; I can discern the secret of His power through faith in Jesus. In the main, my confidence is unshaken in Him, and my joy is sweet; but there are seasons of dimness, which, I think, all are subject to. Do you think it possible for one to live always without a cloud or shadow of a doubt? If so, I am still in the background as to my joy. I am, I know, far behind as to knowledge, but I feel I have as much right to 'joy in God, through Jesus Christ,' as any. *All* things are to me dung and dross, but yet I find I am apt to cling to them. My ambition is to be a servant in the Father's house. Grace has made me a son: do pray, please, that the results of that grace, working effectually in me, may fit me for the servant's part."

FAREWELL.

" According to promise, I pen these lines to you in order to give you my parting letter.

" I merely wish to write to you by way of acknowledgment for the many kindnesses and much good you have been the means, in God's hand, of doing us. The grace of our dear Lord working effectually in your heart, enabled you so to act as to leave deep impressions on each of our hearts, which time or alterations of any kind can never erase. You appeared to us as one the Lord had raised up to act for Himself in the glorious work of calling dead and sleeping souls into life and liberty, the example shown by your unflinching zeal and craving desire for precious souls yet unsaved had a telling effect upon the hearts of the young brothers, and I trust it will result in causing them to follow the soul-gatherer's narrow path, after the examples shown them in their younger days. Your constant visits to the ship in all weathers were beautiful lessons to them, besides the many and various ways in which grace shone out to enlighten and instruct. They could not only hear you say, but they could see you acting, those precious words, 'The love of Christ constraineth me,' and that love was imparting not to live to yourself but to Him who died for you and rose again. Oh, may that power of love still enable you to patiently endure every opposition you may meet in your endeavour to proclaim the name of our dear Lord Jesus! I am writing this just to let you see that the good you have been the means of doing us is not forgotten; it is highly appreciated by us. Do not despond or grow weary of well doing, dear Miss ——, but go on still as before, letting that rich love control your life. The Lord has noticed and acknowledged your labours for him in the past, why not again? If any has a right to feel encouraged in their work for the Lord, it is yourself. What further proof do we require that the Lord's hand is with us, than the conversion of souls? None, surely! Well, then, here are proofs enough to convince you that the Lord's hand was with you in your work. If you have faithfully finished the work the Lord has given you to do amongst sailors perhaps the Lord may again favour you as a channel to convey blessings to others in another line. But ye have need of patience, He tells us, 'Be not weary in well doing: for in due season ye shall reap, if ye faint not.' If your eyes are on the Lord Jesus, *fixed* there, and if we are walking in the sunlight of His presence, within the sound of His still small voice of love, and the language of our hearts is, 'My God, the spring of all my joys,' there is little opportunity of Satan getting us occupied with our own goodness or feelings within, or with our failure or weakness. It is only by a steady, fixed gaze on the Lord Jesus, now living for us within the veil, that we may hope to rise above ourselves or the present scenes of strife and discord through which we are passing. Our desire is to shine as lights, and reflect the glory of our Lord, is it not? Well, then, let us follow the directions in his Word.

"Oh, may we flee from everything that does not come up to the Word of God, or exalt the blessed person of his Son! I am impressed of late with the necessity of following the Word simply and faithfully, even if it is in direct opposition with all our feelings and voices within.* I must close. We shall perhaps leave for Hong Kong at the end of this month. If spared I hope to write again.

"With true Christian love,

"I remain, your brother in Christ."

HALF-HEARTED CHRISTIANITY.

"Mr. Douglas," writes a sailor, "spoke very plainly and pointedly to those who take their stand as teachers and masters. He let them understand what he thought to be the cause of this easy, half-hearted Christianity, which harms nobody and saves nobody. I hope they were benefited by his clear declaration of the truth. I feel, if there was the individual purging and close abiding in Jesus of every individual who professes His Name, it would result in something very different from the present state of things. The 'trumpet would give a certain sound,' and His dear Name be glorified. I am struck with the disorder that reigns around me. In the world all is confusion, because the sceptre is not in the rightful hands. Satan reigns, and the language from the hearts of the majority of his subjects, is rebellion against Him, whose rightful

---

* At this time an unscriptural perfection had reached the shores of China and Japan. So they felt the need of steering clear of quicksands. Our first great trial was the spiritual death that prevailed everywhere. The outpoured blessing among the sailors resulted in calling forth much earnest prayer. Our next season of refreshing all along the coast was through the visit of the Rev. S. D. C. Douglas. The sailors were charmed with his sound and powerful teaching.

place it is to reign. But the time is coming when He will reign; for God will interfere, and with His own hand set things in order, wresting the sceptre from him who now wields it, and placing it in the hands of his dear Son. In this, His time of rejection, we are called to follow Him, glorying in the Cross, and the privileges of suffering for Him."

*　　　*　　　*　　　*　　　*

EXTRACTS FROM THE LETTERS OF A ROYAL MARINE STATIONED AT YOKOHAMA.

I need scarcely tell you that among men situated as we are, almost isolated from the rest of the world, we are left pretty much to our own resources for spiritual instruction; and where there is no shepherd, the sheep are almost sure to be scattered. We number about 300 in our battalion, nearly all young men; and where we have neither the influence of female society, nor the example of godly men to restrain us, morality must sadly suffer. It is true we have a chaplain attached to us, and a good one too, whom we all love and respect; but his duties are so various, and his time so much occupied in attending to them, that we only get the benefit of his instruction for a very small portion of the time. But I thank God one person was induced, and moved by His Holy Spirit, to come among us at last, and by His blessing her efforts have not been unattended with success.

I had been so long grieving the Holy Spirit that I despaired of receiving forgiveness, until I learnt that "He is able to save them to the uttermost that come unto God by Him, seeing He ever liveth to make intercession for them." I felt the Spirit working mightily within me, and I was fearful of any longer refusing to listen to its warning voice, remembering God has said, "My spirit shall not always strive with man." I struggled earnestly with prayers, and tears, for forgiveness, feeling my own unworthiness, but trusting in the atoning blood of Christ which "cleanseth from all sin;" and I thank the Father of all mercies that I felt the truth of that blessed promise of our Saviour, "Him that cometh to me, I will in no wise cast out."

It would be impossible to convey to you an adequate idea of the happiness we feel in serving our blessed Lord and Master Jesus Christ, nor the extent of the blessings wherewith we have been blessed. God has, indeed, been gracious to us, and has added to our number. It is, indeed, a great conquest when one sinner has been drawn from the ranks of Satan to swell the number of our pilgrim band. People who are not acquainted with the interior economy of a body of men in H. M. service, cannot realize the extreme difficulty of doing, or being, different from those by whom one may be surrounded, and the great moral courage it requires to separate from them. Men who would not fear to engage an enemy three times their number, or charge boldly to the cannon's mouth, in the service of their country, shrink like cowards from the bare thought of ridicule; but when once that stronghold is broken down, there is then no difficulty. When we left England, there was not a man, I think, in the whole battalion who openly professed Christ; nor do I think there was one, either officer or private, who would be found at any time reading God's Word. Oh, it was so gratifying on Easter day, to see eight going to receive the Holy Communion* in public, and in presence of their comrades; gratifying not only to those who partook of that sacred feast, but also, above measure, to those who had been, through Christ, instrumental in bringing about such a consummation. My own feelings I cannot describe; there was a time when I looked upon the sacred precincts of the communion table with a kind of superstitious awe, as something unapproachable, unattainable to such as I, and now that I was in reality drawing near—as I felt—God's immediate presence, it was with fear and trembling, but still with unutterable thankfulness, that I was counted worthy. Oh, pray for us, dear friends, that we may be made strong in the grace which is in Christ Jesus, and that our numbers may be increased, remembering that every recruit to our ranks is, indeed, a soul saved from hell, and a great weakening of the picquet chain which Satan has thrown so adroitly round the way of escape for our perishing comrades.

---

* The Royal Battalion of 300 men had their own chaplain, and officiated at Christ Church, Yokohama.

APPENDIX III.

CRUMBS FROM THE LETTERS OF MY SISTER FORMERLY ABUNDANT IN LABOURS AMONG BLUEJACKETS AT SHANGHAI.

I have been feeling like John in the Island of Patmos for a long time. But it is a blessed spot, and only those who are true to the Word of God and to the testimony of Jesus Christ, get sent there. It is there we hear the voice of Jesus in risen power, and the revelation of Jesus Christ is imparted. Have you got "Woman's Work," the January number? Mrs. Pennefather's lesson for February is beautiful, "Death for Jesus' sake." Christians are afraid of the dying daily, and that is the secret of the lack of power; and it is in vain Christians ask to be made powers for God's glory, unless they accept it in the way of the Cross. Paul would say of most Christians of the present day, "They are the enemies of the Cross of Christ." This was said of Christians by Paul: they went certain lengths with him, but when they saw the Cross, they turned aside, for they *minded* earthly things.

It is delightful to hear all you say about the camp and sailors. It seems distinctly given you from God. God will bless it more and more. Weary not! Faint not! "I know thy works, how thou hast laboured, and hast not fainted for my name's sake." The Word of God is a mine of wealth to my soul. I rejoice in it as one that findeth great spoil. I want you to keep before God in prayer, to show me in July whether I can come to Yokohama for a month. I would not think of asking for a reduced rate. Some Christians approve of asking for it; but it seems to me to be unscriptural to do so. The silver and the gold are His. It is one to be *offered* a passage gratuitously, but quite a different thing to *ask* for it. The servant of God should not be under obligation to the world—no, not from a thread to a shoe-latchet. He will only make plain paths for our feet as we are looking to Him for guidance. How much we need the simplicity and confidence of little children! The thought of not being cared for by their parents never crosses their minds.

* * * * *

I have not the least regret for disconnecting myself with the ———; on the contrary, much cause for joy. Few see with me; but I am quite indifferent to man's opinion, so conscious am I of God's leading. . . . I am sure God means we should not trust to, or lean on, man at all. I received your last on Wednesday. I am so glad of what you say about the camp and Sunday-class among the Japanese lads. I think you have a glorious opportunity for spreading the knowledge of the truth. I am sorry I have not a supply of Chinese books to send you. Send to Mr. Mateer for Chinese Bibles. There is much prayer made for you by the sailors. G. G. never forgets you. Mrs. —— has written, asking for incidents of missionary work in Japan that might interest their working parties. I thought you might give a little account of gospel work among the Japanese, only don't sit up late to do it—the sailors say you work so hard.*

* * * * *

I am sorry you made up your mind so much for me to come. I cannot feel it would be right for me to leave Shanghai for any place just now. I should enjoy the change, I have no doubt, if I had distinct guidance from God about it, but I have not: and the visit, consequently, if taken irrespective of such guidance, would prove fruitless, and to be regretted. My present position is one of waiting, and it is

---

* Felt for five years like one wound up by God for a work which He meant me to do at His charges, and I went on unweariedly in it. Praise His name! "Not unto us, O Lord, not unto us, but unto Thy name give glory," &c.—M. McL.

impossible for anyone to judge for me as to my course. It is a path in which our soundest sense and most enlightened judgment can have no verdict ; for God's thoughts are *so far* above *our* thoughts and *His* way above *our* ways. It is the path in which all God's children should ever be found, or failure and disappointment will be the canker that will not fail to sap out the strength which ought to be preserved until God's time of action comes. He leadeth in the paths of righteousness—the path in which we shall not be making mistakes—and He leadeth "for His name's sake." I see very few people. I am kept in perfect peace. It is such a change: the PEACE keeping our hearts and minds, to our trying to keep it! I hope you pray much for me. I need wisdom to walk before God amid an opposing world, and church, too. The writer of the Chinese letter (enclosed) would like to go to Japan as your helper.

* * * * *

I feel sure that God would have his labourers look to him alone for all their wants. I never mean to tell anyone how I am situated, but God alone. He has been tenderly weaning and schooling me of late. It is better to trust in the Lord than to put confidence in man. . . . I think what you say of Lady P—— and other friends wishing to contribute to the support of your work at Yokohama, is very nice. But I think you have acted wisely in declining it. Unless all the contributors were of the same turn of mind as Lady P—— and Mrs. C——, with yourself, it would, sooner or later, as you say, bring you into bondage. We must be prepared to be misunderstood, and even blamed for the truth's sake. I am quite in the dark as to my future proceedings, and I am quite willing to remain so day by day, living according to the Scriptural command, doing *whatsoever my hand findeth to do*, and doing it with my might. How much blessing we lose by not observing this command, viz., "*Take no thought for the morrow*"! It is a positive command, and most Christians break it. I am a wonder to myself what I am facing. . . . But I expect greater trials to my faith than I have yet met with. I am glad you enjoy the meetings with the sailors ashore and afloat. There is nothing real in this world but dealing with souls in communion with Jesus. Oh, to know it more!

With regard to going to Japan, I feel still that I should ilike to spend a month with you; but such changes have come over Mrs. J.'s plans lately, that, for the present, my work is in Shanghai. If the interesting work among the sailors—and which God has so abundantly blessed—is not followed up with a firm hand just now, and set on foot for some time, it might flag, and be difficult to get it re-adjusted. All earthly advantages even health, must be put last. It is such joy to see God at work among the sailors. I have asked Mr. —— to *give* himself to the work (and I will gladly give it up to him), and I will go and work with you in Japan. But this I could not think of doing, unless one *gave* himself *entirely* to it, and did not take it up as a *recreation* only.

I am delighted to think you are having so much blessing in your own soul, and in your work. To be used of God we ought to be dead to everything else but the prosperity of His kingdom. And thus it shall be, if we are yielded up to Him for life-long service. Mrs. C. died the other day: it was like gazing into heaven to witness her departure. I was with her three nights.

* * * * *

I am making book-markers of the kwetzu (Chinese braid) for the sailors' Bibles. Is there any way of getting cheap Bibles at Yokohama? As yet I do not see my way to go to Japan; but I have no doubt it will be made plain if it is right for me to go. The change later on would, I have no doubt, be beneficial, even if I cannot leave the heat of Shanghai this month.

* * * * *

I have not said half of all I wish to write about. Tell me about the temperance movement. I cannot countenance the theatrical style in which it is carried on at Shanghai. I believe in temperance, but not in the way it is conducted. The *Curlew* brethren are now at Tientsin. I get such nice letters from them. They say that there is so much made of Templarism, that they had to take a stand against it; and they are suffering much from Christians on land, who, I think, are not so out-and-out as they are.

* * * * *

I feel strongly that God would have me regard the work among the sailors more as my work. Dear Mrs. J. is likely to be taken up with other work. It will be a trial to me to lose her fellowship, for we have worked with one mind and one soul in the blessed work among the sailors ever since its commencement . . . . . Of course, people will think me out of my mind, as they already do, for *daring* to trust God for all my need. But this is nothing compared to the joy it gives me to see my work cut out for me by God. There are scores of Chinese girls whom I have taught to read God's Word in their own tongue; but nothing has rejoiced my heart like the work God has given me among the men-o'-war's men, especially. I would as soon work at Yokohama with you, except that my school of twenty-five Chinese girls can be carried on just the same if I remain here: and there is no end to what I can do in an indirect way among the Chinese women. My work among the sailors has impressed a good many of the Chinese. My Amah has got greatly blessed through seeing the sailors so happy. She even imagines the cat must be sharing the blessing, because it runs to and fro madly (a bit of Chinese credulity!).

I have great trials from opposition. It is a case of the devil raging, but I have never been in a state to bear it more, though I feel it keenly. I do not expect anyone here, except the sailors, to see with me. I never have felt God's gracious leading as I do now. "He maketh me to lie down in green pastures." I am full of writing always to the various ships that leave. I should very much like to be among the marines in the fulness of blessing. I feel confident that, as soon as God sees right I should go, He will open up my way in a manner worthy of Himself. I will send you a long letter next week, and will begin it this week.

* * * * *

I moved into my new home a fortnight ago to-day. I am beginning to gather a few Chinese girls. The room is large enough to hold eighty or a hundred. I have taken a most important step, and had I not felt God leading me every step I should have broken down long since. My faith is often sorely tested, but I joy in each test for Jesus' sake. I can never regret the step. I could not have taken it without *deep views of God's power and faithfulness*. And it is a step which no one would be justified in taking unless they were led into it by God Himself, though God would have all His children yield themselves to have His perfect will wrought in them. My arm is not strong like the other yet, but the scars on my forehead are all healed (referring to the injury met with in the riot) but I am bearing the heat well.

* * * * *

The brethren on the *Cadmus* have shown me true brotherly kindness: they have papered two rooms; have done carpenter jobs, scrubbed floors, etc. Some of them declared that they got a great deal more blessing by doing it than if they attended meetings. Some of them have wonderfully grown in grace. The *Curlew* men gave me a stove, and helped me in various ways; so, you see, we have all things in common!

* * * * *

I was very glad of your last, especially to hear that ——— takes so much interest in the work among sailors. I can truly say myself, that I have never been engaged in any work for the Lord in which I have been so consciously used by Him; nor have I been so blessed in my own soul since I began, now two years ago, to speak to H.M.S. sailors.

* * * * *

I may say that all my days and hours are taken up with meetings for them, also conversation and writing. I feel fairly launched out in the work! I could not do so much for the sailors had I not disconnected myself from ———. This has been a year of waiting on the Lord, to know what He would have me do, as I told you before. My work among the Chinese girls has been much circumscribed and retarded for lack of funds; and this I see to be wonderfully overruled by God. [This house was set fire to by the rioters, and work among the Chinese entirely broken up for a time.]

* * * * *

I received yours, of no date, yesterday. The *Dwarf* is here. God gives me strength to study His Word, and to speak for hours to the sailors; although I have but little strength for other work. I need a change for my work here; but I am strong on doing as I feel led. God will show His way about it. He opening my way, it would be nice to go to Japan in November, and you to come back with me at Christmas. But we must not be making plans. I have received your last by S.S. *Ulysses*. It is matter of great thankfulness that God is at work, as you state, from time to time. There would be no end of work, I feel convinced, if we were fitted channels, and then willing to remain channels *only*. While self is in the ascendency it will seek its own, and mar the work.

* * * * *

I trust the reason why you have not written so much lately is the same reason that has prevented me from writing to you and nearly all my friends, viz., souls are being gathered; and I feel they must have all my time. My room is crowded almost every evening, as well as the evenings of the regular meetings. Last Sunday morning a friend led three merchant-ship sailors here for me to speak to them. They left deeply impressed. Two decided to follow Christ, but were ashamed to confess it. Two hours later one returned to make confession with his lips of the joy he found; he said he could hardly give himself time to swallow his dinner, he was so ashamed of himself for acting the coward when he saw me in the morning.

* * * * *

My soul triumphs in the Lord daily, even when my faith is tested as with a red-hot iron. God is with me, and for me. Oh, what gain ! I rejoiced in all Mr. M—— told me about your work. As dear Miss Weston says in a letter to hand, "It only wants a wholly surrendered heart in order to realise the power of Christ in work."

Extracts from Letters addressed to Sailors (in H.M. Ships) by my Sister, who daily welcomed them to her Tent.

And many a Sailor has had cause to thank God for the sympathy too rarely shown them in far off parts.

MY DEAR FRIEND AND BROTHER IN JESUS,
    In case you might have an opportunity of distributing tracts on H.M.S. *Thistle*, or other vessels, I send a few ; they will help to pave your way while endeavouring to speak a word for Jesus, or inviting them to come ashore to the meeting. I think a great deal about you in your difficult post ; but ever remember that your position is only difficult while viewing it in the scale of your own strength, which is weakness in the power of the Holy Ghost. I can imagine a ship of war to be a magnificent platform on which to exhibit the life of Jesus. Jesus requires of us to be nothing to Him or for Him at our own charges : it is the power of the Holy Ghost alone acting mightily in us that can enable us to achieve victories over the world, the flesh, and the devil. Oh, then, dear friend, ever yield yourself to be *filled* with the Spirit! I was reading this morning in Mark i. Jesus was in the wilderness with *wild beasts;* but *there* angels ministered to Him. And so with you, or any sailor who ministers for Jesus among untractable, wicked men, angels minister still.

* * * * *

The *Mosquito* is here (Shanghai) on a flying visit. This is the only ship of war in harbour. I believe in just what you say—to be nothing, and Him all in all. We shall be all God wants us to be when we are as *nothing*. Oh, may He teach us this more and more! Love to all the dear brethren afloat. I send a packet of the "Christian."

* * * * *

AT YOKOHAMA.

My sister and I went to the British Legation in Tokyo, on Thursday. I enjoyed the ride in the train. Lady P—— is a genuine Christian. How I wish we had such another lady at Shanghai! After luncheon, Sir H—— and Lady P—— took us to see the Mikado's Park. What a contrast Japan is to China!

* * * *

I do so regret not having written to you since I left Shanghai. The receipt of your letter last Saturday gladdened my heart. It is perfectly delightful to see how God is leading you forth..... The Spirit unites our will to God, or sinks it in His. When the flesh has the reins the liberty it gives brings us into bondage, and we say, "O WRETCHED MAN THAT I AM!" But the Holy Spirit's reign works in accordance with the will of God, and never wounds the conscience, so that we may ever have to say, "BLESSED BE GOD, WHO ALWAYS CAUSETH US TO TRIUMPH IN CHRIST;" and rejoice that there is such a command as, "*Let not sin reign in your mortal bodies.*"

* * * * *

Dear little Ippay is at Osaka for his holiday. My sister misses him very intensely, and she may go to Kobé to fetch him by the 22nd of this month (August). Pray for me, that my visit to Yokohama and Japan ports may not be in vain for souls. Yokohama needs the stirring up a man of God like Mr. Douglas may give it.

* * * * *

AT SHANGHAI.

I was thankful for your very kind letter. I have missed you so much, but I cannot regret that you go about the world a burning and a shining witness. There is good feeling with Christians of the several ships. There are two additions on the *Ringdove*, and four on the *Modeste*. Your words in the Temperance Hall had effect on D. He is really converted now. He came on the following Monday to me, feeling very miserable. To-morrow, Christmas-day, I hope to have about sixty or seventy men from the various ships. I often think of the help you were to me the last tea.

* * * * *

God tries and strengthens my faith from day to day. One of my printed letters was blessed to one of the *Ringdove's* men. I sent about 2,200 printed letters and cards about the shipping and settlement; pray for a blessing on them. There are over thirty Christians in the *Thalia* since she went to Yokohama. My sister goes on board every Sunday.

* * * * *

"Confess your faults one to another."

I received your last kind letter the other day. It was so good of you not to have scolded me for not writing you. You will be glad to hear that I have had great joy of the Christians on —— since I last wrote. I told you I charged —— and —— with hindering the work. —— came half an hour before the meeting to acknowledge the sin with shame, and to ask prayer.* He was quite broken-hearted, poor fellow. Before the meeting began, he asked the brethren for prayer. He owned he grieved the Holy Spirit, and disgraced us all; it was a sweet, unmitigated confession. I felt the Spirit fill the room, and we had great blessing that night.

---

* I believe the besetment of a sailor, at home and abroad, is strong drink. But my only reason for giving this extract to the reader is, in order to show the absolute necessity there is for judging ourselves repeatedly before the Lord, and when the sin becomes known, to acknowledge it to *one another*, before the soul can prosper. Secret *malice, backbiting, jealousies, pride*, &c., are equally calculated to cause a blight, and hinder communion with God and with one another. Why are some of the places of worship and prayer-meetings we attend so dry? It is to be feared that the reason is, we are not honest with ourselves, like the dear brother here referred to.—M. McL.

I sent him a note on board every day after that, to comfort him, and he came every night to see me. Last Sunday night I went on board the ———, and had a word with over a hundred of them. Owing to petty jealousies, some of them kept away from the meeting; this made me very unhappy and sad. When I returned, at ten o'clock, I wrote to each, and asked every one of them to come and confess their faults one to another, and for us all to humble ourselves before God. We went on Tuesday evening. They all came except ———, who was ill, but all right in soul: we had rich blessing. There was tender confession on everyone's part, and much blessing was the result. They all confessed it was of God I invited them. I asked them from six to seven, an hour before the meeting commenced. I told them it would be mockery in us to meet for edification and prayer, as if all were right, until we had the breaches of ill-feeling repaired. Ever since they have been adding cubits to their stature. For the first time there were several of the unsaved from the *Palos* and *Vigilant* here, and I spoke the Gospel to them from Isa. lxv. 3. After they left, I led the *Modeste's* attention to Acts i., and showed them how God would have them, in the strength of the peace and joy He was giving them, wait for power with which to witness for Jesus in their ship. I told them if they would fall in with God's way, He would give them the ship, for she only wanted witnesses; she was already saturated with the Gospel.

* * * * *

I must tell you that again I am like Paul, "without a certain dwelling-place," and this letter and myself are covered with dust and grit. The house is pulled to pieces for alterations. You would feel for me if you were here; but, "strengthened with all might, according to his glorious power, unto all patience and long suffering with joyfulness," works wonders! To be more central, I could wish for another place at once. Pray for me. He answered prayer for the *Modeste*, why not for me? I have no room for the sailors now. I and my things are penned and packed in the little room at the back. Two men from the *Midge* were here for a long time this afternoon; they left deeply impressed. Is it not strange that —— never brings any unsaved to see me? What can I make of it? I am so glad to hope that there is nothing of this mistaken exclusiveness among the *Thalias*. What a refreshing it will be to me to give the whole thing into their hands, if they are truly free, and liberated, not crystallized men! It would be nice if my sister could see her way to meet them here. And I should like to return with her to Yokohama for a month. L. and B. will not join us in our meetings; and when they call, they never seem to be in the spirit for prayer. They puzzle me exceedingly. They want to be set at liberty at meetings. And the worst of it is, they put me into bondage. I heard lately from Mrs. John, who is at Hankow. I am glad to say she was delighted with the *Modeste* Christians, and thinks I must feel "greatly encouraged." Oh, pray for the *Modeste!* All that can be done for a ship has been done for her. She seems lifted up to heaven in privileges. What we want is men valiant for the truth; men who are themselves all they would have others to be. Such only can minister the word of rebuke with power. People are in such ignorance of God's Word; every shortcoming, it seems to me, is to be traced to that. We want ever to steep our souls in the truth. I was so pleased to have learnt from my sister that you remember our Lord's dying love in her room, in pentecostal freshness and power, and not after any human sect. How much I long to have men around me whom I could feel had strength and resolution, and see the necessity of this ordinance, and seek to gather for this purpose, in obedience to His command, and get the blessing which must follow its being ever done in its primitive reality! Without this we should dwindle into formalism, like many Christians who began well. As a woman, I can see how I cannot take the active part which is necessary in this ordinance; and I see none sufficiently strong to regard it in its *simplicity* that I could suggest the matter to. I can see how alone, with a sister like-minded with myself,

I could take that part, but not with brethren.* But in preaching the gospel, or the study of the Word with others, I can say, "*My God helpeth me.*"

* * * * *

There is great cry for union, and I long and pant for *true* unity; but experience has taught me that true unity is not brought about until each believer dares to be first a unit—alone before God. Much of what is accepted as unity is only kept together by what "Anna Shipton" calls "*the honey of Nature*"; and we know well, though Nature's honey is sweet and adhesive, that it cannot stand the storm and rain; and much of what keeps Christians together is some attraction or advantage of NATURE.

---

* My sister here refers to real Christians of any denomination, and not to "Brethren," so named only.

Conclusion.

"And David longed, and said, Oh that one would give me drink of the water of the well of Beth-lehem, that is at the gate!"—1 Chron. xi. 17.

(1) I cannot help feeling that the guilty apathy of the Church of God towards the perishing world, is one reason why ritualism, spiritualism, evil doctrines and infidelity are stalking unblushingly through the land. The great necessity of the times is a force of valiants who will run every risk for Jesus' sake; those who, like David's mighty men, will not count their lives dear unto them, in order to gratify the longings of their King. Oh, why are we not more quick of scent, more ready to apprehend the meaning of the heart-thirst of David's ANTI-TYPE?

Why are not our numberless conferences more productive of the results that characterised the early church, when anointed men and women "went everywhere preaching the WORD"! Oh, how feebly have the most advanced teachers and evangelists drank of the love which is in the heart of Jesus for the sheep for whom he laid down His life! Those who have drank of the living waters deepest ought to be to the fore-front of the battle, and show by their fearlessness and loyalty that they are not their own. May God multiply *conferences and Bible readings* all over the land! such are the spiritual halting-places by the way; but let us beware, lest we fail to hear the warning voice in Ezekiel xxxiv: " *Woe be to the shepherds of Israel that do feed themselves!* SHOULD NOT THE SHEPHERDS FEED THE FLOCKS?" Our abundant knowledge and revelations are not enough, we need tender shepherd hearts, who will seek out the diseased, lame, lost, etc. It is to be feared that many of us lack the power and tact of commanding the companies of tired and hungry souls to sit down on the grass, in order to minister to their necessities.

(2) It would be pessimistic to say that the state of things was better thirty years ago than at present. The forces at work proclaim that a king—OUR KING—is coming! It may be at midnight, at cock-crowing, or in the morning! Yet there are credentials which a waiting church ought to display, but such it seems are covered with the dust and grit of worldly conformity and indifference, as well as with the millinery of rife ritualism. Where are those who weep over this doomed world—those who are moved with compassion towards the "multitudes" in lands still un-evangelised? These were prominent features in the Good Shepherd and His early followers.   M. McLEAN,

c/o Passmore and Alabaster, Paternoster Buildings,
London, E.C.

Alabaster, Passmore, & Sons,
Printers,
Fann Street, Aldersgate Street,
London, E.C.

WORKS BY C. H. SPURGEON.
PUBLISHED BY PASSMORE & ALABASTER,
PATERNOSTER BUILDINGS, E.C.

Expository.

TREASURY OF DAVID: Containing an Original Exposition of the Book of Psalms; a collection of illustrative Extracts from the whole range of Literature; a series of Homiletical Hints upon almost every verse; and list of Writers upon each Psalm. Complete in 7 vols., Cloth 8s. each. May also be had in half-calf and calf bindings.

Vol. I., containing Psalms I. to XXVI.—Twenty-sixth Thousand.
„ II., „ „ XXVII. „ LII.—Twenty-third Thousand.
„ III., „ „ LIII. „ LXXVIII.—Twenty-first Thousand.
„ IV., „ „ LXXIX. „ CIII.—Nineteenth Thousand.
„ V., „ „ CIV. „ CXVIII.—Fifteenth Thousand.
„ VI., „ „ CXIX. „ CXXIV.—Eleventh Thousand.
„ VII., „ „ CXXV. „ CL.—Eighth Thousand.

"If the eloquent Baptist preacher of the Metropolitan Tabernacle had produced nothing but these volumes he would certainly be entitled to the thanks of all Bible readers."—*The Rock.*

THE INTERPRETER; or, Scripture for Family Worship: being selected passages of the Word of God for every morning and evening throughout the year, accompanied by a running comment and suitable Hymns. By C. H. SPURGEON. Cloth 25s., Persian Morocco 32s. Turkey Morocco 42s. Cheap edition, Cloth, 12s. 6d., Imitation Morocco, gilt edges, 21s.

"The impress of Mr. Spurgeon's genius is observable in the very felicitous arrangement of the passages of Scripture as well as in the characteristic running comments in which latter, by the way, Mr. Spurgeon's theological views come prominently to the front."—*The Christian Family.*

THE GOLDEN ALPHABET OF THE PRAISES OF HOLY SCRIPTURE, setting forth the Believer's Delight in the Word of the Lord: being a Devotional Commentary upon the One Hundred and Nineteenth Psalm. By C. H. SPURGEON. Crown 8vo. Cloth, 3s. 6d.

"Our hope is that it will be largely used by devout persons for private reading. We shall be glad if our subscribers will purchase the book, and also make it known among their friends."—*C. H. Spurgeon.*

Homiletical.

THE METROPOLITAN TABERNACLE PULPIT, Containing the Sermons of C. H. SPURGEON, preached during the past thirty-five years. Vols. I. and II., 6s. 6d. each. Vols. III. to VI., 7s. each. Vol. VII., 8s. 6d. Vols. VIII. to XXXV., 7s. each. Whole calf, 17s. 6d. and 21s., and half-calf, 12s. per vol. The Sermons are published every Thursday at 1d.; and will be sent weekly by the Publishers, post free, to any address in the United Kingdom:—Three months, 1s. 11d.; Six months, 3s. 9d.; Twelve months, 7s. 6d.

TWELVE SERMONS ON VARIOUS SUBJECTS. By C. H. SPURGEON. With Portrait, Views of Cottage where Mr. Spurgeon first preached, and of the Metropolitan Tabernacle. Limp Cloth, 1s. Post free 14 stamps.

TWELVE SELECTED SOUL-WINNING SERMONS. Bound in Limp Cloth, 1s. Post free 14 stamps.

TWELVE STRIKING SERMONS. Bound in Limp Cloth, 1s. Post free 14 stamps.

TWELVE CHRISTMAS SERMONS. Price 1s. Post free 1s. 2d.
TWELVE NEW YEAR'S SERMONS. Price 1s. Post free 1s. 2d.
TWELVE SERMONS ON THE DEATH AND PASSION OF CHRIST. Price 1s. Post free 1s. 2d.
TWELVE SERMONS ON THE RESURRECTION OF CHRIST. Price 1s. Post free 1s. 2d.

TYPES AND EMBLEMS: A Collection of Sermons preached on Sunday and Thursday Evenings at the Metropolitan Tabernacle. By C. H. SPURGEON. 3s.
"It will be sure to be a favourite. 'Types and Emblems' are attractive themes, and in Mr. Spurgeon's hands they neither lack suggestiveness nor power. All his well-known qualities as a preacher are in great force throughout this volume."—*General Baptist Magazine.*

TRUMPET CALLS TO CHRISTIAN ENERGY: A Second Series of Sunday and Thursday Evening Sermons. 3s. 6d.
"The aim in each of these addresses is the simple one of rousing Christian men and women to renewed activity for God."—*Rock.*

THE PRESENT TRUTH: A Third Series of Sunday and Thursday Evening Sermons. 3s. 6d.
"Each discourse has the genuine gospel ring that proves it to have been coined in the mint of heaven. No better gift-book could be suggested for an unconverted or backsliding friend."—*The Christian.*

STORM SIGNALS: A Fourth Series of Sunday and Thursday Evening Sermons at the Metropolitan Tabernacle. 3s. 6d.
"Discourses which come upon the soul as the trumpet blast of judgment, but always end with salvation. . . . .'—*Christian Age.*

FARM SERMONS. By C. H. Spurgeon. New Illus- trated Volume. Crown 8vo. 328 pp. 3s. 6d. cloth gilt.
"These sermons are as fresh and fragrant as the newly-ploughed soil, or the new-mown hay."—*The Christian.*

THE ROYAL WEDDING. The Banquet and the Guests. By C. H. SPURGEON. Paper covers, 6d. Cloth, 1s.
"An elegant little book of 80 pages, illustrating the parable of the Wedding Garment, and worthy of the world-wide fame of the author."—*Baptist Messenger.*

Illustrative.

ILLUSTRATIONS AND MEDITATIONS; or, Flowers from a Puritan's Garden. Distilled and Dispensed by C. H. SPURGEON. Price 2s. 6d.
"It is a Garden full of beautiful and useful things, which will yield its delights to many classes of readers."—*Christian World.*

FEATHERS FOR ARROWS; or, Illustrations for Preachers and Teachers, from my Note Book. By C. H. SPURGEON. Price 2s. 6d. 29th Thousand.
"The collection is very varied, but all bearing on the highest themes, and fitted to help the highest purpose of the Christian ministry. There is an admirable index of subjects, and another of texts."—*Evangelical Magazine.*

THE SALT-CELLARS; Being a Collection of Proverbs and Quaint Sayings, with Homely Notes thereon. By C. H. SPURGEON. Vol. I.—A to L. Vol. II.—M to Z. Cloth, gilt, 3s. 6d. each, French morocco, 7s. 6d. each.
"No reader can fail to be interested, instructed, and spiritually benefited by a frequent perusal of the volumes. It should be placed among minister's helps, for it is certainly far more helpful than many vaunted aids."—*Christian Million.*

Extracts.

FLASHES OF THOUGHT; being one Thousand Choice
Extracts from the Works of C. H. Spurgeon. Alphabetically arranged, and with a copious Index. Price 5s.

"A thousand extracts, bright with the light of heaven, sparkling with wit, rich in imagery, beautiful in their setting, forcible in style, and devoutly stimulating in tone, make up a volume of unique merit."—*General Baptist Magazine.*

SPURGEON'S GEMS: being Brilliant Passages Selected
from the Discourses of C. H. Spurgeon. Large Type, 4s.

GLEANINGS AMONG THE SHEAVES. By C. H.
Spurgeon. Cloth, price 1s.

"These extracts are quite Spurgeonic—racy, rich, and rare, both as to style and matter—full of exquisite consolation—faithful advice—clear analogies—poetic touches—and glorious old gospel."—*Weekly Review.*

SPURGEON'S BIRTHDAY BOOK. Cloth, 2s. 6d.,
Calf or Morocco, 5s., Russia, with Photograph, 10s. 6d.

"A metaphor, simile, allegory, or illustration for every day in the year, compiled from the works of C. H. Spurgeon. For thirty pence our readers may possess a book which is as useful as it is handsomely got up."—*Christian Age.*

Devotional.

MORNING BY MORNING; or, Daily Readings for the
Family or the Closet. By C. H. Spurgeon. 3s. 6d. Morocco, 7s. 6d.

"Those who have learned the value of morning devotion, will highly prize these helps. All who love a full-orbed gospel, vigorous, varied thought, and a racy style, will appreciate this volume."—*Rev. J. Angus, D.D.*

EVENING BY EVENING; or, Readings at Eventide for
the Family or the Closet. By C. H. Spurgeon. 3s. 6d. Morocco, 7s. 6d.

"On learning that 'Evening by Evening' was published, how gladly I bade it welcome! And I can humbly commend it in no higher terms than by simply saying that it will be found a fit companion, every way, for its forerunner of the morning."—*Charles J. Brown, D.D., Edinburgh.*

THE CHEQUE BOOK OF THE BANK OF FAITH;
Being Precious Promises arranged for Daily Use; with Brief Experimental Comments. 3s. 6d. Persian Morocco, red and gilt edges, 7s. 6d.

"'The Cheque Book of the Bank of Faith' is suitable for family use, or for solitary prayer. It consists of a series of texts from the Bible, both from the Old and New Testaments, with a short commentary upon them. There is one of these texts for each day in the year. Each of them contains a promise of God, which, as the writer remarks, may be compared to a cheque payable to order, to be endorsed by faith, and presented in due time. There is much that is comforting in the volume, which will, doubtless, be largely used in households."
The Morning Post.

For Students.

LECTURES TO MY STUDENTS; A Selection from
Addresses delivered to the Students of the Pastors' College, Metropolitan Tabernacle. By C. H. Spurgeon, President. First and Second Series. Price 2s. 6d. each.

"We have read this work with a feeling very nearly approaching to delight. Nothing that Mr. Spurgeon has printed has so thoroughly pleased us, and few of his works are calculated to be of greater practical service. It abounds in words of wisdom; it is rich in humour, but richer in human and spiritual experience."—*Nonconformist.*

COMMENTING AND COMMENTARIES: Two Lec-
tures addressed to the Students of the Pastors' College, together with a Catalogue of Bible Commentaries and Expositions. Price 2s. 6d.

"Every candid reader will admit that, in impartiality, in terse and telling brevity, in wisdom sharpened into wit, in unaffected zeal for Christ's cause, and, above all, in robust common sense, this volume has few equals, if any."
Literary World.

MY SERMON-NOTES. A Selection from Outlines of
Discourses delivered at the Metropolitan Tabernacle. Part I. Genesis to Proverbs—I. to LXIV. Part II. Ecclesiastes to Malachi—LXV. to CXXIX. 2s. 6d. each. Parts I. and II. bound together in one Volume, Cloth, 5s. Part III. Matthew to Acts—CXXX. to CXCV. Part IV. Romans to Revelation. CXCVI. to CCLXIV. 2s. 6d. each. Parts III. and IV. bound together in one volume, price 5s.

When a preacher, be he lay or regular, finds himself severely pressed for a subject, he will find here an outline clearly drawn, a good deal of filling up and a little lot of stories or pithy bits to season the whole.

SPEECHES by C. H. SPURGEON AT HOME and
Abroad. In Paper covers, 1s. Cloth, 2s.

The pieces are in the main given as they originally appeared; in the majority of instances the author is made to speak in the first person; but this is not the case throughout. The reader will also find that the principal subjects are admirably reported.

Periodical.

THE SWORD AND THE TROWEL: A Monthly
Magazine, Price 3d. Yearly vols., 5s. Cases for binding, 1s. 4d.

It commands a large circulation among almost all classes of Christians, and as a religious periodical, it now occupies a position second to none. It records the works of faith and labours of love which are the honour of the various sections of the Church, and it contends most unsparingly against the errors of the times. It is an accurate record of the religious movements which emanate from the Metropolitan Tabernacle, but its advocacy is far from being confined within that area. No pains will be spared to render the Magazine growingly worthy of the widest circulation.—Editor, C. H. SPURGEON.

Historical.

THE METROPOLITAN TABERNACLE: its History
and Work. With 33 Illustrations. By C. H. SPURGEON. Price, in paper covers, 1s. Bound in cloth, 2s.

"Profusely illustrated with portraits, *fac-similes* of forgotten caricatures, and other engravings, quaint and otherwise, is likely to rival 'John Ploughman' in popularity. Containing between one and two hundred octavo pages, the matter might easily have been spread out into a five or six shilling volume; but, as Mr. Spurgeon desires to write for the people, he publishes his works at prices to suit the pockets even of the poor."—*Christian World.*

MEMORIAL VOLUME. Containing Sermons and
Addresses delivered on the completion of the Twenty-fifth year of the Pastorate of C. H. SPURGEON. Price 1s., cloth.